THE LIVINGSTONE TOUCH

THE
LIVINGSTONE
TOUCH

Philip Birkinshaw

MACDONALD · LONDON

First published in Great Britain in 1973 by
Macdonald & Jane's
St Giles House, 49/50 Poland Street,
London W1

First published in South Africa by
Purnell & Sons (S.A.) (Pty) Ltd
70 Keerom Street,
Cape Town

ISBN   0 356 04718 0

Printed and bound in South Africa by
Galvin & Sales (Pty) Ltd, Cape Town

Foreword

I hope this is a responsible book but it is more an act of hero-worship than a piece of scholarship.

I first read Livingstone in 1955, after making a TV film in the Gwembe Valley, east of the Victoria Falls, in what is now the bottom of Lake Kariba. I was charmed by the tribe that lived there, the Valley Tonga, and found the only person who seemed to have written of them was David Livingstone, whose books I immediately bought. From the sinew of his prose I was drawn to the whole cut of his life, especially his relationship with blacks, whom I had learned to like during service with the King's African Rifles in World War II.

My presentation is thus literary and not historical. I have not read the Letters, even, because my aim is not to try to summarise the man who lived between 1813 and 1873 but the self he chose through his books to project into the future. Some will think this image less truthful, but those whose field is literature are used to greater discrepancies by far between the lives men lead and the books they publish than the historians are able to show in Livingstone. His flesh and its frailties I leave to the resurrection men; it is the spirit he drove them with that speaks in this book.

I have scarcely been critical, either, *wapi faida*, as the Swahili say, where's the profit? When Livingstone is more widely read will be the time to sift his pretensions. My few Freudian excursions are hazardous, but they temper (and somewhat explain) the hero-worship. I simply confess to thinking Livingstone's style and content worth recommending. Africa has stood for many romantic and subtle things to whites – Conrad, Greene, Heuser, Dinesen/Blixen, Hemingway, Van der Post – but here is the dawn view.

Least of all have I ventured to interpret Livingstone politically. He was not a politician and it would be rash to claim him for a party. He yearned for the peace and prosperity of Africa but, while he has the patience of a saint, he is far too resolute to be a martyr. He can confidently be recommended to 'all civilized men south – and north – of the Zambezi'; with the plea that enough of them be found to practise his touch in good time.

Thanks are due to Cooper Partridge, who encouraged the idea of this book; to Mrs. Edwards, who supervised its typing; and to my publishers for their invariable courtesy and efficiency.

P.C.B.
Cape Town,
7th April, 1973.

Contents

The Map

(facing page 55)

The routes marked are approximate only but anyone who wished to follow them exactly could use them as a rough guide between Livingstone's own maps in his first editions and such detailed modern maps as Bartholomew's *South Africa and Madagascar, 1:4 000 000*, which I used.

While wonderfully accurate, Livingstone's maps present certain minor difficulties. Many of his place-names — Linyanti, for example — seem to have proved impermanent, for they are no longer marked. Sometimes a town on today's map is miles away from where he indicates it; the modern Sesheke, for instance, is further up the Zambezi than Livingstone's could have been, and Xassangue in Angola is well south of what he calls 'Cassange's'. Finally, perhaps from his desire to include detail, his routes sometimes appear actually longer than they do when placed on a modern map.

While modern towns, roads, game-reserves etc., are marked for convenience, few will need reminding that Livingstone's paths often pass through areas of confrontation — around Tete, for instance and on the Caprivi Strip — that are highly dangerous today. I have included Game Reserves as these may be the simplest means of seeing Livingstone's Africa both now (when they are in peaceful areas) and in the hopeful future.

P.C.B.

List of Illustrations

Book List and Key to Symbols

I have used certain books regularly and, since the list is short, I give it here in place of a bibliography.

These books are referred to in the text or in footnotes by the author's name only. Livingstone's own works are referred to respectively as:

MT *Missionary Travels.*
ZT *Zambezi and its Tributaries.*
LJ *Last Journals* (with date of entry).

1. COUPLAND, Sir R. *Livingstone's Last Journey.* Collins, London, 1945.
2. FANON, F. *Black Skin White Masks.* Paladin Books, London, 1970.
3. FLETCHER, I. M. *David Livingstone.* Occasional Papers of the Rhodes-Livingstone Museum, Number Nine. Livingstone, N. Rhodesia, 1950.
4. LIVINGSTONE, David. *Missionary Travels and Researches in South Africa,* including a sketch of sixteen years' residence in the interior of Africa and a journey from the Cape of Good Hope to Luanda on the West Coast; thence across the continent, down the River Zambezi, to the Eastern Ocean. John Murray, London, 1857.
    Narrative of an Expedition to the Zambezi and its Tributaries and of the Discovery of Lakes Shirwa and Nyassa, 1858–1864. John Murray, London, 1865.
    The Last Journals of David Livingstone in Central Africa from 1865 to his Death. Continued by a Narrative of his last moments and sufferings obtained from his faithful servants Chuma and Susi by Horace Waller, F.R.G.S. In Two Volumes, etc., John Murray, London, 1874.
5. MACNAIR, Dr. J. I. (Editor). *Livingstone's Travels.* With geographical sections by Dr. R. Miller. Maps, etc. Dent, London, 1954.
6. SCHAPERA, I. *Livingstone's Private Journals 1851–1853.* Chatto & Windus, London, 1960.
7. SILLERY, A. *Sechele.* George Ronald, Oxford, 1954.
8. TABLER, E. C. *The Far Interior.* Balkema, Cape Town, 1955.
9. WALLIS, J. R. P. *Thomas Baines.* Cape, London, 1941.

CHAPTER 1

The Uncanny Scot

Livingstone's is the first western imagination to fall in love with Africa without condescending to it. He holds a Victorian mirror to the infancy of the world's youngest continent and describes his passion for it in prose often perfect in its clarity. Between the day in 1873 when his body left Zanzibar for the nave of Westminster Abbey, and the 21st March, 1841, when he set foot in Simonstown at the age of 27, lie thirty-three years of almost continuous safari. He mapped Capricorn Africa, its peoples with his heart, its territories with his compass, his sextant, his untiring feet and his canny Scots eye. His heart still lies in a flour-box beneath the tree in Zambia where it was put five days after his death into an earth to which it profoundly belongs.

It was agreed that all honours should be shown to the dead and the customary mourning was arranged forthwith. At the proper time, Chitambo, leading his people and accompanied by his wives, came to the new settlement. All carried bows, arrows and spears but no guns were seen. Two

1

drummers joined in the loud wailing lamentation, whilst the servants fired volley after volley in the air according to the strict rule of the Portuguese and Arabs on such occasions.

As yet nothing had been done to the corpse.

A separate hut was now built in such a manner that it should be open to the air at the top and sufficiently strong to defy the attempts of any wild beast to break through it. Boughs and saplings were planted side by side and bound together so as to make a stockade. Close to this building the men constructed their huts, and finally, the whole settlement had another high stockade carried completely around it.

Arrangements were made to treat the corpse on the following morning. One of the men had bought a large quantity of salt: this was purchased of him for sixteen strings of beads. There was besides some brandy in the Doctor's stores, and with these few materials they hoped to succeed in their object.

Farijala was appointed to the necessary task. He had picked up some knowledge of post-mortem examinations whilst servant to a doctor at Zanzibar, and at his request, Carras, one of the Nassick boys, was told off to assist him. Previous to this, however, a special mourner arrived. He came with the anklets that are worn on these occasions, composed of rows of hollow seed-vessels fitted with rattling pebbles and, in low monotonous chant, sang, whilst he danced, as follows:

> *Lelo Kwa Engerese*
> *Muana sis oa konda:*
> *Tu kamb' tamb' Engerese*

which translated is:

> *Today the Englishman is dead*
> *Who has different hair from ours:*
> *Come round to see the Englishman.*

His task over, the mourner and his son, who accompanied him in the ceremony, retired with a suitable present of beads.

The emaciated remains of the deceased traveller were soon afterwards taken to the place prepared. Over the heads of Farijala and Carras, a thick blanket was held as a kind of screen under which the men performed their duties. They say his frame was little more than skin and bone. Through an incision carefully made, the viscera were removed and a quantity of salt was placed in the trunk. All noticed one very significant circumstance in the autopsy. A clot of coagulated blood as large as a man's hand lay in the left side, whilst Farijala pointed to the state of the lungs, which they describe as dried up and covered with black and white patches. The heart and the other parts removed were placed in a tin box which had formerly contained flour and decently and reverently buried in a hole dug some four feet deep on the spot where they stood. Jacob was then asked to read the Burial Service which he did in the presence of all. The body was left fully exposed to the sun. No other means were taken to preserve it beyond placing some brandy in the mouth and some on the hair. The men kept watch day and night to see that no harm came to their sacred charge. Once a day the position of the body was changed but at no other time was any one allowed to approach it.

No molestation of any kind took place during the fourteen days' exposure. At the end of this period, preparations were made for retracing their steps. The corpse, by this time tolerably dried, was wrapped round in some calico, the legs being bent inwards at the knees to shorten the package. The next thing was to plan something in which to carry it and, in the absence of planking or tools, a substitute was found by stripping from a *myonga* tree enough of the bark in one piece to form a cylinder. In it their master was laid. Over this case a piece of sailcloth was sewn and the whole package was lashed securely to a pole so as to be carried by two men.

Jacob Wainwright was asked to carve an inscription on the large *mvula* tree which stands by the place where the body rested, stating the name of Dr. Livingstone and the date of his death. Before leaving, the men gave strict injunctions to Chitambo to keep the grass cleared away so as to save it from the bush-fires which annually sweep over the country and destroy so many trees. Beside this, they erected close to the spot, two high thick posts with an equally strong cross-piece, like a lintel and door-posts in form, which they painted thoroughly with the tar that was intended for the boat: this sign they think will remain a long time from the solidity of the timber. Before parting with Chitambo, they gave him a large tin biscuit-box and some newspapers, which would serve as evidence to all future travellers that a white man had been to his village.

The chief promised to do all he could to keep both the tree and the timber sign-posts from being touched but added that he hoped the English would not be long in coming to see him because there was always risk of an invasion of Mazitu, when he would have to fly, and the tree might be cut down for a canoe by someone and then all trace would be lost. The homeward march was then begun.

It took eight months and 1 500 miles to the coast, one of the most famous of African journeys, of which the end is less creditable than the beginning:

At last the coast town of Bagamoio came in sight and, before many hours were over, one of Her Majesty's cruisers conveyed the Acting Consul, Captain Prideaux, from Zanzibar to the spot which the cortege had reached. Arrangements were quickly made for transporting the remains of Dr. Livingstone to the Island some thirty miles distant, and then it became rather too painfully plain to the men that their task was finished. ... No sooner did they arrive at their journey's end than they were so far frowned out of notice that not so much as a passage to the Island was offered them when their burden was borne away.[2]

South Africa, where this book is written, is an authoritarian state where whites and blacks are more socially polarized than anywhere else in the world. And yet there is an enormous concern, some of it lipservice only, perhaps, for interracial dialogue, within South Africa itself and with the states beyond its borders. Livingstone was a man with an extraordinary gift in such dialogue and the intuitive skill recorded in this book may somehow — for who knows how literature works? — promote a higher synthesis, whatever shape that may assume, of black-white interests in the country.

It would be simplistic to think of such dialogue as a local matter. There is a South Africa in every country and in most peoples' hearts. The world is not wrong in seeing a plank in South Africa's eye but there is not so little sawdust flying round that we can't all benefit from Livingstone's mirror and his healing touch, whether it be in Detroit or Wolverhampton or Durban.

The foundation of Livingstone's African experience was laid in South Africa, at Kuruman, in the Northern Cape. This mission, the most famous in Africa until Lambarene, was founded in 1817 and taken over by its virtual creator, Robert Moffat, in 1821. The little settlement that Livingstone knew as his home base between 1840 and 1850 is still there, its buildings, gardens, canals, even the register of the original converts who came in to communion the first Sunday of July, 1829. It was in a poor state when I visited it in 1969. Plaster was crumbling from walls, and junk accumulating in the little yard where Livingstone proposed to Moffat's daughter, Mary. A chimney-stack had begun to totter and weeds were climbing through wind-strewn thatch. The church, built between 1831 and 1838 for a thousand people, was golden and sunlit – it was restored in 1958 – but around it burned silence and neglect.

Livingstone was never stationed at Kuruman but he always regarded it as a model and a touchstone for his thinking and policies and it inspired his life and aims in Africa in the same way as Rancho La Rosa guided Che Guevara's very different ones in South America.

> This place has been what the monasteries of Europe are said to have been when pure. The monks did not disdain to hold the plough. They introduced fruit trees, flowers and vegetables in addition to teaching and emancipating the serfs. ... Monasteries were mission-stations, which resembled ours in being dispensaries for the sick, alms-houses for the poor and nurseries of learning.[3]

Thus it is to South Africa that Livingstone turns for memories of the formative years of his professional, and some of the tenderest of his private life. When he looks home, of course, it is to Scotland: he sees the streams of the Congo as 'burns', the valleys of Angola as 'straths' and 'glens'. The very porridge he was brought up on gave him a feeling of kinship with the maize, millet and cassava-eaters he moved amongst. He compares the agonies of Central African slavery with those of the Scottish Lowlanders in the twelfth and thirteenth centuries, torn by Sassenach and Celtic rievers. The stories he hears 'sitting by the African evening fires' remind him 'wonderfully' of tales of the clans told him by a favourite grandfather whose own father had fallen with the Highlanders at Culloden.

But no less impressive are his references to the Dutch colonists who have effectively ruled South Africa for over 300 years, as settled farmers in the Cape and (in Livingstone's time) as the filibusters of the Transvaal. South Africa is not alone in having a certain North-South polarisation in its politics. Blood being thicker than water, and both ends of the country being Afrikaner-Dutch, there is more homogeneity than disagreement in the ideas of the governing stock: but such powers to evolve as it shows stem from the slight oscillation of ideas between Pretoria and Cape Town.

Livingstone came in on the ground floor of this development. He travelled through the Cape countryside and admired the colonists he found there for their religion – many of their pastors were Scotsmen like himself – their patriarchal way of life and their practical skills. His references to them are familiar and favourable. 'The inhabitants of Natal and the Cape Colony will understand perfectly when we say the low belt adjacent to the East Coast . . . is *zour velt* and well suited for cattle.' And 'if men like the Cape farmers owned this country, their energy and enterprise would soon render the crops independent of rain'.

His views on the still-pioneering Transvalers, when he came across them in the Magalaiesberg and the Marico, however, were very different. He was as tough and outspoken as they and I have described his spat with them at Kolobeng in Chapter 6.

The root of his difference with them was slavery. The abolition of slavery was proclaimed by the British in Cape Town on the 1st December, 1834. Little over a year later, groups of dissatisfied Dutch burghers took their own families, belongings and practices into the wilderness beyond the Orange and the Vaal Rivers, and it was these groups, in the full flush of their slaving self-righteousness, that Livingstone encountered when he was prospecting for mission stations along the border of what is now the Western Transvaal. They regarded him, as many in South Africa still do, as a *Kaffir-boetie* or Kaffir-lover, which means a white Uncle Tom, or one who goes along with another race at the expense of his own. Now Livingstone is certainly an African-lover: a man of love who spent his life among Africans could hardly be otherwise. He accepts the title and is proud of it:

> After a considerable time, two old men made their appearance and said they had come to enquire who I was. I replied 'I am an Englishman'. They said 'We don't know that tribe. We suppose you are a *Mzungu*, the tribe with which we have been fighting.' As I was not yet aware that the term *Mzungu* was applied to a Portuguese, and thought they meant halfcaste, I asked if the *Mzungu* had skin and hair like mine. As the Portuguese have the custom of cutting their hair close and are also somewhat darker than we are, they answered 'No: we never saw skin so white as that' and added 'Ah, you must be one of the tribe that loves the black men'. I, of course, gladly replied in the affirmative.[4]

I do not think a fair reading will find much prejudice one way or the other in Livingstone. He casts a cool eye on English, Scot, Arab, Boer, Portuguese alike and, of course, on the very varied behaviour of Africans. Each and all disgust him on occasion but his fault, if any, is generosity; criticism is never hasty, resentment quite absent. It is said he got on worse with white men than he did with blacks.[5] If so, there is no evidence for it in his books. His standards for whites were higher than those for blacks, because he considered their opportunities had been greater. He seems to have judged men impartially, making less allowance the higher their positions and the whiter their skins. When a generous person writes of people he has come to love, one ought to be on one's guard, in case his affection, given at the expense of others equally deserving, becomes disproportionate and sentimental. But Livingstone would certainly agree with Fanon, who says 'The man who adores the negro is as sick as the man who abominates him'[6]. He was above the sub-humanities of commerce and the distortions and fears of politics. He was a priest, and had he belonged to a canonizing church, I think he would have been a saint. His efforts in all his human dealings were to be like the God he served, 'no respecter of persons'.

He soon left the Great Trekkers behind and drove north towards the deepening horrors of the Central African slave trade, that 'open sore of the world', draining through Portuguese and Arab territories at Tete-Quelimane and Zanzibar. This became his moral *hate,* and the negative compass of his heart had always one point in London and the other in a Royal Naval squadron off the East African coast that should suppress slavery as effectively in the Indian Ocean as the Lagos Squadron had, since 1808, in the Atlantic.

In this matter, his thoughts were British, and it is primarily for them that he lies in Westminster Abbey. But his affection was for Africa, its loveliness, its unique and fragile ecology, the exhilaration of safari through it, the kaleidoscope of its tribes and characters, the vision of its future. 'I am no dreamer', he writes, but he was. He dreamed the ruins we inherit, though I speak of the British here, not the Afrikaners. The year, 1870, that Stanley sailed from New York in search of Livingstone was that in which Cecil Rhodes landed in Durban: and the ruins I am thinking of are the East African High Commission and the Central African Federation of Rhodes's dreams. The tragic currents that wrecked them are seen at their source in Livingstone's writings and are still of prime concern to the world. It would be fair to say that Livingstone's *love* was the civilizing of Africa. Some will recoil at this word, considering Africa has its own civilization and that all Livingstone did was help open its doors to an alien one. But it is futile to romanticize tribalism, primitive or sophisticated. There must be a culture of the heart that rises above hysteria and confrontation to a mutual sympathy. Frantz Fanon (in an early book) still speaks with the moderation that is anathema to revolutionaries and reactionaries alike but which pre-exists their crises, passes through them, and has to stitch up their wounds in the end:

I recognise I have one right alone, that of demanding human behaviour from the other . . .

I am not a prisoner of history . . . I am not the slave of the slavery that dehumanized my ancestors. The disaster of the man of colour lies in the fact that he was once enslaved. The disaster and the inhumanity of the white man lies in the fact that somewhere he has killed man.

Superiority? Inferiority? Why not the quite simple attempt to touch the other, to sense the other, to explain the other to myself?

I have no wish to be the victim of the *fraud* of a black world. My life should not be devoted to drawing up the balance-sheet of negro values.

There is no white world, there is no white ethic, any more than there is a white intelligence. There are in every part of the world men who search.[7]

Livingstone reaches this position by the short-cut of Christianity but the spirit of the two men is one, and, in the long run, the one that has to prevail among whites as well as blacks:

I hope to finish my work among those who have not been abused . . . and who still retain their natural kindness of disposition. . . . The education of the world is a terrible one and it has come down in relentless rigour on Africa from remote times. What the African will become after this hard lesson is learned is among the future developments of Providence. . . . This will be a wonderful country, and again something like what it was of old, when Zerah and Tirhaka flourished and were great.[8]

To this aspect of Livingstone, his most creative, his most contemporary and visionary, we in Southern Africa and we alone are the immediate heirs. From this point of view, and with all its implications, the positive compass of Livingstone's heart rested one foot in Kuruman and the Cape, while the other described wider and wider arcs to the north. This part of his story is neither historical nor geographical, but an existential admonition for our times, the continuous, casual revelation of the reciprocal humanity of black and white. He does not preach this: it comes, like all the best things, indirectly. How he manages it is something that can only rub off in the reading and in no other way. His flair in what we nervously call race relations is so extraordinary that I have stolen my title from another courageous and unorthodox genius and called it 'the Livingstone touch'. It is at once mysterious and extremely simple. The Africans thought Livingstone 'uncanny' but at the same time, they credited him with that mere human kindness they call *ubuntu*. He always treated people (as the Irish say, with sad irony) as if they were human beings. He himself called his practice 'diffusive philanthropy', which sounds ghastly. But it is wrong to snatch such a phrase from one who seldom philosophises. He says little, he does much. His books record action, they reflect principle. He is aware that his ideals and practices coexist with many others, to which he gives courteous hearing, even to the slavers', some of them. He thinks his way is the best and he acts accordingly, and one delights to find him quoting, in the *Last Journals*, that wisest of St. Paul's maxims, 'patient continuance in well-doing'. Perhaps his is not the only way for a world of frightened people, but it is one ignorance of which is fearfully impoverishing. It is their content of practical love, given and received in Africa, that make his books 'the precious life-blood of a master spirit, treasured up to a purpose beyond death.'

The aim of this book being to present Livingstone, not to write about him, it is a work of affection rather than scholarship. There are eight sections. The first is on his *Prose*. Then come chapters, each with its short preamble, on *Safari* through the *Black Arcady* of the *African Ecology*, with its gallery of *Chiefs and Commoners*, not overlooking (in the hour of Women's Lib) *Venus in Black*. A section on slavery, *The Open Sore*, could not be omitted, and certain extracts offer data on what has been called *The Livingstone Touch*. Apart from the chronology of his explorations at the head of *Safari*, no attempt has been made to write a biography that was even more adventurous and certainly more celebrated than these selections recount. The details are easily available in libraries. A book I have profited from with great pleasure for years, is the selection by Dr. James Macnair, published in 1954 by Dent to celebrate the centenary of the discovery of the Victoria Falls. Its title declares its emphasis — *Livingstone's Travels* — and I recommend it heartily. *The Livingstone Touch*, however, does intend to reveal the quality of a life, and I must not omit some brief account of the mould in which it was cast.

David Livingstone was a child of the Industrial Revolution. He was born, the second of three brothers, at Blantyre, near Glasgow, in 1813 (Darwin — 1809, Marx — 1812, Dickins — 1812). At ten he went to work in a cotton mill, working six days a week from 6 a.m. to 8 p.m. From 8 to 10 at night he attended the factory school — an institution the English had not thought of — and from 10 to midnight he read Latin and books of travels, science and theology. Inconceivably, he not only makes no complaint about this life (which strikes me as vile) but he glories in it. Blantyre is 'beautiful', his schoolmaster 'a blessing'. His work and studies were so absorbing that he combined them by putting his books on his spinning-jenny so that he could pick up their meaning sentence by sentence as he passed about his work in the psychedelic din of a textile factory.

This leaves two features for us to ponder. The first is the cheerful response of an apt child to conditions severe to the point of cruelty; the second is the demoralising economic conditions themselves. When Livingstone ran into a comparable socio-economic disaster in the form of slavery, he dimly perceived the parallel, and on several occasions (in very muted tones) compares the common 'degradation' of the industrial poor in Britain and the slaves in Africa. But he was too uncritically committed to the Protestant ethic to pursue the hint. Socially, there is a trace of the Victorian lickspittle about him that surprises in a man so independent and outspoken. Stracheyan hindsight, however, is not really profitable with the Victorians. They were mistaken but they were powerfully and genuinely mistaken. Livingstone was not a Marxist with a lie in the soul, but a man cast in the stern mould of the Reformation in general and the thirteenth chapter of *Romans* in particular:

> Let every soul be subject unto the higher powers. For there is no power but of God: the powers that be are ordained of God, etc.

We have the right to criticise this doctrine but it is trifling to ignore its power in the world. The Victorian in Livingstone makes him neither less nor more than us, just different. He could not grasp that the system his talents alone enabled him to scramble out of was 'degrading' nine out of ten of his fellows. To him, an Africa full of Blantyres and decorous missions, running northwards from Kuruman to the Congo, along the great plateau of Zambia into the highlands of Tanzania, was a beatific vision. We may laugh but, if we wholly dismiss Livingstone with the dream of his times, we throw out the baby with the bathwater.

On Sundays, the Livingstone family used to walk some miles from Blantyre to worship in the kirk of the Independents in Hamilton. Presumably it was on the way back that David, with his brothers or alone (which he rather preferred), found time for the excursions that built up his collection of rocks, fossils and herbs. No doubt (as I. M. Fletcher suggests[9]) a poached trout or salmon frequently graced the Livingstones' table as a result of his rambles. To help classify his specimens he read all the scientific books he could find, harrassed by his mother on the one hand, anxious to get him off to bed before midnight, and his father on the other, who was liable to thrash him for not reading theology. On the whole, however, his home life, if strenuous, seems to have been very happy. He writes more warmly of his father than his mother, whom he simply mentions as 'an anxious housewife striving to make both ends meet'. His father died while Livingstone was finishing his first journey down the Zambezi in 1856. 'I revere his memory', he wrote, and travelled 'expecting no greater pleasure than sitting by our cottage fire and telling him my travels'.

Blantyre was a conventional Scottish village but its two thousand inhabitants were of a stock that has made a rich contribution to Southern Africa and to the world at large, and Livingstone's remarks on them are quaint and sturdy:

> Looking back now on that life of toil, I cannot but feel thankful that it formed such a material part of my early education – and, were it possible, I should like to begin life over again in the same lowly style, and to pass through the same hardy training.
>
> Time and travel have not effaced the feelings of respect I imbibed for the inhabitants of my native village. For morality, honesty and intelligence, they were in general good specimens of the Scottish poor. . . . Much intelligent interest was felt by the villagers on all public questions and they furnish a proof that . . . education did not render them an unsafe portion of the popula-

tion. They felt kindly towards each other and much respected those of the neighbouring gentry who, like the late Lord Douglas, placed some confidence in their sense of honour. Through the kindness of that nobleman, the poorest of us could stroll at pleasure over the ancient domains of Bothwell and other spots hallowed by associations of which our school-books and local traditions made us well aware — and few of us could view the memorials of the past without feeling that these carefully-kept monuments were our own. The masses of the working people of Scotland have read history, and are no revolutionary levellers. They rejoice in the memories of Wallace and Bruce ... who are still revered as the champions of freedom. And while foreigners imagine that we want the spirit only to overturn capitalist and arisocracy, we are content to respect our laws till we can change them, and hate those stupid revolutions which might sweep away time-honoured institutions dear alike to rich and poor.[10]

Certain men — one a veteran of the Napoleonic Wars in Spain — and certain books — especially those that showed 'that religion and science are not hostile but friendly to each other' — kept alive religious tendencies that might have been killed by his father's fanaticism. The fresh wave of confusion that comes to most teenagers was transcended by powerful identifications with Christ and (I would guess) St. Paul. In his middle teens, at any rate, and 'in the glow of love that Christ inspires, I ... resolved to devote my life to the alleviation of human misery'. Therefore, as soon as his wages could cover his fees, he began to walk nine miles each way to winter classes at the University of Glasgow. It was 1836, he was in his early twenties, and in South Africa the ox-waggons were about to roll out of Grahamstown to begin the Great Trek. Two years later, in London to discuss a missionary future in China, he came across his father-in-law-to-be, Robert Moffat, drumming up support for his work among the Tswana: and with 'the smoke of a thousand villages north of Kuruman' in his eyes, Livingstone returned to Glasgow, was ordained, took his diploma in medicine, and sailed in 1840 for the Cape.

1   LJ, Vol. II, pp. 314–319. The tree perished but the part of the trunk with the inscription was brought to London in 1900 and is at the headquarters of the Royal Geographical Society. (Coupland, p. 249.)
2   LJ, Vol. II, p. 344.
3   MT 117.
4   MT 593. The incident took place on the Zambezi, near Zumbo.
5   See Kirk on the Zambezi, Sir R. Coupland, Clarendon Press, Oxford, 1928.
6   Fanon, p. 8.
7   Fanon, pp. 163–165.
8   LJ 11 November 1870.
9   Fletcher, p. 6.
10   MT 6.

CHAPTER 2

The African Cobbett

Livingstone's touch must endure because he writes well enough to rank as an artist. Not always: he has characteristic faults and he can write badly. At the same time a current of excellence runs through all his pages and often clears their Victorian sedge in passages of brilliant, shallow simplicity that are the very staple of English prose. His qualities do not excite today's academic tastes, which incline to the Alexandrian,[1] but they continue a pure, old and durable tradition.

Here is a paragraph of typically good Livingstone:

We passed through the patch of the tsetse, which exists between Linyanti and Shesheke, by night. The majority of our company went on by daylight, in order to prepare our beds. Sekeletu and I, with about forty young men, waited outside the tsetse till dark. We then went forward, and about ten o'clock it became so pitchy dark that both horses and men were completely blinded. The lightning spread over the sky, forming eight or ten branches at

11

a time, in shape exactly like those of a tree. This, with great volumes of sheet lightning, enabled us at times to see the whole country. The intervals between the flashes were so densely dark, as to convey the idea of stone-blindness. The horses trembled, cried out, and turned round, as if searching for each other, and every new flash revealed the men taking different directions, laughing and stumbling against each other. The thunder was of that tremendously loud kind only to be heard in tropical countries, and which, friends in India have assured me, is louder in Africa than any they have ever heard elsewhere. Then came a pelting rain, which completed our confusion. After the intense heat of the day, we soon felt miserably cold, and turned aside to a fire we saw in the distance. This had been made by some people on their march; for this path is seldom without numbers of strangers passing to and fro from the capital. My clothing having gone on, I lay down on the cold ground, expecting to spend a miserable night, but Sekeletu kindly covered me with his own blanket and lay uncovered himself. I was much affected by this little act of genuine kindness.[2]

This is very simple prose, unselfconscious and slightly loose – the two 'each others' in the middle, for instance. The simplicity is that of basic English, in which only eight percent also of words have over two syllables. I have often sampled the sentence length of contemporary English journalism and found it to be around twenty words, just Livingstone's average here. Clearly he keeps close to the grain of his medium.

The Livingstone staple will be found to be plain words, short sentences, unpretentious, easy rhythms, quick, apt similes. He can write with such a perfect ear as this:

As I sat in the rain a little tree-frog, about half an inch long, leaped on to a grassy leaf, and began a tune as loud as that of many birds, and very sweet; it was surprising to hear so much music out of so small a musician.

Or with this kind of precision:

The under north-west stratum of clouds is composed of fluffy cottony masses, the edges spread out as if on an electrical machine – the upper or south-east is of broad fields like striated cat's hair.

And with this quiet although never very enterprising elasticity:

We observed among the people of Katema a love for singing-birds. One pretty little songster, named 'cabazo', a species of canary, is kept in very neatly made cages, having traps on the top to entice its still free companions. On asking why they kept them in confinement, 'Because they sing sweetly', was the answer. They feed them on the *lotsa,* of which great quantities are cultivated as food for man, and these canaries plague the gardeners here, very much in the same way as our sparrows do at home.

Everything is bright, clear, sharp and, thanks to Africa, strange:

> Their songs are intermixed with several curious abrupt notes unlike any-
> thing English. One utters deliberately 'peek, pak, pok'; another has a single
> note like a stroke on a violin-string. The *mokwa reza* gives forth a screaming
> set of notes like our blackbird when disturbed, then concludes with what the
> natives say is 'pula, pula' (rain, rain), but more like 'weep, weep, weep'. Then
> we have the loud cry of francolins, the 'pumpuru, pumpuru' of turtle-doves,
> and the 'chiken, chiken, chik, churr, churr' of the honey-guide. Occasionally
> near villages we have a kind of mocking bird, imitating the calls of domestic
> fowls. These African birds have not been wanting in song, they have only
> lacked poets to sing their praises.

One shares in his books the outer life of an observant, enterprising, brave,
simple, compassionate man. Of the man within one shares nothing but the pale
sometimes pawky humour, the unquestioned faith, the expected response to
good and bad. Few conflicts are shared, few intimacies broached. That there
was an inward life is certain but it was for private prayer not public prose.
When his heart is sore with disappointment, he is not emotionally indulgent:
the steady reel of facts is hardly interrupted:

> ... being now within three miles of the end of the Lake, we could see the
> whole plainly. There we first saw the Shire emerge, and there also we first
> gazed on the broad waters of Nyassa. Many hopes have been disappointed
> here. Far down on the right bank of the Zambezi lies the dust of her whose
> death changed all my future prospects; and now, instead of a check being
> given to the slave-trade by lawful commerce on the Lake, slave-dhows
> prosper. ... It is impossible not to regret the loss of good Bishop Mackenzie,
> who sleeps far down the Shire, and with him all hope of the Gospel being
> introduced into Central Africa. The silly abandonment of all the advantages
> of the Shire route by the Bishop's successor I shall ever bitterly deplore, but
> all will come right some day, though I may not live to participate in the joy,
> or even see the commencement of better times.
> In the evening we reached to village of Cherekalongwa, on the brook Pam-
> chololo [3] ...

Prose is furthest from poetry and therefore most itself when it does not
charge the word 'with the divers states of our consciousness'[4] but keeps as
close as may be to a one-to-one, word-thing, word-act basis; when it conveys
common experience rather than 'more delicate modes';[4] and when it follows the
habits of simple, practical, purposeful, everyday speech. Such a style is cen-
trally Cobbett's;[5] although there is no mention of him, Livingstone was seventeen when *Rural Rides* appeared, and he may well have read it.
The resemblances between the two, although limited, are central. Livingstone lacks Cobbett's dauntless loquacity, he is taut where Cobbett is eruptive
and, of course, he has a piety foreign to Cobbett, which some cannot stomach.

But when they are simply depicting, as Livingstone usually is, the two men share an appetite for detail, an equal briskness of pace, and a certain happy extroversion. When Hazlitt says that Cobbett 'places us in the same situation with himself and makes us see all that he does', he might have been writing of Livingstone. *Rural Rides* and *Missionary Travels* have much in common. Both are documentary, both have practical aims, both are confronted by a monstrous injustice. It is the latter that differentiates the two most: the System that whips Cobbett into rage is the slavery that makes Livingstone grim and laconic. To call Livingstone the African Cobbett is not to ignore historical and temperamental differences but to stress technical affinities and, of course, to suggest a revaluation, for Cobbett's prose is justly admired.

Once linked with Cobbett, Livingstone's place is clear. He belongs at his best – and he is commonly close to it – to the oldest and central tradition of English prose, not only the factual prose of ordinary journalism but that of chronicles and logs, with their transparency and impersonality, and of diaries and letters, with their trust in colloquial directness, their tendency 'to express on paper exactly what one would say to the same person by word of mouth'.[6] The style has the balance natural to its precipitancy and tolerates looseness as the price of uncalculating sincerity. Its great practitioners – Tindale, Bunyan, Swift, Defoe and, in this century, Orwell, Hemingway, Hersey, for example – are aware of its merits and cunningly heighten its purity and/or innocence. Livingstone is not up to this and when he polishes he brings in emotionalism and a slight stiffness. But he has a right to be his Victorian self, it is amusing; and the core is sound.

To his temperament and circumstances two influences must be added inclining his prose always to simplicity. He was a doctor and as conscious as Chekhov of the virtues of a medical education. Hence his style is not only plain, brisk and earnest but 'close, naked, natural', aspiring, as Sprat put it in 1666, to the 'clear, simple prose' of the best science.

A famous entry in the *Last Journals* runs

> 3rd October 1871: I read the whole Bible through four times whilst I was in Manyuema.

This habit formed Livingstone's prose as well as his life. Under the dust of archaism there is in the Bible a style of timeless energy, economy and music. This does not rub off directly on Livingstone's writing – his manner is more scientific than Biblical – so much as give it a quality of driving, self-sacrificing simplicity that powers the best prose as well as, perhaps, the best lives.

The one author Livingstone refers to several times is Defoe. He had even read *Captain Singleton* and was alert to catch any reference to an original for this hero in Central Africa. Comparison quickly reveals the longer sinew of Defoe's sentences (as of Cobbett's) but the limpidity common to all three is usually prominent.

I suspect Livingstone idolised Robinson Crusoe less for the prose in which he is presented than for his self-sufficiency and ingenuity: he says life on an

African mission station must be something of a Robinson Crusoe existence. His own resourcefulness on the march with his Makololo Man Fridays reminds one of Crusoe's, and occasionally the resemblance in content of the prose, no doubt quite fortuitous, is amusing:

> My losses are more than made up by Mr. Stanley, who has given me twelve bales of calico; nine loads = fourteen and a half bags of beads; thirty-eight coils of brass wire; a tent; boat; bath; cooking pots; twelve copper sheets; air beds; trousers; jackets, &c. Indeed, I am again quite set up, and as soon as he can send men, not slaves, from the coast I go to my work with a fair prospect of finishing it.
>
> *19th February.* – Rest. Receive 38 coils of brass wire from Mr. Stanley, $14\frac{1}{2}$ bags of beads, 12 copper sheets, a strong canvas tent, boat-trousers, nine loads of calico, a bath, cooking pots, a medicine chest, a good lot of tools, tacks, screw nails, copper nails, books, medicines, paper, tar, many cartridges, and some shot.
>
> *20th February.* – To my great joy I got four flannel shirts from Agnes, and I was delighted to find that two pairs of fine English boots had most considerately been sent by my friend Mr. Waller. Mr. Stanley and I measured the calico and found that $733\frac{3}{4}$ yards were wanting, also two frasilahs of samsam, and one case of brandy.

This extract is from the *Last Journals* (1872) and the prose is in a relatively raw state. Livingstone was a compulsive recorder. He carried small, hard-back notebooks in his pocket, using them for instant annotations and thumbnail sketches as freely as a modern would use a Leica. On Sundays and in periods of enforced leisure on safari he wrote up his notes 'in large, strongly bound, locked volumes of the size of a family Bible'.[7] A third stage of polishing supervened before publication.

Before venturing on his first book, he was tempted to employ a ghost. 'Greater smoothness of diction, and a saving of time might have been secured by the employment of a person accustomed to compilation, but my journals having been kept for my own private purposes, no one else could have made use of them or have entered with intelligence into the circumstances in which I was placed in Africa.' So, 'in the absence of any excellence in literary composition', Livingstone committed himself to a book of 687 pages, and might be excused a note of weariness and petulance at the end of it: 'I think I would rather cross Africa again than write another book'. This should not deceive us. He was a tireless correspondent, of whom his younger daughter said 'I can only remember him as always writing letters'. He rose from his second book – 608 pages – cheered by the success of his first and by 'the conviction that very many readers will receive this narrative with the kindly consideration and allowances of friends'. The preface to the second book has an altogether new vehemence, acerbity and self-confidence, and in its introduction he allows us a glimpse of his literary judgement when he incorporates the journal of his brother, Charles, who had accompanied him, 'for the sake of the freshness which usually attaches to first impressions'. The same criterion must have operated when he drew upon his own notebooks for his journals, and journals for his published works; and to this taste for freshness we owe all that is best in him. So when he says he finds 'composition irksome and laborious' we should take it with a pinch of salt. He read hard, wrote voluminously, and reveals certain standards: in spite of his disclaimers it is fair to judge him as an author.

Naturally the selections that form the bulk of this book are from good Livingstone and as far as possible from the best. If his style, his content, his message, lead to a desire to read his books in full, then a mild warning must be entered. He excels in letting facts speak for themselves. When these facts imply emotions, and sometimes, in the context of his adventurous life, deep emotions, the outcome is a native understatement of the over-experience quite admirable. The account of the famous meeting with Stanley is an example, to which Stanley's own version makes an interesting contrast. But Livingstone's success often seems in inverse ratio to his effort. Two situations regularly tempt him to conscious literary endeavour and then you almost hear his heavy breathing and observe a certain fatuous Victorian satisfaction in the result. The first is when he feels he must achieve the emotional level he feels an incident deserves. The result is a supercharge of sentiment that spoils the strength of such an account as this of the near loss of his children's lives in Northern Botswana, east of the Okavango, in 1851:

> Shobo gave us no hope of water in less than a month. Providentially, how-
> ever, we came sooner than we expected to some supplies of rain-water in a
> chain of pools. It is impossible to convey an idea of the dreary scene on
> which we entered after leaving this spot: the only vegetation was a low scrub
> in deep sand; not a bird or insect enlivened the landscape. It was without
> exception the most uninviting prospect I ever beheld; and, to make matters
> worse, our guide Shobo wandered on the second day. We coaxed him on at
> night, but he went to all points of the compass on the trails of elephants
> which had been here in the rainy season; and then would sit down in the
> path, and in his broken Sichuána say, 'No water, all country only; – Shobo
> sleeps; – he breaks down; – country only;' – and then coolly curl himself up
> and go to sleep. The oxen were terribly fatigued and thirsty; and on the
> morning of the fourth day Shobo, after professing ignorance of everything,
> vanished altogether. We went on in the direction in which we last saw him,
> and about eleven o'clock began to see birds; then the trail of a rhinoceros.
> At this we unyoked the oxen, and they, apparently knowing the sign, rushed
> along to find the water in the river Mabábe, which comes from the Tamu-
> nak'le, and lay to the west of us. The supply of water in the waggons had
> been wasted by one of our servants, and by the afternoon only a small
> portion remained for the children. This was a bitterly anxious night; and
> next morning the less there was of water, the more thirsty the little rogues
> became. The idea of their perishing before our eyes was terrible. It would
> almost have been a relief to me to have been reproached with being the
> entire cause of the catastrophe, but not one syllable of upbraiding was

uttered by their mother, though the tearful eye told the agony within. In the afternoon of the fifth day, to our inexpressible relief, some of the men returned with a supply of that fluid of which we had never before felt the true value.

I find the often-quoted accounts of the Victoria Falls marred by emotionalism and have omitted them for this reason.

Livingstone's other temptation is to be funny. He has a dry wit, by-product of his reserve, but when over-writing and forced humour combine, the effect is disastrous:

> There must be something in the appearance of white men, frightfully repulsive to the unsophisticated natives of Africa; for, on entering villages previously unvisited by Europeans, if we met a child coming quietly and unsuspectingly towards us, the moment he raised his eyes, and saw the men in trousers, he would take to his heels in an agony of terror, such as we might feel if we met a live Egyptian mummy at the door of the British Museum. Alarmed by the child's outcries, the mother rushes out of her hut, but darts back again at the first glimpse of the same fearful apparition. Dogs turn tail, and scour off in dismay; and hens, abandoning their chickens, fly screaming to the tops of the houses. The peaceful village becomes a scene of confusion and hubbub, until calmed by the laughing assurance of our men, that white people do not eat black folks; a joke having oftentimes greater influence in Africa than solemn assertions. Some of our young swells, on entering an African village, might experience a collapse of self-inflation, at the sight of all the pretty girls fleeing from them, as from hideous cannibals; or by witnessing the mammas holding naughty children away from them, and saying 'Be good, or I shall call the white man to bite you'.

At times his fault is syntactic and we seem to be reading a paragraph of the factory school's star pupil, eager to show off his new constructions. He is prone, especially, to a dreary Latinate participle:

> ... in a pleasant valley we met some of the people of the country, who were miserably poor and hungry. The women were gathering wild fruits in the woods. A young man, having consented for two yards of cotton cloth to show us a short path to the cataract, led us up a steep hill to a village perched on the edge of one of its precipices; a thunderstorm coming on at the time, the headman invited us to take shelter in a hut until it had passed. Our guide having informed him of what he knew and conceived to be our object, was favoured in return with a long reply in well-sounding blank verse; at the end of every line the guide, who listened with deep attention, responded with a grunt, which soon became so ludicrous that our men burst into a loud laugh.

It is rare for facts to overwhelm him but with African proper names he some-

times achieves self-parody that from Edward Lear we should accept as happy
nonsense:

> All the Arabs are loud in his praises, but they have a bad opinion of the
> Queen Moäri or Ngombé or Kifuta. The Garaganza people at Katanga
> killed a near relative of Casembe and herself, and when the event happened,
> Fungafunga, one of the Garaganza or Banyamwezi being near the spot, fled
> and came to the Mofwé: he continued his flight as soon as it was dark
> without saying anything to anyone, until he got north to Kabiuré. The
> Queen and Casembe suspected Mpamari of complicity with the Baynyam-
> wezi, and believed that Fungafunga had communicated the news to him
> before fleeing further. A tumult was made; Mpamari's eldest son was killed;
> and he was plundered of all his copper, ivory, and slaves: the Queen loudly
> demanded his execution, but Casembe restrained his people as well as he
> was able and it is for this injury that he now professes to be sorry.

A complicating feature of his second book, *The Zambezi and its Tributaries*, is the tacit interweaving of Charles Livingstone's journals. David's
horrors, like his felicities, have a transparent honesty of purpose about them,
but such calculated stylism, such smooth artifice as this does not strike me as
his: the scene is the Zambezi delta:

> For sixty or seventy miles before reaching Mazaro, the scenery is tame
> and uninteresting. On either hand is a dreary uninhabited expanse, of the
> same level grassy plains, with merely a few trees to relieve the painful mono-
> tony. The round green top of the stately palm-tree looks at a distance, when
> its grey trunk cannot be seen, as though hung in mid-air. Many flocks of
> busy sandmartins, which here, and as far south as the Orange River, do not
> migrate, have perforated the banks two or three feet horizontally, in order to
> place their nests at the ends, and are now chasing on restless wing the
> myriads of tropical insects. The broad river has many low islands, on which
> are seen various kinds of waterfowl, such as geese, spoonbills, herons, and
> flamingoes. Repulsive crocodiles, as with open jaws they sleep and bask in
> the sun on the low banks, soon catch the sound of the revolving paddles and
> glide quietly into the stream. The hippopotamus, having selected some still
> reach of the river to spend the day, rises from the bottom, where he has been
> enjoying his morning bath after the labours of the night on shore, blows a
> puff of spray out of his nostrils, shakes the water out of his ears, puts his
> enormous snout up straight and yawns, sounding a loud alarm to the rest of
> the herd, with notes as of a monster bassoon.

There is an ant-piece in this section from the *Missionary Travels* and therefore free from any possible contamination by Charles, that sums up the failings
of Livingstone's prose – tactlessness of vocabulary *(seriatim, rencontre)*,
Latinism in word and construction, superfluities, literariness, archness, jocu-
larity, and adjectives that come in like Victorian hands, jabbing the implicit.

And yet the very facts take over, force themselves through the style, and capture the interest.

It is not unnatural to suspect that, when these faults occur, Livingstone is over-dressing his field notes to meet his starchy Victorian public. I have concluded with two continuous passages from the *Last Journals*, therefore, as examples of his field work. When it is possible to compare his raw notes with their worked-up form in official correspondence the inherent simplicity always carries through and it is evident that his stylistic inflation is at least not caused by social pretentiousness. Livingstone is a good but uncritical writer: his lapses are as naive as his natural level is high. It is as well to be prepared for them and the previous specimens may be taken as prophylactics against disappointment for any who intend to take the pleasure of reading him further than the selections that follow.

The four volumes themselves are so protracted, so full of vitality in observation and action, that they correspond to the journeys they describe. Reading them through is a mixed experience. One cannot dodge the naïvetés of cliché and pietism, the failures of rhythmic control, the injections of emotion as if in shame of being simple. But the prose is always adequate, always with momentum, and often of a purity I rank with the best. It is like the surface of Central Africa, predominantly high, flat, thin-aired and bright, with sog, peak and jungle. It reflects the fitness of his relentlessly driven body, and the zest that can still grip anyone confronting the wilderness, wherever it remains:

> The mere animal pleasure of travelling in a wild unexplored country is very great. When on lands of a couple of thousand feet elevation, brisk exercise imparts elasticity to the muscles, fresh and healthy blood circulates through the brain, the mind works well, the eye is clear, the step is firm . . . The effect on a man whose heart is in the right place is that the mind is made more self-reliant: it becomes more confident of its own resources — there is greater presence of mind. The body is soon well-knit; the muscles of the limbs grow as hard as a board, and seem to have no fat; the countenance is bronzed, and there is no dyspepsia . . .
>
> LJ 26 March 1866

A brief editorial note seems honest. I have not hesitated to make minor alterations in Livingstone's text, to modernise a word occasionally — I did feel that *balls* should be changed to *bullets* sometimes — to telescope the narrative, to clarify a passage torn from its context or very rarely indeed, to touch out a flaw which I felt embarrassed the writing. In the whole section following, apart from a cut or two, only half a dozen words have been changed: it is 99,9 per cent pure Livingstone. I have arranged the selections from short to long, and I hope they will tickle the appetite like one of those refreshing salads which the Americans still begin their main meals with, as the British used to long ago. The Livingstone touch is not only in the content but the style: if he is a suitable and at his best a model writer, it is because the style is so thoroughly the man.

8th July. – Hard travelling through a depopulated country. The trees are about the size of hop-poles with abundance of tall grass; the soil is sometimes a little sandy, at other times that reddish, clayey sort which yields native grain so well. The rock seen uppermost is often a ferruginous conglomerate, lying on granite rocks. The gum-copal tree is here a mere bush, and no digging takes place for the gum: it is called *Mchenga,* and yields gum when wounded, as also bark, cloth, and cordage when stripped. Mountain masses are all around us; we sleep at Linata mountain.

LJ 7 Jul 1866

Although we were in doubt as to our reception by Mpende, I could not help admiring the beautiful country as we passed along. There is, indeed, only a small part under cultivation in this fertile valley, but my mind naturally turned to the comparison of it with Kolobeng, where we waited anxiously during months for rain, and only a mere thunder-shower followed. I shall never forget the dry, hot east winds of that region; the yellowish, sultry, cloudless sky; the grass and all the plants drooping from drought, the cattle lean, the people dispirited, and our own hearts sick from hope deferred. There we often heard in the dead of the night the shrill whistle of the rain-doctor calling for rain that would not come, while here we listened to the rolling thunder by night and beheld the swelling valleys adorned with plenty by day. We have rain almost daily, and everything is beautifully fresh and green. The hills are covered with forests, and there is often a long line of fleecy cloud lying on them about midway up; they are very beautiful.

MT 590

The direction of the prevailing wind of this region is well marked on the islands in Lake Bangweolo: the trunks are bent away from the south-east, and the branches on that side are stunted or killed; while those on the north-west run out straight and make the trees appear lopsided. The same bend away from the south-east is seen on all exposed situations, as in the trees covering the brow of a hill. At Kizinga, which is higher than the Lake, the trees are covered with lichens, chiefly on the south-east sides, and on the upper surfaces of branches, running away horizontally to or from the north-west. Plants and trees, which elsewhere in Africa grow only on the banks of streams and other damp localities, are seen flourishing all over the country: the very rocks are covered with lichens, and their crevices with ferns.

LJ 29 Aug 1868

We met with native travellers occasionally. Those on a long journey carry with them a sleeping-mat and wooden pillow, cooking-pot and bag of meal, pipe and tobacco-pouch, a knife, bow, and arrows, and two small sticks, of from two to three feet in length, for making fire, when obliged to sleep away from human habitations. Dry wood is always abundant, and they get fire by the following method. A notch is cut in one of the sticks, which, with a close-grained outside, has a small core of pith, and this notched stick is laid horizontally on a knife-blade on the ground; the operator squatting, places his great toes on each end to keep all steady, and taking the other wand, which is of very hard wood cut to a blunt point, fits it into the notch at right angles; the upright wand is made to spin rapidly backwards and forwards between the palms of the hands, drill fashion, and at the same time is pressed downwards; the friction, in the course of a minute or so, ignites portions of the pith of the notched stick, which, rolling over like live charcoal on the knife-blade, are lifted into a handful of fine dry grass, and carefully blown, by waving backwards and forwards in the air. It is hard work for the hands to procure fire by this process, as the vigorous drilling and downward pressure requisite soon blister soft palms.

ZT 174

The shields are made of hides partially dried in the sun, and then beaten with hammers until they are stiff and dry. Two broad belts of a differently-coloured skin are sewed into them longitudinally, and sticks inserted to make them rigid and not liable to bend easily. The shield is a great protection in their way of fighting with spears, but they also trust largely to their agility in springing aside from the coming javelin. The shield assists when so many spears are thrown that it is impossible not to receive some of them. Their spears are light javelins; and, judging from what I have seen them do in elephant-hunting, I believe, when they have room to make a run and discharge them with the aid of the jerk of stopping, they can throw them between forty and fifty yards. They give them an upward direction in the discharge, so that they come down on the object with accelerated force. I saw a man who in battle had received one in the shin; the excitement of the moment prevented his feeling any pain; but, when the battle was over, the blade was found to have split the bone, and become so impacted in the cleft that no force could extract it. It was necessary to take an axe and press the split bone asunder before the weapon could be taken out.

MT 193

Pottery seems to have been known to the Africans from the remotest times, for fragments are found everywhere, even among the oldest fossil bones in the country. Their pots for cooking, holding water and beer, are made by the women, and the form is preserved by the eye alone, for no sort of machine is ever used. A foundation or bottom is first laid, and a piece of bone or bamboo used to scrape the clay or to smooth over the pieces which are added to increase the roundness; the vessel is then left a night: the next morning a piece is added to the rim – as the air is dry several rounds may be added – and all is then carefully smoothed off; afterwards it is thoroughly sun-dried. A light fire of dried cow-dung, or corn-stalks, or straw, and grass with twigs, is made in a hole in the ground for the final baking. Ornaments are made on these pots of black lead, or before being hardened by the sun they are ornamented for a couple or three inches near the rim, all the tracery being in imitation of plaited basket work. LJ 24 Jun 1866

St. Paul de Loanda has been a very considerable city, but is now in a state of decay. It contains about twelve thousand inhabitants, most of whom are people of colour. There are various evidences of its former magnificence, especially two cathedrals, one of which, once a Jesuit college, is now converted into a workshop; and in passing the other we saw with sorrow a number of oxen feeding within its stately walls. Three forts continue in a good state of repair. Many large stone houses are to be found. The palace of the governor and government offices are commodious structures; but nearly all the houses of the native inhabitants are of wattle and daub. Trees are planted all over the town for the sake of shade; and the city presents an imposing appearance from the sea. It is provided with an effective police; and the custom-house department is extremely well managed. All parties agree in representing the Portuguese authorities as both polite and obliging; and if ever any inconvenience is felt by strangers visiting the port, it must be considered the fault of the system, and not of the men.

MT 394

It is remarkable that I never met with an Albino in crossing Africa, though, from accounts published by the Portuguese, I was led to expect that they were held in favour as doctors by certain chiefs. I saw several in the south: one at Kuruman is a full-grown woman, and a man having this peculiarity of skin, was met with in the colony. Their bodies are always blistered on exposure to the sun, as the skin is more tender than that of the blacks. The Kuruman woman lived some time at Kolobeng, and generally had on her bosom and shoulders the remains of large blisters. She was most anxious to be made black, but nitrate of silver, taken internally, did not produce its usual effect. During the time I resided at Mabotsa, a woman came to the station with a fine boy, an Albino. The father had ordered her to throw him away, but she clung to her offspring for many years. He was remarkably intelligent for his age. The pupil of the eye was of a pink colour, and the eye itself was unsteady in vision. The hair, or rather wool, was yellow, and the features were those common among the Bechuanas. After I left the place, the mother is said to have become tired of living apart from the father, who refused to have her while she retained the son. She took him out one day, and killed him close to the village of Mabotsa, and nothing was done to her by the authorities. From having met with no Albinos in Londa, I suspect they are there also put to death. We saw one dwarf only in Londa, and brands on him showed he had once been a slave; and there is one dwarf woman at Linyanti. The general absence of deformed persons, is partly owing to their destruction in infancy, and partly to the mode of life being a natural one, so far as ventilation and food are concerned. In several tribes a child which is said to 'tlola', transgress, is put to death. 'Tlolo', or transgression, is ascribed to several curious cases. A child who cut the upper front teeth before the under, was always put to death among the Bakaa, and, I believe, also among the Bakwains. In some tribes, a case of twins renders one of them liable to death; and an ox, which, while lying in the pen, beats the ground with its tail, is treated in the same way. It is thought to be calling death to visit the tribe. When I was coming through Londa, my men carried a great number of fowls, of a larger breed than any they had at home. If one crowed before midnight, it had been guilty of 'tlolo', and was killed. The men often carried them sitting on their guns, and, if one began to crow in a forest, the owner would give it a beating, by way of teaching it not to be guilty of crowing at unseasonable hours.

MT 576

At the Loangwa of Zumbo we came to a party of hereditary hippopotamus hunters, called Makombwé. They follow no other occupation, but when their game is getting scanty at one spot they remove to some other part of the Loangwa, Zambesi, or Shiré, and build temporary huts on an island, where their women cultivate patches: the flesh of the animals they kill is eagerly exchanged by the more settled people for grain. They are not stingy, and are everywhere welcome guests. I never heard of any fraud in dealing, or that they had been guilty of an outrage on the poorest: their chief characteristic is their courage. Their hunting is the bravest thing I ever saw. Each canoe is manned by two men; they are long light craft, scarcely half an inch in thickness, about eighteen inches beam, and from eighteen to twenty feet long. They are formed for speed, and shaped somewhat like our racing boats. Each man uses a broad short paddle, and as they guide the canoe slowly down stream to a sleeping hippopotamus not a single ripple is raised on the smooth water; they look as if holding in their breath, and communicate by signs only. As they come near the prey the harpooner in the bow lays down his paddle and rises slowly up, and there he stands erect, motionless, and eager, with the long-handled weapon poised at arm's length above his head, till coming close to the beast he plunges it with all his might in towards the heart. During this exciting feat he has to keep his balance exactly. His neighbour in the stern at once backs his paddle, the harpooner sits down, seizes his paddle, and backs too to escape: the animal surprised and wounded seldom returns the attack at this stage of the hunt. The next stage, however, is full of danger.

The barbed blade of the harpoon is secured by a long and very strong rope wound round the handle: it is intended to come out of its socket, and while the iron head is firmly fixed in the animal's body the rope unwinds and the handle floats on the surface. The hunter next goes to the handle and hauls on the rope till he knows that he is right over the beast: when he feels the line suddenly slacken he is prepared to deliver another harpoon the instant the hippo's enormous jaws appear with a terrible grunt above the water. The backing by the paddles is again repeated, but hippo often assaults the canoe, crunches it with his great jaws as easily as a pig would a bunch of asparagus, or shivers it with a kick by its hind foot. Deprived of their canoe the gallant comrades instantly dive and swim to the shore under water: they say that the infuriated beast looks for them on the surface, and being below they escape his sight. When caught by many harpoons the crews of several canoes seize the handles and drag him hither and thither till, weakened by loss of blood, he succumbs.

I have seen our dragoon officers perform fencing and managing their horses so dexterously that every muscle seemed trained to its fullest power and efficiency, and perhaps had they been brought up as Makombwé they might have equalled their daring and consummate skill: but we have no sport, except perhaps Indian tiger shooting, requiring the courage and coolness this enterprise demands. The danger may be appreciated if one remembers that no sooner is blood shed in the water than all the crocodiles below are immediately drawn up stream by the scent, and are ready to act the part of thieves in a London crowd, or worse.

LJ 7 Jul 1872

25th July. – Having paid the canoe-men amply for four days with beads, and given the chief a hoe and beads too, we embarked at 11.40 a.m. in a fine canoe, 45 feet long, 4 feet deep, and 4 feet broad. The waves were high, but the canoe was very dry, and five stout men propelled her quickly towards an opening in Lifungé Island, on our S.E. Here we stopped to wood, and I went away to look at the island, which had the marks of hippopotami and a species of jackal on it: it had hard wiry grass, some flowers, and a species of Capparidaceous tree. The trees showed well the direction of the prevailing wind to be south-east, for the branches on that side were stunted or killed, while those on the north-west ran out straight, and made the trees appear, as sailors say, lopsided: the trunks too were bent that way.

The canoe-men now said that they would start, then that they would sleep here, because we could not reach the Island Mpabala before dark, and would not get a hut. I said that it would be sleeping out of doors in either case, so they went. We could see the island called Kisi on our east, apparently a double island, about 15 miles off, and the tops of the trees barely visible on Mpabala on our south-east. It was all sea horizon on our south and north, between Lifungé and Mpabala, and between Lifungé and Kisi. We could not go to Kisi, because, as the canoe-men told us, they had stolen their canoe thence. Though we decided to go, we remained awhile to let the sea go down. A hammerhead's nest on one of the trees was fully four feet high. Coarse rushes show the shoals near the islands. Only one shell was seen on the shores. The canoe ships much less water in this surf than our boat did in that of Nyassa. The water is of a deep sea-green colour, probably from the reflection of the fine white sand of the bottom; we saw no part having the deep dark blue of Nyassa, and conjecture that the depth is not great; but I had to leave our line when Amoda absconded. On Kisi we observed a dark square mass, which at first I took to be a low hill: it turned out to be a mass of trees (probably the place of sepulture, for the graveyards are always untouched), and shows what a dense forest this land would become were it not for the influence of men.

We reached Mpabala after dark. It was bitterly cold, from the amount of moisture in the air. I asked a man who came to see what the arrival was, for a hut; he said, 'Do strangers require huts, or ask for them at night?' he then led us to the public place of meeting, called Nsaka, which is a large shed, with planks around and open spaces between, instead of walls; here we cooked a little porridge, and ate it, then I lay down on one side, with the canoe-men and my attendants at the fire in the middle, and was soon asleep, and dreamed that I had apartments in Mivart's Hotel. This made me feel much amused next day, for I never dream unless I am ill, or going to be ill; and of all places in the world, I never thought of Mivart's Hotel in my waking moments; a freak of the fancy surely, for I was not at all discontented with my fare, or apartment, I was only afraid of getting a stock of vermin from my associates.

27th July. – The canoe-men now got into a flurry, because they were told here that the Kisi men had got an inkling that their canoe was here, and were coming to take it; they said to me that they would come back for me, but I could not trust thieves to be so honest. I thought of seizing their paddles, and appealing to the headmen of the island; but aware from past experience how easy it is for acknowledged thieves like them to get up a tale to secure the cheap sympathy of the soft-headed, or tender-hearted, I resolved to bear with meekness, though groaning inwardly, the loss of two of the four days for which I had paid them. I had only my coverlet to hire another canoe, and it was now very cold; the few beads left would all be required to buy food on the way back. I might have got food by shooting buffaloes, but that on foot and through grass, with stalks as thick as a goose quill, is dreadfully hard work; I had thus to return, and trust to the distances as deduced from the time taken by the natives in their canoes for the size of the Lake.

LJ 1868 (Lake Bangweulu)

During our stay at Tala Mungongo, our attention was attracted to a species of red ant, which infests different parts of this country. It is remarkably fond of animal food. The commandant of the village having slaughtered a cow, slaves were obliged to sit up the whole night, burning fires of straw around the meat, to prevent them from devouring most of it. These ants are frequently met with in numbers, like a small army. At a little distance, they appear as a brownish-red band, two or three inches wide, stretched across the path, all eagerly pressing on in one direction. If a person happens to tread upon them, they rush up his legs and bite with surprising vigour. The first time I encountered this by no means contemptible enemy, was near Cassange. My attention being taken up in viewing the distant landscape, I accidentally stepped upon one of their nests. Not an instant seemed to elapse, before a simultaneous attack was made on various unprotected parts, up the trousers from below, and on my neck and breast above. The bites of these furies were like sparks of fire, and there was no retreat. I jumped about for a second or two, then in desperation tore off all my clothing, and rubbed and picked them off seriatim as quickly as possible. Ugh! they would make the most lethargic mortal look alive. Fortunately no one observed this rencontre, or word might have been taken back to the village that I had become mad. I was once assaulted in a similar way, when sound asleep at night in my tent, and it was only by holding my blanket over the fire that I could get rid of them. It is really astonishing, how such small bodies can contain so large an amount of ill-nature. They not only bite, but twist themselves round after the mandibles are inserted, to produce laceration and pain, more than would be effected by the single wound. Frequently while sitting on the ox, as he happened to tread near a band, they would rush up his legs to the rider, and soon let him know that he had disturbed their march. They possess no fear, attacking with equal ferocity the largest as well as the smallest animals. When any person has leaped over the band, numbers of them leave the ranks and rush along the path, seemingly anxious for a fight. They are very useful in ridding the country of dead animal matter, and, when they visit a human habitation, clear it entirely of the destructive white ants and other vermin. They destroy many noxious insects and reptiles. The severity of their attack is greatly increased by their vast numbers, and rats, mice, lizards, and even the *python natalensis*, when in a state of surfeit from recent feeding, fall victims to their fierce onslaught. These ants never make hills like the white ant. Their nests are but a short distance beneath the soil, which has the soft appearance of the abodes of ants in England. Occasionally they construct galleries over their path to the cells of the white ant, in order to secure themselves from the heat of the sun during their marauding expeditions.

MT 430

7th August. – Some of my people went down to Karambo and were detained by the chief, who said 'I won't let you English go away and leave me in trouble with these Arabs'.

A slave had been given in charge to a man here and escaped, the Arabs hereupon went to Karambo and demanded payment from the chief there; he offered clothing, but they refused it, and would have a man; he then offered a man, but this man having two children they demanded all three. They bully as much as they please by their firearms. After being spoken to by my people the Arabs came away. The chief begged that I would come and visit him once more, for only one day, but it is impossible, for we expect to move directly. I sent the information to Hamees, who replied that they had got a clue to the man who was wiling away their slaves from them. My people saw others of the low squad which always accompanies the better-informed Arabs bullying the people of another village, and taking fowls and food without payment. Slavery makes a bad neighbourhood!

Hamees is on friendly terms with a tribe of Mazitu who say that they have given up killing people. They lifted a great many cattle, but have very few now; some of them came with him to show the way to Kasonso's.

Slaves are sold here in the same open way that the business is carried on in Zanzibar slave-market. A man goes about calling out the price he wants for the slave, who walks behind him; if a woman, she is taken into a hut to be examined in a state of nudity.

Some of the Arabs believe that meteoric stones are thrown at Satan for his wickedness. They believe that cannon were taken up Kilimanjaro by the first Arabs who came into the country, and there they lie. They deny that Van der Decken did more than go around a portion of the base of the mountain.

The information one can cull from the Arabs respecting the country on the north-west is very indefinite. They magnify the difficulties in the way by tales of the cannibal tribes, where anyone dying is bought and no one ever buried, but this does not agree with the fact, which also is asserted, that the cannibals have plenty of sheep and goats. The Rua is about ten days west of Tanganyika, and five days beyond it a lake or river ten miles broad is reached; it is said to be called Logarawa. All the water flows northwards, but no reliance can be placed on the statements. Kiombo is said to be chief of Rua country.

Another man asserts that Tanganyika flows northwards and forms a large water beyond Uganda, but no dependence can be placed on the statements of these half Arabs; they pay no attention to anything but ivory and food.

25th August. – Nsama requested the Arabs to give back his son who was captured; some difficulty was made about this by his captor, but Hamees succeeded in getting him and about nine others, and they are sent off today. We wait only for the people, who are scattered about the country. Hamees presented cakes, flour, a fowl and leg of goat, with a piece of eland meat: this animal goes by the same name here as at Kolobeng – 'Pofu'.

A fig-tree here has large knobs on the bark, like some species of acacia; and another looks like the Malolo of the Zambesi magnified. A yellow wood gives an odour like incense when burned.

A large spider makes a nest inside the huts. It consists of a piece of pure white paper, an inch and a half broad, stuck flat on the wall; under this some forty or fifty eggs are placed, and then a quarter of an inch of thinner paper is put round it, apparently to fasten the first firmly. When making the paper the spider moves itself over the surface in wavy lines; she then sits on it with her eight legs spread over all for three weeks continuously, catching and eating any insects, as cockroaches, that come near her nest. After three weeks she leaves it to hunt for food, but always returns at night: the natives do not molest it.

A small ant masters the common fly by seizing a wing or leg, and holding on till the fly is tired out; at first the fly can move about on the wing without inconvenience, but it is at last obliged to succumb to an enemy very much smaller than itself.

A species of Touraco, new to me, has a broad yellow mask on the upper part of the bill and forehead; the topknot is purple, the wings the same as in other species, but the red is roseate. The yellow of the mask plates is conspicuous at a distance.

A large callosity forms on the shoulders of the regular Unyamwesi porters, from the heavy weights laid on them. I have noticed them an inch and a half thick along the top of the shoulders. An old man was pointed out to me who had once carried five frasilahs (= 175 lbs.) of ivory from his own country to the coast.

LJ 1867 (Zambia)

The plain extending from the Lundé to the town of Casembe is level, and studded pretty thickly with red ant-hills, from 15 to 20 feet high. Casembe has made a broad path from his town to the Lundé, about a mile-and-a-half long, and as broad as a carriage-path. The chief's residence is enclosed in a wall of reeds, 8 or 9 feet high, and 300 yards square, the gateway is ornamented with about sixty human skulls; a shed stands in the middle of the road before we come to the gate, with a cannon dressed in gaudy cloths. A number of noisy fellows stopped our party, and demanded tribute for the cannon; I burst through them, and the rest followed without giving anything: they were afraid of the English. The town is on the east bank of the Lakelet Mofwé, and one mile from its northern end. Mohamad bin Saleh now met us, his men firing guns of welcome; he conducted us to his shed of reception, and then gave us a hut till we could build one of our own. Mohamad is a fine portly black Arab, with a pleasant smile, and pure white beard, and has been more than ten years in these parts, and lived with four Casembes: he has considerable influence here, and also on Tanganyika.

An Arab trader, Mohamad Bogarib, who arrived seven days before us with an immense number of slaves, presented a meal of vermicelli, oil, and honey, also cassava meal cooked, so as to resemble a sweet meat (I had not tasted honey or sugar since we left Lake Nyassa, in September 1866): they had coffee too.

Neither goats, sheep, nor cattle thrive here, so the people are confined to fowls and fish. Cassava is very extensively cultivated, indeed, so generally is this plant grown, that it is impossible to know which is town and which is country: every hut has a plantation around it, in which is grown cassava, Holcus sorghum, maize, beans, nuts.

Mohamad gives the same account of the River Luapula and Lake Bemba that Jumbe did, but he adds, that the Chambezé, where we crossed it, *is* the Luapula before it enters Bemba or Bangweolo: on coming out of that Lake it turns round and comes away to the north, as Luapula, and, without touching the Mofwé, goes into Moero; then, emerging thence at the north-west end it becomes Lualaba, goes into Rua, forms a lake there, and afterwards goes into another lake beyond Tanganyika.

The Lakelet Mofwé fills during the rains and spreads westward, much beyond its banks. Elephants wandering in its mud flats when covered are annually killed in numbers: if it were connected with the Lake Moero the flood would run off.

Many of Casembe's people appear with the ears cropped and hands lopped off: the present chief has been often guilty of this barbarity. One man has just come to us without ears or hands: he tries to excite our pity making a chirruping noise, by striking his cheeks with the stumps of his hands.

A dwarf also, one Zofu, with backbone broken, comes about us: he talks with an air of authority, and is present at all public occurrences: the people seem to bear with him. He is a stranger from a tribe in the north, and works in his garden very briskly: his height is 3 feet 9 inches.

LJ 21 Nov 1867 (Lake Mweru)

1   Cf. *The Art of Victorian Prose*, ed. G. Levine and W. Madden, Oxford University Press, New York, 1969, p. xvii.
2   MT 515.
3   LJ 13 September 1866.
4   The snippets are from 'How to Read', in *Literary Essays of Ezra Pound*, ed. T. S. Eliot, Faber and Faber, London, 1954, p. 26.
5   Cf. *Grammar of the English Language* (1818), Letter XXI.
6   Jane Austen to Cassandra, January 3rd, 1801.
7   Macnair, p. xvi. See Waller's Introduction to the *Last Journals* for further details.

CHAPTER 3

Safari

Livingstone's safaris are his chosen way of life. He must have adored the morning's get-up-and-go, the day's surprises, the exhilaration, the beauty, the repose of a good day's march, ride, sail, paddle. This is what I have chosen to illustrate, for while his explorations are history, safari is what this vast and lovely continent still offers those who still enjoy it. The terrain and climate from the Cape to the Equator are the finest on earth for climbing, shooting, camping, right down to the weekend barbecue or *braaivleis,* as we call it here. Four years after Retief left Grahamstown on his Great Trek, Livingstone made his own first long African journey, over the wagon-route from Port Elizabeth through Graaff Reinet and Colesberg, across the Orange and along its north bank to the Vaal near Douglas, and over the veld to Kuruman. He called it 'a protracted system of picnickings, excellent for health and agreeable to those who are not fastidious about trifles and who delight in fresh air'. As his family grew up, he took them wherever their great Cape wagon could go. Their fun is reflected when he writes 'no one who has visited this region fails to remember with pleasure the wild, healthy, gypsy life of wagon travelling'.[2] They went with him on his second trip to Lake Ngami in April, 1850: their wagon can be seen where the family pickup would be today in the exquisitely Victorian sketch[3] made by young Alfred Ryder, who died soon afterwards of the fever from which this expedition had to turn back. It was during the next trip, a year later, that the children themselves almost died of thirst, but they made it to Linyanti, north of the Okavango, and barely a hundred miles from the Zambezi. In these projects Livingstone was silently opposed by his mother-in-law, and Mary herself seems to have dreaded their hazards, though she sits bravely enough in Ryder's sketch. It must have been with a measure of relief that she took the children back to Scotland in 1852, leaving her husband at the Cape.[4] to organise his trans-continental journey.

The usual way of regarding Livingstone's safaris is as the first scientific survey of Central Africa. So many books have been written on this subject that I was tempted to omit it; but it is a background I do tacitly assume, and which the reader may miss, if not reminded of it at least in outline.

The explorations fall into four main phases, each one distinctively motivated.

The first phase, lasting from 1845 to 1852, pushed the famous Missionaries Road west of the Marico up to the Zambezi. Livingstone's homes during this decade were with the Moffats at Kuruman, 1841–1843; forty miles further on at Mabotsa, north of Mafeking, near Zeerust, 1844–1845; forty miles north again, at Tshongwane, 1845–1847; and finally just across the present Botswana border at Kolobeng, 1848–1852. Livingstone pioneered all these except Kuruman, taking Mary Moffat as his bride to their first home, Mabotsa, early in 1845. Their four children were born and raised on the mission stations. The family left Kolobeng for the Cape in 1852; when Livingstone returned it had been destroyed in a border raid.

The still unexplored tribal areas north of Kuruman were swarming with elephant, and Livingstone's arrival coincided with the start of a big-game rush that by his death had extracted hundreds of tons of ivory and depopulated the herds as far as Barotseland. In the 1840s the hunters were 'traders frankly in quest of gain, Indian Civil Servants, Army Officers, men of family bored with deer-stalking and salmon-fishing and seeking a new excitement that, with luck, might be made to pay. All had one thing in common, an almost insatiable blood-lust.'[5] Livingstone, educated, eager, hardy, and knowing the country, people and language, was a godsend to these gentleman butchers and he made lasting friends among them: three acted as pall-bearers at the Abbey in 1874. As a missionary, his salary was £100 a year, but his friends were generous with the spoils he led them to and this made his life and his family's much easier.

In these circumstances and sometimes with his family he made a number of minor expeditions and two major discoveries. In 1849 he reached Lake Ngami, the sump of the Okavango Swamps. This was in the realm of the Makololo, which became his favourite tribe. In 1851 he took his family to their royal kraal at Linyanti and, leaving them with the dying chief, Sebituane, made the electrifying discovery of the Zambezi, some 1 000 miles inland from the east and west coasts. This lit a cluster of dreams that guided his life.

Phase two of his explorations was the ocean-to-ocean journey of 1853–1856. After leaving his family, he spent three unhappy and unpopular months in Cape Town, before setting off with a coloured trader for Linyanti, where he persuaded the new chief, Sekeletu, to support a primitive trade mission to the Portuguese in Angola. Taking four tusks to compare their value with Cape Town prices, he set off up the Zambezi with twenty-seven warriors, whom he presciently called 'Zambezians'. Near the source of the river he entered the colossal, ambivalent watershed between the Zambezi and the Congo systems. Turning west, towards the borders of Angola, he strikes a Quangle-Wangle country of demoralised tribes, wet, corrupt and threatening, that took all his coolness and cunning to negotiate. At the border he was amused to be asked for his passport but found great kindness among 'our ancient allies'. He arrived at Luanda on 31st May, 1854. His men were ecstatic, and as for the sea, 'We marched along with our father believing what the elders had also told us, that the world had no end. But, all at once, the world said to us "I am finished. There is no more of me" '.

Livingstone toured around indefatigably. He sold Sekeletu's tusks at far better than Cape prices, and collected trade samples and presents, including a full-dress colonel's uniform for the chief. He set off back – a hard and honourable decision – on 1 January, 1855, his last news from Europe of the Charge of the Light Brigade, his last fears for his soldier friends in the Crimea. His experiences are now reversed, as he follows the same trail back, on his surly ox Sinbad. He is reduced to a shadow by malaria, fights off marauding tribes, kills an angry buffalo at five yards, and on re-entering Barotseland is almost speechified to death, a hazard that became increasingly occupational. His men, now in white ducks and red bonnets, rose to great heights, singing the songs they had composed on the way back. ' "The Argonauts are nothing to us," they remarked impressively to me. "It is well you come with the Makololo. For no tribe could have accomplished what we have done in coming to the white man's country. We are the true ancients who can tell wonderful things." '

The route to the west having proved difficult and unfriendly, Livingstone makes a diptych of this phase of his explorations and decides to follow the Zambezi eastward to its mouth. Sekeletu's mother fried him peanuts in cream with salt, a chief's food, and Sekeletu himself accompanied him beyond the falls which he named Victoria. It was on the first night of this journey that the episode of Sekeletu's blanket occurred which has such mythical charm. Livingstone's party was now armed with guns from Luanda and the original splendour of their spears and shields has departed. He passes, with many adventures, north of Matabeleland and the now drowned Gwembe Valley, and past the confluence of the Kafue. With a negligence almost euphoric in one who, above all, was surveying a good waterway, he not only marches off the Zambezi for long stretches but makes no attempt to assess the rumoured 'small rapids' at Kariba and Caborabasa. Long before Tete he meets 'the first symp-

tom of the slave-trade on this side of the country': traversing Portuguese territory to Quelimane, he thinks it far more demoralised than Angola, attributing
this, of course, to the practice of slavery. In his waiting mail he finds differences of opinion with the London Missionary Society, which could not share
his opinion that 'the geographical feat is the beginning of the missionary enterprise'. He left his men in good hands enjoying themselves in Tete, and recupe-
rated a while in Mauritius. When he landed in England he was a national hero.
The Duke of Argyll claimed kinship with him, the Queen asked him to tea. He
politely resigned from the London Missionary Society and when he returned to
Quelimane in 1858 it was in his famous blue peaked cap as Consul of the
Eastern Coast of Africa.

The six year reconnaissance of Malawi, 1858–1864, was a phase almost
wholly wretched. Livingstone was a loner. He was capable of friendship but
not of official relationships: he could lead but not *use* men. His best work was
done in his own way and at his own expense. Now he was tied to the Foreign
Office and the Treasury. Everything was pompous and accountable. Just as
when he tries hardest to write he succeeds least, so, as leader of an official expedition, he grows rigid and absurd. Not wholly. Inside the frustration is the
irresponsibly happy individual, snatching at the Africa he loves. In this phase
we have to put up with two men in parallel, a fact curiously emphasised in the
style of *The Zambezi and its Tributaries*, in which, to distinguish him from his
brother and co-author, Charles, he always appears self-consciously as 'Dr.
Livingstone'.

He arrived back in Cape Town on the 21st April, 1858. Six years before he
could 'plainly perceive we are in bad odour in Cape Town': now he was feted.
'The town gave him a rousing welcome, presenting him with a silver casket containing 800 guineas and entertaining him to a banquet whereat all the resources
of colonial oratory were exhausted'.[6] His reception at Tete was more spon-
taneous:

> The ship anchored in the stream on the 8th September, 1858, and I went
> ashore in the boat. No sooner did the Makololo recognise me than they
> rushed to the water's edge and manifested great joy at seeing me again.
> Some were hastening to embrace me, but others cried out 'Don't touch him,
> you will spoil his new clothes'.

What ensued is highly complex. Essentially his instructions were to explore
the Zambezi and the Shire rivers as commercial routes to the interior. *And* as
missionary routes; this aspect he had explicitly preserved.

His supply base was the malarial delta of the Zambezi, from its two main
mouths, at Chinde (north of Beira) and Quelimane, to Tete, where the hills
begin, 250 miles upstream. About halfway between Tete and the coast the
Shire joins the Zambezi from its source in Lake Malawi, 300 miles and 2 000
feet up in the mountains to the north.

Politically, the situation was chaotic. In theory the Portuguese governed the
territory from Quelimane. In fact the land south of the river was controlled by

the 'Landeens', a Zulu tribe from Mashonaland, who exacted regular tribute from its traders. North of the river, when Livingstone arrived, a monstrous slaver called Mariano was in full rebellion, with his headquarters at the Shire confluence. The forward headquarters of the Portuguese forces was 80 miles south of this at Chupanga, a name to be seared on Livingstone's heart. The Portuguese commander lived in 'a one-storeyed stone house on the prettiest site on the river. In front a sloping lawn, with a fine mango orchard leading down to the broad Zambezi, whose green islands repose on the sunny bosom of the tranquil waters. Beyond, northwards, lie vast fields and forests of palms and tropical trees, with the massive mountain of Morambala towering amidst the white clouds and further away more distant hills appear on the blue horizon'. Livingstone continues: 'The Chupanga house was the headquarters of the Governor during the Mariano war. He told us that the Province of Mozambique costs the Home Government between £5 000 and £6 000 annually, and yields no reward in return to the mother country.'[7] The situation has a certain familiarity.

He had brought out with him a small steam-launch. It would only burn logs of the finest and hardest woods, ebony, for example, and it scoffed these like eclairs. Water came in everywhere. It was a Jumbly-boat, a disaster, called by the Makololo the Ma-Robert, by the whites the Asthmatic, and by Livingstone, using it as best he could, 'this wretched little steamer'.

He tackled the Zambezi, in the first of three trips to the Caborabasa Rapids. One good look at them was, as Wallis puts it, 'the annihilation of his hopes'. He turned to the Shire to find a precisely similar barrier in five rapids that bring the river down 1 200 feet over 40 miles and which he named the Murchison Falls. What was beating Livingstone, of course, was the configuration of Africa, whereby its serene and sunny highveld descends in two or three majestic steps to the sea, over whose edge (as Dr. Miller writes) 'the rivers tumble, either in sheer falls like those Livingstone called Victoria, or in cataracts none the less prohibitive to transport'.[8]

Livingstone made six trips in all up the Shire, returning to Tete between them. He reported on the lovely Highlands where Blantyre-Limbe and Zomba are today, and sailed round the large and dangerous lake in a four-oared gig, almost losing to the water the charmed life the land could not win. He had ordered a new ship from England and, in the six-month interval of waiting for it, led his Makololo triumphantly back home, taking his second look at the Falls. He found Sekeletu dying, as he had found Sebituane, his father, before him.

In January, 1861 the new *Pioneer* arrived at Quelimane escorted by two of HM. cruisers together with the personnel of the Universities Mission under Bishop Mackenzie. Livingstone immediately took the boat 500 miles up the coast in the first of three ascents of the Rovuma River. Once again he was fooled. The Rovuma begins magnificently with a deep-water harbour but runs through impassable rocks 160 miles upstream and, unlike the Shire, never reaches Lake Malawi.

The Universities Mission was established on Livingstone's fourth trip up the

Shire, inland from the Murchison Falls at Magomero. He had originally found Lake Malawi a sink of slavery but now discovered to his horror, that the scourge had spread in a single year, into the paradise of the Upper Shire. For the first time he took the initiative, released a party of slaves winding down to Tete and repulsed the Portuguese agents, the Ajawa, with firearms at the little battle of Magomero. In these unsettled circumstances he left Mackenzie and his flock and returned to Quelimane to greet the half-dozen ladies of the mission and his own Mary, who had arrived on 30th January, 1862, on *HMS. Gorgon*. A naval gig took the ladies up to their rendezvous with Mackenzie, only to hear that he and others with him were dead. Mary stopped off at Chupanga, as the stricken mission withdrew to the Cape; but in little over three weeks she died of delta malaria in Livingstone's arms. He buried her remains under a baobab at Chupanga and her memory very deep in his reticent heart. He had had a new ship brought out on *Gorgon*, the little *Lady Nyasa*, which he had commissioned himself for £6 000. He took her up the Rovuma again, and then up the Shire, but before he could get her on to the lake the whole expedition was cancelled by the Foreign Office, all salaries ceasing w.e.f. 31st December, 1863. He was able to make an important reconnaissance west of the lake while waiting for the Shire floods, but had to turn back before sighting Lake Bangweulu. He then actually did a Chichester with his little boat, sailing it 2 500 miles across the Indian Ocean to Bombay, in order to make a Scottish bargain of it. His crew were seven Zambezians 'who before volunteering had never seen the sea; three whites and myself as navigator'. They beat the monsoon by two days. It was his craziest action, but how much of the man is in it!

When he returned to England in 1864 his reception was publicly warm but officially cold. He had offended the Portuguese with his anger at the slave trade. The King of Portugal was the Prince Consort's cousin, and there was no invitation to the Palace.

The secret of the enduring response to Livingstone's life is not in its surface detail, rich though that is, but in its tragic rhythm. It is such as must attend any daemonic idealism caught in 'the world's great snare'. The third phase of his life begins to stir this response and soon the others catch its echo, the first and second phases now appearing brilliant with hope, the third shadowed with torment, and the fourth tragically dark, although nerved with fire and forming a marvellous background for his apotheosis.

Livingstone's last exploration was for the source of the Nile. What was known was that the river seemed to flow north out of *both* of Uganda's lakes, the Victoria (Speke, 1862) and the Albert (Baker, 1864). The questions were, did it flow *into* their southern ends and if so, where from? From the top of Lake Tanganyika (Burton & Speke, 1858) never yet seen? Or from even further west and south? Here it was confidently and decoratively sited by seventeenth-century cartographers. I have in my study a large map from an atlas of 1820. The scientific spirit has swept it bare of conjecture. The centre of

Africa, south of the (still) mythical Mountains of the Moon, is virgin white, with a single exception: a little box of guesses from James Bruce (1770) – on the source of the Nile.

Livingstone arrived in Zanzibar in 1866 from Bombay (where he had sold the *Lady Nyasa* at a loss), bringing with him the compliments of the Governor to the Sultan and the gift of a luxury yacht. The Sultan was so pleased he held a great reception with *God save the Queen* and *The British Grenadiers* ('although *Wee Willie Winkie* would have been more appropriate', remarked the 5′ 8″ explorer). Worth far more than the ceremony, however, was a *firman* or open injunction of welcome from the Sultan, which ensured Livingstone respect wherever Arabic was spoken.

Livingstone's joy at being back is as famous as it was to prove ironic (p. 19). He set off with a nucleus of old friends, including Susi and Chuma, who were with him to the end, a zoo of draught animals for tsetse research and, though he little knew it at the time, a gang of delinquents. He had shed most of them by the time he had reached Lake Malawi from the Rovuma and looked sadly south towards Chupanga. He rounded the familiar end of the Lake and headed north-west across Zambia on the Chipata (Fort Jameson) – Mpika – Mbala (Abercorn) line, between what are now the two Luangwa Game Reserves. It was a geography of violence and beauty, a sociology of chaos, a gangrene of slavery, and an Indo-Arab commercial empire. In the new year of 1867 his medicine-chest was stolen (p. 49), and from then to the end he slowly lost his battle with chronic dysentery and malaria. He reached Lake Tanganyika in April but turned south to discover Lake Mweru and a huge river flowing north from it. It was called the Lualaba. It is, in fact, the great southern tributary of the Congo but it became for Livingstone the false Nile. He heard it came from a lake further south, and, passing Casembe's town, he reached Lake Bangweulu and found it did. Logically he should have explored south again but he unaccountably left that as unfinished business and turned north to replenish his stores across Lake Tanganyika, at Kigomo (Ujiji). They had been plundered. He rested and set off into the central Congo to the country called Manyuema, lying west of the upper half of the Lake. In March, 1870 he struck his false Nile again at Nyangwe. It was nearly two miles broad and flowing north. His head full of dreams, he was raising canoes to go towards Katanga with it, when all hell broke loose around him.

> The terrible scenes of man's inhumanity to man brought on severe headache which might have been serious had it not been relieved by a copious discharge of blood; I was laid up all yesterday afternoon with the depression the bloodshed made. It filled me with unspeakable horror. 'Don't go away', say the Manyuema chiefs to me; but I cannot stay here in agony.

Almost despairing, he gave up and returned, down and out, to Kigoma, to find the country between him and Tabora in flames, and all hopes of fresh supplies cut off.[9] He sat there waiting (Stanley wrote) 'on the verandah of his house, with his face turned eastward, the direction from which I was coming'.

Had I this, had I that, etc., 'I might have lost him and I began to recognise the hand of an overruling and kindly Providence'.

'Bales of goods, baths of tin, huge kettles, cooking pots, tents, etc.' – American supplies, American generosity, what an injection of hope they can be! Within a month the pair had rounded the north of Lake Tanganyika and confirmed there was neither Nile nor Congo to be found there. Livingstone journeyed with Stanley back to Tabora but resisted his persuasions to hurl in. All that was required, he thought, to finish the job he had been set, was six months; and he turned back to the unfinished business south of Lake Bangweulu.

He had left his false Nile at Nyangwe in 1870, and on the map at the end of his *Last Journals* it heads on in his dreams, a double dotted line, into nothing. From the Bible, memories of Herodotus, and Congo hearsay he had established a concept of its source. He knew, with hallucinatory vividness, what he was looking for, the only problem was where it should be. His expedition was strong, large – 62 men – and well-equipped. He was on his own again. In firm control, in good heart, but with ravaged physique, he headed his last safari into the rains.

'A bleaker, gloomier, more monotonous scene could not be imagined', says Coupland of the area near Lake Bangweulu he reached early in 1873. He had no resistance and was soon fatally ill. 'I am pale, bloodless, and weak from bleeding ... an artery gives off a copious stream and takes away all my strength. Oh how I long to be permitted by the Over Power to finish my work.' He sought a mountain with twin peaks where four rivers rise. 'Nothing earthly will make me give up', he wrote on March 25th. 'I encourage myself in the Lord my God and go forward.'

On 21st April he was lifted on to a litter and the decision seems to have been made to get him off the water-table of the Lake and build him a dry hut where he could rest and recuperate. The nearest possibility was the village of the chief, Chitambo. It was against his will, but he was beyond speech. He lay in the hut with fires burning until the night of the 30th April. After midnight he contrived to die on his knees, where his young servant, Majwara, found him before dawn.

It is hard to resist re-phrasing this story, however often it has been told, by Livingstone and Waller, Blaikie, Coupland, MacNair, how often more in the centenary year. I wished not to repeat it, since it ends on a note of defeat. But although a doctor, and as precise in observing his own symptoms as anything external, Livingstone is the least valetudinarian of men; and, since he makes light of hardships too, his actual writing retains its buoyancy and vividness until the pen literally falls from his hand. That extraordinary encounter with the ants, for instance (p. 49), takes place at a period of constant haemorrhage. He wages a long battle of wits with the wily Matipa within a few weeks of his death, never once losing his pale humour, his sharp eye and ear, his long vision. In this mood one returns to the texture of a way of life to which his discoveries are a mere grid of reference.

A local trip with Sekeletu, June, 1853.

It was pleasant to look back on the long-extended line of our attendants, as it twisted and bent according to the curves of the footpath, or in and out behind the mounds, the ostrich-feathers of the men waving in the wind. Some had the white ends of ox-tails on their heads, hussar fashion, and others great bunches of black ostrich-feathers, or caps made of lions' manes. Some wore red tunics, or various-coloured prints which the chief had bought from Fleming; the common men carried burdens; the gentlemen walked with a small club of rhinoceros horn in their hands, and had servants to carry their shields; while the 'Machaka', battle-axe men, carried their own, and were liable at any time to be sent off a hundred miles on an errand, and expected to run all the way.   MT 204

We always follow the native paths, though they are generally not more than fifteen inches broad, and so often have deep little holes in them, made for the purpose of setting traps for small animals, and are so much obscured by the long grass, that one has to keep one's eyes on the ground more than is pleasant. In spite, however, of all drawbacks, it is vastly more easy to travel on these tracks, than to go straight over uncultivated ground, or virgin forest. A path usually leads to some village, though sometimes it turns out to be a mere game track leading nowhere.   ZT 469

Stores for the trip to Angola, November, 1853.

I had three muskets for my people, a rifle and double-barrelled smooth bore for myself; and, having seen such great abundance of game, I imagined that I could easily supply the wants of my party. Wishing also to avoid the discouragement which would naturally be felt if my companions were obliged to carry heavy loads, I took only a few biscuits, a few pounds of tea and sugar, and about twenty of coffee, which, as the Arabs find, though used without either milk or sugar, is most refreshing after fatigue or exposure to the sun. We carried one small tin canister, about fifteen inches square, filled with spare shirting, trousers, and shoes, to be used when we reached civilised life, and others in a bag, which were expected to wear out on the way; another of the same size for medicines; and a third for books, my stock being a Nautical Almanac, Thomson's Logarithm Tables, and a Bible; a fourth box contained a magic lantern, which we found of much use. The sextant and artificial horizon, thermometer and compasses, were carried apart. My ammunition was distributed in portions through the whole luggage, so that, if an accident should befall one part, we could still have others to fall back upon. Our chief hopes for food were upon that, but in case of failure I took about 20 lbs. of beads, worth 40s., which still remained of the stock I brought from Cape Town; a small gipsy tent, just sufficient to sleep in; a sheepskin mantle as a blanket, and a horse-rug as a bed. As I had always found that the art of successful travel consisted in taking as few impedimenta as possible, and not forgetting to carry my wits about me, the outfit was rather spare, and intended to be still more so when we should come to leave the canoes. Some would consider it injudicious to adopt this plan, but I had a secret conviction that if I did not succeed it would not be for lack of the knicknacks, but from want of pluck, or because a large array of baggage excited the cupidity of the tribes through whose country we wished to pass.

MT 230

A note of Waller's (Livingstone's friend, who edited the *Last Journals*).

We may here add a few particulars concerning beads, which form such an important item of currency all through Africa. With a few exceptions they are all manufactured in Venice. The greatest care must be exercised, or the traveller – ignorant of the prevailing fashion in the country he is about to explore – finds himself with an accumulation of beads of no more value than tokens would be if tendered in this country for coin of the realm.

Thanks to the kindness of Messrs. Levin & Co., the bead merchants, of Bevis Marks, E.C., we have been able to get some idea of the more valuable beads, through a selection made by Susi and Chuma in their warehouse. The Waiyou prefer exceedingly small beads, the size of mustard-seed, and of various colours, but they must be opaque: amongst them dull white chalk varieties, called 'Catchokolo', are valuable, besides black and pink, named, respectively, 'Bububu' and 'Sekundereché' = the 'dregs of pombe'. One red bead, of various sizes, which has a white centre, is always valuable in every part of Africa. It is called 'Sami-sami' by the Suahélé, 'Chitakaraka' by the Waiyou, 'Mangazi', = 'blood', by the Nyassa, and was found popular even amongst the Manyuéma, under the name of 'Masokantussi' = 'bird's eyes'. Whilst speaking of this distant tribe, it is interesting to observe that one peculiar long bead, recognised as common in the Manyuéma land, is only sent to the West Coast of Africa, and *never* to the East. On Chuma pointing to it as a sort found at the extreme limit explored by Livingstone, it was at once seen that he must have touched that part of Africa which begins to be within the reach of the traders in the Portuguese settlements. 'Machua Kanga' = 'guinea fowl's eyes', is another popular variety; and the 'Moiompio' = 'new heart', a large pale blue bead, is a favourite amongst the Wabisa; but by far the most valuable of all is a small white oblong bead, which, when strung, looks like the joints of the cane root, from which it takes its name, 'Salani' = cane. Susi says that 1 lb. weight of these beads would buy a tusk of ivory, at the south end of Tanganyika, so big that a strong man could not carry it more than two hours.

LJ 24 Jan 1867

In Barotseland, en route to Luanda, November, 1853.

When under weigh our usual procedure is this: We get up a little before five in the morning; it is then beginning to dawn. While I am dressing, coffee is made; and, having filled my pannikin, the remainder is handed to my companions. The servants are busy loading the canoes, while the principal men are sipping the coffee, and, that being soon over, we embark. The next two hours are the most pleasant part of the day's sail. The men paddle away most vigorously; the Barotse, being a tribe of boatmen, have large, deeply-developed chests and shoulders, with indifferent lower extremities. They often engage in loud scolding of each other, in order to relieve the tedium of their work. About eleven we land, and eat any meat which may have remained from the previous evening meal, or a biscuit with honey, and drink water.

After an hour's rest we again embark and cower under an umbrella. The heat is oppressive, and, being weak from the last attack of fever, I cannot land and keep the camp supplied with flesh. Sometimes we reach a sleeping-place two hours before sunset, and, all being troubled with languor, we gladly remain for the night. Coffee again, and a biscuit, or a piece of coarse bread made of maize meal, or that of the native corn, make up the bill of fare for the evening, unless we have been fortunate enough to kill something, when we boil a potful of flesh.

The cooking is usually done in the natives' own style, and, as they care-fully wash the dishes, pots, and the hands before handling food, it is by no means despicable. Sometimes alterations are made at my suggestion, and then they believe that they can cook in thorough white man's fashion. The cook always comes in for something left in the pot, so all are eager to obtain the office.

I taught several of them to wash my shirts, and they did it well, though their teacher had never been taught that work himself. Frequent changes of linen and sunning of my blanket kept me more comfortable than might have been anticipated, and I feel certain that the lessons of cleanliness rigidly instilled by my mother in childhood, helped to maintain that respect which these people entertain for European ways. It is questionable if a descent to barbarous ways ever elevates a man in the eyes of savages.

MT 243

A trip up the Zambezi from Sesheke, July, 1853.

I had six paddlers, and the larger canoe of Sekeletu had ten. They stand upright, and keep the stroke with great precision, though they change from side to side as the course demands. The men at the head and stern are selected from the strongest and most expert of the whole. The canoes, being flat-bottomed, can go into very shallow water; and whenever the men can feel the bottom they use the paddles, which are about eight feet long, as poles to punt with. Our fleet consisted of thirty-three canoes, and about one hundred and sixty men. It was beautiful to see them skimming along so quickly, and keeping the time so well. On land the Makalaka fear the Makololo; on water the Makololo fear them, and cannot prevent them from racing with each other, dashing along at the top of their speed, and placing their masters' lives in danger.

MT 211

Returning the Makololo from Tete, June, 1860.

Having now entered a country where lions were numerous, our men began to pay greater attention to the arrangements of the camp at night. As they are accustomed to do with their Chiefs, they place the white men in the centre; Kanyata, his men, and the two donkeys, camp on our right; Tuba Mokoro's party of Bashubia are in front, Masakasa, and Sininyane's body of Batoka, on the left, and in the rear six Tette men have their fires. In placing their fires they are careful to put them where the smoke will not blow in our faces. Soon after we halt, the spot for the English is selected, and all regulate their places accordingly, and deposit their burdens. The men take it by turns to cut some of the tall dry grass, and spread it for our beds on a spot, either naturally level, or smoothed by the hoe; some, appointed to carry our bedding, then bring our rugs and karosses, and place the three rugs in a row on the grass; Dr. Livingstone's being in the middle, Dr. Kirk's on the right, and Charles Livingstone's on the left. Our bags, rifles, and revolvers are carefully placed at our heads, and a fire made near our feet. We have no tent nor covering of any kind except the branches of the tree under which we may happen to lie; and it is a pretty sight to look up and see every branch, leaf, and twig of the tree stand out, reflected against the clear star-spangled and moonlit sky.

The men cut a very small quantity of grass for themselves, and sleep in *fumbas* or sleeping-bags, which are double mats of palm-leaf, six feet long by four wide, and sewn together round three parts of the square, and left open only on one side. They are used as a protection from the cold, wet, and mosquitoes, and are entered as we should get into our beds, were the blankets nailed to the top, bottom, and one side of the bedstead. When they are all inside their *fumbas,* nothing is seen but sacks lying all about the different fires. At times two persons sleep inside one, which is, indeed, close packing. Matonga, one of the men, has volunteered to take the sole charge of our fire, and is to receive for his services the customary payment of the heads and necks of all the beasts we kill; and, except on the days when only guinea-fowl are shot, he thus gets abundance of food. He bears our fowl diet resignedly for a few days, and then, if no large game is killed, he comes and expostulates: 'Morena, my lord, a hungry man cannot fill his stomach with the head of a bird; he is killed with hunger for want of meat, and will soon, from sheer weakness, be unable to carry the wood for the fire; he ought to have an entire bird to save him from dying of starvation'. His request being reasonable, and guinea-fowl abundant, it is of course complied with.

A dozen fires are nightly kindled in the camp; and these, being replenished from time to time by the men who are awakened by the cold, are kept burning until daylight. Abundance of dry hard wood is obtained with little trouble; and burns beautifully. After the great business of cooking and eating is over, all sit round the camp-fires, and engage in talking or singing. Every evening one of the Batoka plays his *sansa,* and continues at it until far into the night; he accompanies it with an extempore song, in which he rehearses their deeds ever since they left their own country. At times animated political discussions spring up, and the amount of eloquence expended on these occasions is amazing. The whole camp is aroused, and the men shout to one another from the different fires; whilst some, whose tongues are never heard on any other subject, now burst forth into impassioned speech. The misgovernment of Chiefs furnishes an inexhaustible theme. 'We could govern ourselves better', they cry, 'so what is the use of Chiefs at all? They do not work. The Chief is fat, and has plenty of wives; whilst we, who do the hard work, have hunger, only one wife, or more likely none; now this must be bad, unjust, and wrong.' All shout to this a loud 'ēhē', equivalent to our 'hear, hear'. Next the headman, Kanyata, and Tuba with his loud voice, are heard taking up the subject on the loyal side. 'The Chief is the father of the people; can there be people without a father, eh? God made the Chief. Who says that the Chief is not wise? He is wise; but his children are fools.' Tuba goes on generally till he has silenced all opposition; and if his arguments are not always sound, his voice is the loudest, and he is sure to have the last word.

As a specimen of our mode of marching, we rise about five, or as soon as dawn appears, take a cup of tea and a bit of biscuit; the servants fold up the blankets and stow them away in the bags they carry; the others tie their *fumbas* and cooking-pots to each end of their carrying-sticks, which are borne on the shoulder; the cook secures the dishes, and all are on the path by sunrise. If a convenient spot can be found we halt for breakfast about nine a.m. To save time, this meal is generally cooked the night before, and has only to be warmed. We continue the march after breakfast, rest a little in the middle of the day, and break off early in the afternoon. We average from two to two-and-a-half miles an hour in a straight line, or, as the crow flies, and seldom have more than five or six hours a day of actual travel. This in a hot climate is as much as a man can accomplish without being oppressed; and we always tried to make our progress more a pleasure than a toil. To hurry over the ground, abuse, and look ferocious at one's companions, merely for the foolish vanity of boasting how quickly a distance was accomplished, is a combination of silliness with absurdity; while kindly consideration for the feelings of even blacks, the pleasure of observing scenery and everything new as one moves on at an ordinary pace, and the participation in the most delicious rest with our fellows, render travelling delightful. Though not given to over haste, we were a little surprised to find that we could tire our men out; and even the headman, who carried but little more than we did, and never, as we often had to do, hunted in the afternoon, was no better than his comrades. Our experience tends to prove that the European constitution has a power of endurance, even in the tropics, greater than that of the hardiest of the meat-eating Africans.

After pitching our camp, one or two of us usually go off to hunt, more as a matter of necessity than of pleasure, for the men, as well as ourselves, must have meat. We prefer to take a man with us to carry home the game, or lead the others to where it lies; but as they frequently grumble and complain of being tired, we do not particularly object to going alone, except that it involves the extra labour of our making a second trip to show the men where the animal that has been shot is to be found. When it is a couple of miles off it is rather fatiguing to have to go twice; more especially on the days when it is solely to supply their wants that, instead of resting ourselves, we go at all. Like those who perform benevolent deeds at home, the tired hunter, though trying hard to live in charity with all men, is strongly tempted to give it up by bringing only sufficient meat for the three whites and leaving the rest; thus sending the 'idle ungrateful poor' supperless to bed. And yet it is only by continuance in well-doing, even to the length of what the worldly-wise call weakness, that the conviction is produced anywhere, that our motives are high enough to secure sincere respect.

ZT 175

Christmas 1855, on the way down the Zambezi to Tete.

We tried to leave one morning, but the rain coming on afresh brought us to a stand, and after waiting an hour, wet to the skin, we were fain to retrace our steps to our sheds. These rains were from the east, and the clouds might to be seen on the hills, exactly as the 'Table-cloth' on Table Mountain. This was the first wetting we had got since we left Sesheke, for I had gained some experience in travelling. In Londa we braved the rain, and as I despised being carried in our frequent passage through running water, I was pretty constantly drenched; but now, when we saw a storm coming, we invariably halted. The men soon pulled grass sufficient to make a little shelter for themselves by placing it on a bush, and having got my camp-stool and umbrella, with a little grass under my feet, I kept myself perfectly dry. We also lighted large fires, and the men were not chilled by streams of water running down their persons, and abstracting the heat, as they would have been had they been exposed to the rain. When it was over, they warmed themselves by the fires, and we travelled on comfortably. The effect of this care was, that we had much less sickness than with a smaller party in journeying to Loanda. Another improvement made from my experience, was avoiding an entire change of diet. In going to Loanda I took little or no European food, in order not to burden my men and make them lose spirit, but trusted entirely to what might be got by the gun, and the liberality of the Balonda; but on this journey I took some flour which had been left in the waggon, with some got on the island, and baked my own bread all the way in an extemporaneous oven made by an inverted pot. With these precautions, aided, no doubt, by the greater healthiness of the district over which we passed, I enjoyed perfect health.

MT 572

Near the Makarikiri Depression, Northern Botswana, February, 1853.

The Bechuanas put their milk into sacks made of untanned hide, with the hair taken off. Hung in the sun, it soon coagulates; the whey is then drawn off by a plug at the bottom, and fresh milk added, until the whole sack is full of a thick sour curd, which, when one becomes used to it, is delicious. The rich mix this in the porridge into which they convert their meal, and, as it is thus rendered nutritious and strength-giving, an expression of scorn is sometimes heard respecting the poor or weak, to the effect that 'they are mere water-porridge men'.

MT 160

Near Caborabasa, on the way home with the Makololo, early June, 1860.

We had the elephant's fore-foot cooked for ourselves, in native fashion. A large hole was dug in the ground, in which a fire was made; and, when the inside was thoroughly heated, the entire foot was placed in it, and covered over with the hot ashes and soil; another fire was made above the whole, and kept burning all night. We had the foot thus cooked for breakfast next morning, and found it delicious. It is a whitish mass, slightly gelatinous, and sweet, like marrow. A long march, to prevent biliousness, is a wise precaution after a meal of elephant's foot. Elephant's trunk and tongue are also good, and, after long simmering, much resemble the hump of a buffalo, and the tongue of an ox; but all the other meat is tough, and, from its peculiar flavour, only to be eaten by a hungry man. The quantities of meat our men devour is quite astounding. They boil as much as their pots will hold, and eat till it becomes physically impossible for them to stow away any more. An uproarious dance follows, accompanied with stentorian song; and as soon as they have shaken their first course down, and washed off the sweat and dust of the after performance, they go to work to roast more: a short snatch of sleep succeeds, and they are up and at it again; all night long it is boil and eat, roast and devour, with a few brief interludes of sleep. Like other carnivora these men can endure hunger for a much longer period than the mere porridge-eating tribes. Our men can cook meat as well as any reasonable traveller could desire; and, boiled in earthern pots, it tastes much better than when cooked in iron ones.

Their porridge is a failure, at least for a Scotch digestion that has been impaired by fever. When on a journey, unaccompanied by women, as soon as the water is hot, they tumble in the meal by handfuls in rapid succession, until it becomes too thick to stir about, when it is whipped off the fire, and placed on the ground; an assistant then holds the pot, whilst the cook, grasping the stick with both hands, exerts his utmost strength in giving it a number of circular turns, to mix and prevent the solid mass from being burnt by the heat. It is then served up to us, the cook retaining the usual perquisite of as much as can be induced to adhere to the stick, when he takes it from the pot. By this process, the meal is merely moistened and warmed, but not boiled; much of it being raw, it always causes heartburn. This is the only mode that the natives have of cooking the mapira meal. They seldom, if ever, bake it into cakes, like oatmeal; for, though finely ground and beautifully white, it will not cohere readily. Maize meal is formed into dough more readily, but that too is inferior to wheaten flour, or even oatmeal, for baking. It was rather difficult to persuade the men to boil the porridge for us more patiently; and they became witty, and joked us for being like women, when the weakness of fever compelled us to pay some attention to the cooking, evidently thinking that it was beneath the dignity of white men to stoop to such matters. They look upon the meal and water porridge of the black tribes as the English used to do upon the French frogs, and call the eaters 'mere water-porridge fellows', while the Makololo's meal and milk porridge takes the character of English roast-beef.

ZT 168

There is an interest, often bizarre, in Livingstone's acceptance of life off the land, sometimes in plenty, sometimes so famished that he dreams of roast beef until, although 'I scarcely ever dream, the saliva runs from the mouth, and the pillow is wet with it in the mornings'. He enjoyed much hospitality:

Panzo, the headman of the village east of Kebrabasa, received us with great kindness. After the usual salutation he went up the hill, and, in a loud voice, called across the valley to the women of several hamlets to cook supper for us. About eight in the evening he returned, followed by a procession of women, bringing the food. There were eight dishes of *nsima*, or porridge, six of different sorts of very good wild vegetables, with dishes of beans and fowls; all deliciously well cooked, and scrupulously clean. The wooden dishes were nearly as white as the meal itself.

ZT 335

At other times he had what the Americans in the South-West call 'a Mexican lunch':

Simon gave me a little more of his meal this morning, and went without himself: I took my belt up three holes to relieve hunger.

His drink was water, sometimes 'swarming with insects, thick with mud and putrid with other mixtures.' He took no spirits 'except a spoonful in hot water before going to bed, to fend off a chill or a fever', and considered coffee or tea, usually without sugar, his 'greatest luxury'.

He tackled everything with gusto, including caterpillars, frogs and lizards but not human flesh – for which, however, he suggests the only *recipe* I have ever seen:

The men here deny that cannibalism is common: they eat only those killed in war, and, it seems, in revenge, for, said Mokandira, 'the meat is not nice; it makes one dream of the dead man'. Some west of Lualaba eat even those bought for the purpose of a feast; but I am not quite positive on this point: all agree that human flesh is saltish and needs little condiment. The only feasible reason I can discover is a depraved appetite, giving an extraordinary craving for meat which we call 'high'. They are said to bury a dead body for a couple of days in the soil in a forest, and in that time, owing to the climate, it soon becomes putrid enough for the strongest stomachs. The party that came through from Mamalulu found that a great fight had taken place at Muanampunda's, and they saw the meat cut up to be cooked with bananas.

LJ 21 Apr and 10 Aug, 1871

I cannot resist a few more extracts from the African *Escoffier:*

The mission at Kolobeng, Botswana, 1850.

Locusts are strongly vegetable in taste, the flavour varying with the plants on which they feed. There is a physiological reason why locusts and honey should be eaten together. Some are roasted and pounded into meal, which eaten with a little salt is palatable. It will keep thus for months. Boiled they are disagreeable; but when they are roasted, I should much prefer locusts to shrimps, though I would avoid both if possible.

In travelling we sometimes suffered considerably from scarcity of meat, though not from absolute want of food. This was felt more especially by my children; and the natives, to show their sympathy, often gave them a large kind of caterpillar, which they seemed to relish; these insects could not be unwholesome, for the natives devoured them in large quantities themselves.

Another article of which our children partook with eagerness was a very large frog, called Matlamétlo: when cooked, they look like chickens.

MT 42

December, 1855, first trip down the Zambezi, near the Kafue confluence.

They are obliged to make pitfalls, to protect the grain against the hippopotami. As these animals had not been disturbed by guns, they were remarkably tame, and took no notice of our passing. We again saw numbers of young ones, not much larger than terrier dogs, sitting on the necks of their dams, the little saucy-looking heads cocking up between the old one's ears; as they become a little older, they sit on the withers. Needing meat, we shot a full-grown cow. It is a coarse-grained meat something like pork and beef — pretty good when one is hungry and can get nothing better.

MT 569

Kolobeng, Botswana, 1850.

While swarming these ants appear like snow-flakes floating about in the air, and dogs, cats, hawks, and almost every bird, may be seen busily devouring them. The natives, too, collect them for food, they being about half an inch long, as thick as a crow-quill, and very fat. When roasted they are said to be good, and somewhat resemble grains of boiled rice fried in delicious fresh oil. An idea may be formed of this dish by what once occurred on the banks of the Zouga. The Bayeiye chief Palani visiting us while eating, I gave him a piece of bread and preserved apricots; and as he seemed to relish it much, I asked him if he had any food equal to that in his country. 'Ah,' said he, 'did you ever taste white ants?' As I never had, he replied, 'Well, if you had, you never could have desired to eat anything better'. The general way of catching them is to dig into the ant-hill, and wait till all the builders come forth to repair the damage; then brush them off quickly into a vessel, as the ant-eater does into his mouth.

MT 464

With the returned Makololo at Sesheke, September, 1860.

Our visit to Sesheke broke in upon the monotony of their daily life, and we had crowds of visitors both men and women; especially at meal-times, for then they had the double attraction, of seeing white men eat, and of eating with them. The men made an odd use of the spoon in supping porridge and milk, employing it to convey the food to the palm of the left hand, which passed it on to the mouth. We shocked the over-refined sensibilities of the ladies, by eating butter on our bread. 'Look at them, look at them, they are actually eating *raw* butter, ugh! how nasty!' or pitying us, a good wife would say, 'Hand it here to be melted, and then you can dip your bread into it decently'. They were as much disgusted as we should be by seeing an Esquimaux eating raw whale's blubber. In their opinion butter is not fit to be eaten until it is cooked or melted. The principal use they make of it is to anoint the body, and it keeps the skin smooth and glossy.

ZT 287

Lake Malawi, in the four-oared gig, August, 1861.

During a portion of the year, the northern dwellers on the lake have a harvest which furnishes a singular sort of food. As we approached our limit in that direction, clouds, as of smoke rising from miles of burning grass, were observed bending in a south-easterly direction, and we thought that the unseen land on the opposite side was closing in, and that we were near the end of the lake. But next morning we sailed through one of the clouds on our own side, and discovered that it was neither smoke nor haze, but countless millions of minute midges called 'kungo' (a cloud or fog). They filled the air to an immense height, and swarmed upon the water, too light to sink in it. Eyes and mouth had to be kept closed while passing through this living cloud: they struck upon the face like fine drifting snow. The people gather these minute insects by night, and boil them into thick cakes, to be used as a relish – millions of midges in a cake. A kungo cake, an inch thick and as large as the blue bonnet of a Scotch ploughman was offered to us; it was very dark in colour and tasted not unlike caviare or salted locusts.

ZT 373

This seems the appropriate moment to include the less famous account of the memorable meeting with H. M. Stanley:

23rd Sept. – I was sorely knocked up in this march back to Ujiji. In the latter part of it I felt as if dying on my feet. Almost every step was in pain, the appetite failed and a little bit of meat caused violent diarrhoea, whilst the mind, sorely depressed, reacted on the body. All the traders were returning successful: I alone had failed and experienced worry, thwarting, baffling, when almost in sight of the end towards which I strained.

3rd October. – I read the whole Bible through four times whilst I was in Manyuema.

8th October. – The road covered with angular fragments of quartz was very sore to my feet, which are crammed into ill-made French shoes. How the bare feet of the men and women stood out, I don't know; it was hard enough on mine though protected by the shoes. . . .

23rd October. – At dawn, off and go to Ujiji. Welcomed by all the Arabs, particularly by Moenyegheré. I was now reduced to a skeleton, but the market being held daily, and all kinds of native food brought to it, I hoped that food and rest would soon restore me, but in the evening my people came and told me that Shereef had sold off all my goods, and Moenyegheré confirmed it by saying, 'We protested, but he did not leave a single yard of calico out of 3 000, nor a string of beads out of 700 lbs.' This was distressing. I had made up my mind, if I could not get people at Ujiji, to wait till men should come from the coast, but to wait in beggary was what I never contemplated, and I now felt miserable. Shereef was evidently a moral idiot, for he came without shame to shake hands with me, and when I refused, assumed an air of displeasure, as having been badly treated. I felt in my destitution as if I were the man who went down from Jerusalem to Jericho, and fell among thieves; but I could not hope for Priest, Levite, or good Samaritan to come by on either side, but one morning Syed bin Majid said to me, 'Now this is the first time we have been alone together; I have no goods, but I have ivory; let me, I pray you, sell some ivory, and give the goods to you.' This was encouraging; but I said, 'Not yet, but by-and-bye'. I had still a few barter goods left, which I had taken the precaution to deposit with Mohamad bin Saleh before going to Manyuema, in case of returning in extreme need. But when my spirits were at their lowest ebb, the good Samaritan was close at hand, for one morning Susi came running at the top of his speed and gasped out, 'An Englishman! I see him!' and off he darted to meet him. The American flag at the head of a caravan told of the nationality of the stranger. Bales of goods, baths of tin, huge kettles, cooking pots, tents, &c., made me think 'This must be a luxurious traveller, and not one at his wits' end like me'. *(28th October.)* It was Henry Moreland Stanley, the travelling correspondent of the *New York Herald.* The news he had to tell to one who had been two full years without any tidings from Europe made my whole frame thrill. The terrible fate that had befallen France, the telegraphic cables successfully laid in the Atlantic, the election of General Grant, the death of good Lord Clarendon and many other points of interest, revived emotions that had lain dormant in Manyuema. Appetite returned, and instead of the spare, tasteless, two meals a day, I ate four times daily, and in a week began to feel strong. I am not of a demonstrative turn; as cold, indeed, as we islanders are usually reputed to be, but this disinterested kindness was simply overwhelming.

LJ 1871

Livingstone's marches were attended by every kind of African pest and para-site, to which he gives his usual imperturbable attention. The single extract that follows is given less for the ants than for the coolness and complete lack of complaint of their target, then near Lake Bangweulu and within a few weeks of his death:

Suffered a furious attack at midnight from the red Sirafu or Driver ants. Our cook fled at their first onset. I lighted a candle, and remembering Dr. Van der Kemp's idea that no animal will attack man unprovoked, I lay still. The first came on my foot quietly, then some began to bite between the toes, then the larger ones swarmed over the foot and bit furiously, and made the blood start out. I went out of the tent, and my whole person was instantly covered as close as small-pox on a patient. Grass fires were lighted, and my men picked some off my limbs and tried to save me. After battling for an hour or two they took me into a hut not yet invaded, and I rested till they came and routed me out there too!

LJ 17 Feb 1873

Equally remarkable for its fortitude is his famous account of the theft of his medicine-chest in Eastern Zambia, over the Luangwa river, not far from Mpika:

20th January. – The two Waiyau, who joined us at Kandé's village, now deserted. Knowing the language well, they were extremely useful, and no one thought that they would desert, for they were free men – their masters had been killed by the Mazitu – and this circumstance, and their uniform good conduct, made us trust them more than we should have done any others who had been slaves. But they left us in the forest, and heavy rain came on, which obliterated every vestige of their footsteps. To make the loss the more galling, they took what we could least spare – the medicine-box, which they would only throw away as soon as they came to examine their booty. One of these deserters exchanged his load that morning with a boy called Baraka, who had charge of the medicine-box, because he was so careful. This was done because with the medicine-box were packed five large cloths and all Baraka's clothing and beads, of which he was very careful. The Waiyau also offered to carry this burden a stage to help Baraka, while he gave his own load, in which there was no cloth, in exchange. The forest was so dense and high, there was no chance of getting a glimpse of the fugitives, who took all the dishes, a large box of powder, the flour we had purchased dearly to help us as far as the Chambezé, the tools, two guns, and a cartridge-pouch; but the medicine-chest was the sorest loss of all!

All the other goods I had divided in case of loss or desertion, but had never dreamed of losing the precious quinine and other remedies; other losses and annoyances I felt as just parts of that undercurrent of vexation which is not wanting in even the smoothest life, and certainly not worthy of being moaned over by an explorer anxious to benefit a country and people –

but this loss I feel most keenly. It is difficult to say from the heart, 'Thy will be done'; but I shall try. These men had few advantages: sold into slavery in early life, they were in the worst possible school for learning to be honest and honourable. They behaved well for a long time; but, having had hard and scanty fare in Lobisa, wet and misery in passing through dripping forests, hungry nights and fatiguing days, their patience must have been worn out, and they had no sentiments of honour, or at least none so strong as we ought to have; they gave way to the temptation which their good conduct had led us to put in their way. Some we have come across in this journey seemed born essentially mean and base — a great misfortune to them and all who have to deal with them, but they cannot be so blamable as those who have no natural tendency to meanness, and whose education has taught them to abhor it. True; yet this loss of the medicine-box gnaws at the heart terribly. I felt as if I had now received the sentence of death, like poor Bishop Mackenzie.

LJ 20 Jan 1867

Like Burns, Livingstone had a feeling for 'nature's social union', that comes out clearly in his notes on various pets who accompanied his safaris.

Our poodle Chitané chased the dogs of this village with unrelenting fury. His fierce looks inspired terror entirely owing to its being difficult to distinguish at which end his head or tail lay. He enjoyed the chase of the yelping curs immensely, but if one of them had turned he would have bolted the other way.

LJ 3 May 1866

This was on the Rovuma River on the way inland in 1866: the next year Chitané was lost:

15th January. — We had to cross the Chimbwé at its eastern end, where it is fully a mile wide. The guide refused to show another and narrower ford up the stream, which emptied into it from the east; and I, being the first to cross, neglected to give orders about the poor little dog, Chitané. The water was waist deep, the bottom soft peaty stuff with deep holes in it, and the northern side infested by leeches. The boys were — like myself — all too much engaged with preserving their balance to think of the spirited little beast, and he must have swam till he sunk. He was so useful in keeping all the country curs off our huts; none dare to approach and steal, and he never stole himself. He shared the staring of the people with his master, then in the march he took charge of the whole party, running to the front, and again to the rear, to see that all was right. He was becoming yellowish-red in colour; and, poor thing, perished in what the boys all call Chitané's water.

LJ 15 Jan 1867

Whether Sinbad the ox was a pet or a pest seems an open question. Naliele was the chief kraal of the Barotse, reached on the return march from Luanda in June/July, 1855:

In passing through these narrow paths, I had an opportunity of observing the peculiarities of my ox 'Sinbad'. He had a softer back than the others, but a much more intractable temper. His horns were bent downwards and hung loosely, so he could do no harm with them; but as we wended our way slowly along the narrow path, he would suddenly dart aside. A string tied to a stick put through the cartilage of the nose serves instead of a bridle: if you jerk this back, it makes him run faster on; if you pull it to one side, he allows the nose and head to go, but keeps the opposite eye directed to the forbidden spot, and goes in spite of you. The only way he can be brought to a stand is by a stroke with a wand across the nose. When Sinbad ran in below a climber stretched over the path, so low that I could not stoop under it, I was dragged off and came down on the crown of my head; and he never allowed an opportunity of this kind to pass without trying to inflict a kick, as if I neither had nor deserved his love.

Before reaching the Makondo, we came upon the tsetse in such numbers, that many bites were inflicted on my poor ox, in spite of a man with a branch warding them off. The bite of this insect does not affect the donkey as it does cattle. The next morning, the spots on which my ox had been bitten, were marked by patches of hair, about half an inch broad, being wetted by exudation. Poor Sinbad had carried me all the way from the Leeba to Golungo Alto, and all the way back again, without losing any of his peculiarities, or ever becoming reconciled to our perversity, in forcing him away each morning from the pleasant pasturage on which he had fed. I wished to give the climax to his usefulness, and allay our craving for animal food at the same time, but, my men having some compunction, we carried him to end his days in peace at Naliele.

MT 345 and 487

Livingstone is is too much himself to do quite what one expects, and I have left till last what is perhaps the most significant detail of his safaris, the coffee ritual he practised with Sekeletu in 1853:

They are eminently gregarious in their eating; and, as they despise any one who eats alone, I always poured out two cups of coffee at my own meals, so that the chief, or some one of the principal men, might partake along with me.

MT 206

Only at work was he one with his Africans; at rest he had his own area. Needless to say, it was small and not rigidly defined, but it is challenging that this most tactful and unpretentious of men should have thought fit to practise a certain degree of apartheid. Mere racial fusion is certainly not encouraged by Livingstone's example (although he had no objection to mixed marriages).

There seems an extent to which each individual and (I think he might have argued today) each race requires its own solitude. Moreover, to read the parable more closely, races mix not indiscriminately but on common class-levels. The whole of Livingstone's record is there to prove that this stems from no supercilious pride of race. Like Sekeletu's blanket, the coffee ritual takes on a mythical quality in Livingstone's explorations of territories more important even than the Zambezi or the Congo.

1   Macnair, p. 33.
2   MT 94.
3   The sketch is signed by J. W. Whymper, to whom (on second thoughts) I think the 'exquisite Victorian' quality must be credited. Rider or Ryder's sketch was only of the Lake, and it was probably lent by his mother (see MT 75) to be worked up to its present form by Whymper under Livingstone's directions. As the Bakwena chief, Sechele, was present at Lake Ngami on the second trip, it is conceivable that he is the impressive figure behind Livingstone; though it is odd that he is not named.
4   His cottage, The Lodge, Harfield Place, Claremont, was sold in 1973 without anyone's realising whose it had been.
5   Sillery, p. 84.
6   Wallis, p. 147.
7   ZT 31.
8   Macnair, p. 15.
9   This is the present Rwanda-Burundi, where 200 000 were reported dead in tribal warfare in 1972.

CHAPTER 4

The African Ecology

In the early days of the Industrial Revolution in Great Britain factory workers were not urbanised. Machines ran on water-power and many industries, including cotton, stood where streams fell sharply from the unpolluted hills. Factory boys could thus remain naturalists, if the taste was in them as it was in Livingstone. His 'intense love of Nature' arose from the usual psychological sources and gave him response to grandeur, broad, flowing lines and to all kinds of activities; as well as a delicate sensitivity worthy of Burns. This taste took a scientific direction and refinement, and came to be embraced by Christian pantheism. He copies in, as epigraph to his first notebook, Coleridge's

> He prayeth well who loveth well
> Both man and bird and beast;
> He prayeth best who loveth best
> All things both great and small;
> For the dear God who loveth us,
> He made and loves us all.

The variety of African wild life far surpasses that of Europe and America. Even in Southern Africa – to use figures given by the naturalist James Clarke in the *Cape Argus*, 24 June, 1972 – there are nearly 400 different types of mammal, including 80 game animals; 550 different reptiles and amphibians; almost 1 000 kinds of birds; 18 000 plant species, including nearly 1 000 trees; and of insects, well, 800 kinds of butterfly alone. To put Livingstone in the midst of such plenty, fresh from his rambles in the Grampian Hills, was like putting a cat in a dairy.

It is not merely to the details of the African scene that Livingstone responds but to its totality, the ecosystem in all its harmony, including man; and he often calls it Eden. Hence I have started with a few of his descriptions of the great face of Africa, passing to his encounters with big game and other fauna, and concluding with something of his sympathy with and apprehension for the animals.

The final extracts show that he would have been a conservationist today. Before Livingstone's time man had exterminated 300 species of animal and since 1873 170 more have joined them in oblivion, including (in Africa) the quagga, the Cape lion, Burchell's Zebra and several kinds of antelope. All over the world today, 817 species are slated for extinction. By the year 2000, it is said, there will be no wild animals outside the reserves, and those subject to grievous poaching.

On the way down the Zambezi, May, 1855.

When we came to the top of the outer range of the hills, we had a glorious view. At a short distance below us we saw the Kafue, wending away over a forest-clad plain to the confluence, and on the other side of the Zambesi beyond that, lay a long range of dark hills. A line of fleecy clouds appeared lying along the course of that river at their base. The plain below us, at the left of the Kafue, had more large game on it than anywhere else I had seen in Africa. Hundreds of buffaloes and zebras grazed on the open spaces, and there stood lordly elephants feeding majestically, nothing moving apparently but the proboscis. I wished that I had been able to take a photograph of a scene, so seldom beheld, and which is destined, as guns increase, to pass away from earth.

MT 570

Zambezi delta, early 1859.

At the end of the hot season everything is dry and dusty; the atmosphere is loaded with blue haze, and very sultry. After the rains begin, the face of the country changes with surprising rapidity for the better. The air becomes cleared of the smoky-looking haze, and one sees to great distances with ease; the landscape is bathed in a perfect flood of light, and a delightful sense of freshness is given from everything in the morning before the glare of noon overpowers the eye. On asking one of the Bechuanas once, what he understood by the word used for 'holiness' (boitsépho)? he answered, 'When copious showers have descended during the night, and all the earth and leaves and cattle are washed clean, and the sun rising shows a drop of dew on every blade of grass, and the air breathes fresh, that is holiness.'

ZT 64

Plains west of Tete, south-west of Caborabasa, going up the Zambezi, June, 1860.

Our path leads frequently through vast expanses of apparently solitary scenery; a strange stillness pervades the air; no sound is heard from bird or beast or living thing; no village is near; the air is still, and earth and sky have sunk into a deep, sultry repose, and like a lonely ship on the desert sea is the long winding line of weary travellers on the hot, glaring plain. We discover that we are not alone in the wilderness; other living forms are round about us, with curious eyes on all our movements. As we enter a piece of woodland, an unexpected herd of pallahs, or waterbucks, suddenly appears, standing as quiet and still, as if constituting a part of the landscape; or, we pass a clump of thick thorns, and see through the bushes the dim phantom-like forms of buffaloes, their heads lowered, gazing at us with fierce untameable eyes. Again a sharp turn brings us upon a native, who has seen us from afar, and comes with noiseless footsteps to get a nearer view.

ZT 196

The Zambezi (Barotseland)–Angola border, April, 1854.

Below us lay the valley of the Quángo. If you sit on the spot where Mary Queen of Scots viewed the battle of Langside, and look down on the vale of Clyde, you may see in miniature the glorious sight which a much greater and richer valley presented to our view. It is about a hundred miles broad, clothed with dark forest, except where the light-green grass covers meadow-lands on the Quango, which here and there glances out in the sun as it wends its way to the north. The opposite side of this great valley appears like a range of lofty mountains, and the descent into it about a mile, which, measured perpendicularly, may be from a thousand to twelve hundred feet. Emerging from the gloomy forests of Londa, this magnificent prospect made us all feel as if a weight had been lifted off our eyelids. A cloud was passing across the middle of the valley, from which rolling thunder pealed, while above all was glorious sunlight; and when we went down to the part where we saw it passing, we found that a very heavy thunder-shower had fallen under the path of the cloud: and the bottom of the valley, which from above seemed quite smooth, we discovered to be intersected and furrowed by great numbers of deep-cut streams. Looking back from below, the descent appears as the edge of a table-land, with numerous indented dells and spurs jutting out all along, giving it a serrated appearance. Both the top and sides of the sierra are covered with trees, but large patches of the more perpendicular parts are bare, and exhibit the red soil, which is general over the region we have now entered.

MT 360

Going north through the Bamangwato Hills, Botswana, January, 1853.

These hills are the last we shall see for months. The country beyond consisted of large patches of trap-covered tufa, having little soil or vegetation except tufts of grass and wait-a-bit thorns, in the midst of extensive sandy plains. These yellow-coloured grassy plains, with *Moretloa* and *mahatla* bushes, form quite a characteristic feature of the country. The yellow or dun-colour prevails during a great part of the year. The Bakwain hills are an exception, for they are covered with green trees to their tops, and the valleys are often of the most lovely green. If you look north from the hills we are now leaving, the country partakes of this latter character. It appears as if it were a flat covered with a forest of ordinary-sized trees from 20 to 30 feet high, but when you travel over it they are not so closely planted but that a waggon with care may be guided among them. The grass grows in tufts of the size of one's hat, with bare soft sand between.

MT 150

South of the Caprivi Strip, March, 1853.

This being the only hill we had seen since leaving the Bamangwato, we felt inclined to take off our hats to it. It is three or four hundred feet high, and covered with trees. I may mention that the valley on its northern side, named Kandehái, is as picturesque a spot as is to be seen in this part of Africa. The open glade, surrounded by forest trees of various hues, had a little stream meandering in the centre. A herd of reddish-coloured antelopes (pallahs) stood on one side, near a large baobab, looking at us, and ready to run up the hill; while gnus, tsessebes, and zebras gazed in astonishment at the intruders. Some fed carelessly, and others put on the peculiar air of displeasure which these animals sometimes assume before they resolve on flight. A large white rhinoceros came along the bottom of the valley with his slow sauntering gait without noticing us; he looked as if he meant to indulge in a mud bath. Several buffaloes, with their dark visages, stood under the trees on the side opposite to the pallahs. It being Sunday, all was peace, and, from the circumstances in which our party was placed, we could not but reflect on that second stage of our existence which we hope will lead us into scenes of perfect beauty.

MT 172

On the way to Nyangwe, near Kindu, E. Congo, March, 1871.

Our path lay through dense forest, and again, on the 5th, our march was in the same dense jungle of lofty trees and vegetation that touch our arms on each side. We came to some villages among beautiful tree-covered hills, called Basilañgé or Mobasilangé. The villages are very pretty, standing on slopes. The main street generally lies east and west, to allow the bright sun to stream his clear hot rays from one end to the other, and lick up quickly the moisture from the frequent showers which is not drained off by the slopes. A little verandah is often made in front of the door, and here at dawn the family gathers round a fire, and, while enjoying the heat needed in the cold that always accompanies the first darting of the light or sun's rays across the atmosphere, inhale the delicious air, and talk over their little domestic affairs. The various-shaped leaves of the forest all around their village and near their nestlings are bespangled with myriads of dewdrops. The cocks crow vigorously, and strut and ogle; the kids gambol and leap on the backs of their dams quietly chewing the cud; other goats make believe fighting. Thrifty wives often bake their new clay pots in a fire, made by lighting a heap of grass roots: the next morning they extract salt from the ashes, and so two birds are killed with one stone. The beauty of this morning scene of peaceful enjoyment is indescribable.

LJ 2–5 Mar 1871

South-west Malawi near Lilongwe, 29 October, 1866.
    The morning was lovely, the whole country bathed in bright sunlight, and not a breath of air disturbed the smoke as it slowly curled up from the heaps of burning weeds, which the native agriculturist wisely destroys. The people generally were busy hoeing in the cool of the day. One old man in the village where we rested had trained the little hair he had left into a tail, which, well plastered with fat, he had bent on itself and laid flat on his crown; another was carefully paring a stick for stirring the porridge, and others were enjoying the cool shade of the wild fig-trees which are always planted at villages.

LJ 29 Oct 1866

South of Caborabasa, February, 1856.
    While waiting by the elephant, I observed a great number of insects, like grains of fine sand, moving on my boxes. On examination with a glass, four species were apparent; one of green and gold preening its wings, which glanced in the sun with metallic lustre, another clear as crystal, a third of the colour of vermilion, and a fourth black. Almost every plant has its own peculiar insect, and when the rains are over, very few seeds remain untouched; even the fiery bird's-eye pepper, is itself devoured by a maggot. I observed here, what I had often seen before, that certain districts abound in centipedes. Here they have light reddish bodies and blue legs; great myriapedes are seen crawling everywhere. Although they do no harm, they excite in man a feeling of loathing. Perhaps our appearance produces a similar feeling in the elephant and other large animals. When they have been much disturbed, they certainly look upon us with great distrust. In the quietest parts of the forest there is heard a faint but distinct hum, which tells of insect joy. One may see many whisking about in the clear sunshine in patches among the green glancing leaves; but there are invisible myriads working with never-tiring mandibles on leaves, and stalks, and beneath the soil. They are all brimful of enjoyment. Indeed the universality of organic life may be called a mantle of happy existence encircling the world, and imparts the idea of its being caused by the consciousness of our benignant Father's smile on all the works of His hands.

MT 609

The Animals: Lions.

Having tangled with lions at close quarters, Livingstone is perhaps entitled to take the disparaging view of them he does. The fractured shoulder he sustained never perfectly knit and was one of the ways in which his remains were identified.

South of the Caprivi Strip, March, 1853.

Lions here are not often heard. They seem to have a wholesome dread of the Bushmen, who, when they observe evidence of a lion's having made a full meal, follow up his spoor so quietly that his slumbers are not disturbed. One discharges a poisoned arrow from a distance of only a few feet, while his companion simultaneously throws his skin cloak on the beast's head. The sudden surprise makes the lion lose his presence of mind, and he bounds away in the greatest confusion and terror. Our friends here showed me the poison which they use on these occasions. It is the entrails of a caterpillar called N'gwa, half an inch long. They squeeze out these, and place them all around the bottom of the barb, and allow the poison to dry in the sun. They are very careful in cleaning their nails after working with it, as a small portion introduced into a scratch acts like morbid matter in dissection wounds. The agony is so great that the person cuts himself, calls for his mother's breast as if he were returned in idea to his childhood again, or flies from human habitations a raging maniac. The effects on the lion are equally terrible. He is heard moaning in distress, and becomes furious, biting the trees and ground in rage.

MT 171

Mabotsa, near Zeerust, Western Transvaal, 1844.

It is well known that if one in a troop of lions is killed the others take the hint and leave that part of the country. So the next time the herds were attacked, I went with the people, in order to encourage them to rid themselves of the annoyance by destroying one of the marauders. We found the lions on a small hill about a quarter of a mile in length, and covered with trees. Going round the end of the hill I saw one of the beasts sitting on a piece of rock with a little bush in front. Being about thirty yards off, I took a good aim at his body through the bush, and fired both barrels into it. The men then called out, 'He is shot, he is shot!' Others cried, 'He has been shot by another man too!' I saw the lion's tail erected in anger behind the bush, and, turning to the people, said, 'Stop a little till I load again'. When in the act of ramming down the bullets I heard a shout. Starting, and looking half round, I saw the lion just in the act of springing upon me. I was upon a little height; he caught my shoulder as he sprang, and we both came to the ground below together. Growling horribly close to my ear, he shook me as a terrier dog does a rat. The shock produced a stupor similar to that which seems to be felt by a mouse after the first shake of the cat. It caused a sort of dreaminess, in which there was no sense of pain nor feeling of terror, though quite conscious of all that was happening. It was like what patients partially under the influence of chloroform describe, who see all the operation, but feel not the knife. This singular condition was not the result of any mental process. The shake annihilated fear, and allowed no sense of horror in looking round at the beast. This peculiar state is probably produced in all animals killed by the carnivora; and if so, is a merciful provision by our benevolent Creator for lessening the pain of death. Turning round to relieve myself of the weight, as he had one paw on the back of my head, I saw his eyes directed to Mebalwe, who was trying to shoot him at a distance of ten or fifteen yards. His gun, a flint one, missed fire in both barrels; the lion immediately left me, and, attacking Mebalwe, bit his thigh. Another man, whose life I had saved before, after he had been tossed by a buffalo, attempted to spear the lion while he was biting Mebalwe. He left Mebalwe and caught this man by the shoulder, but at that moment the bullets he had received took effect, and he fell down dead. The whole was the work of a few moments, and must have been his paroxysm of dying rage. In order to take out the charm from him, the Bakatla on the following day made a huge bonfire over the carcase, which was declared to be that of the largest lion they had ever seen. Besides crunching the bone into splinters, he left eleven teeth wounds on the upper part of my arm.

MT 11

Eastern Kalahari, Botswana, 1853.

Lions get lean and perish miserably by reason of the decay of the teeth. When a lion grows too old to catch game, he frequently takes to killing goats in the villages; a woman or child happening to go out at night falls a prey too; and as this is his only source of subsistence now, he continues it. From this circumstance has arisen the idea that the lion, when he has once tasted human flesh, loves it better than any other. A man-eater is invariably an old lion; and when he overcomes his fear of man so far as to come to villages for goats, the people remark, 'His teeth are worn, he will soon kill men'. They at once acknowledge the necessity of instant action, and turn out to kill him. When living far away from population, or when, as is the case in some parts, he entertains a wholesome dread of the tribesmen, as soon as either disease or old age overtakes him, he begins to catch mice and other small rodents, and even to eat grass; the natives, observing undigested vegetable matter in his droppings, follow up his trail in the certainty of finding him scarcely able to move under some tree, and despatch him without difficulty.

When a lion is met in the daytime, a circumstance by no means unfrequent to travellers in these parts, if preconceived notions do not lead them to expect something very 'noble', or 'majestic', they will see merely an animal somewhat larger than the biggest dog they ever saw, and partaking very strongly of the canine features; the face is not much like the usual drawings of a lion, the nose being prolonged like a dog's; not exactly such as our painters make it, their ideas of majesty being usually shown by making their lions' faces like old women in nightcaps. When encountered in the day-time, the lion stands a second or two gazing, then turns slowly round, and walks as slowly away for a dozen paces, looking over his shoulder; then begins to trot, and, when he thinks himself out of sight, bounds off like a greyhound. By day there is not, as a rule, the smallest danger of lions which are not molested attacking man, nor even on a clear moonlight night, except when they are breeding; this makes them brave almost any danger; and if a man happens to cross to the windward of them, both lion and lioness will rush at him, in the manner of a bitch with whelps. So general, however, is the sense of security on moonlight nights that we seldom tied up our oxen, but let them lie loose by the waggons; while on a dark rainy night, if a lion is in the neighbourhood, he is almost sure to venture to kill an ox. His approach is always stealthy, except when wounded; and any appearance of a trap is enough to cause him to refrain from making the last spring.

Nothing that I ever learned of the lion would lead me to attribute to it either the ferocious or noble character ascribed to it elsewhere. It possesses none of the nobility of the Newfoundland or St. Bernard dogs. With respect to its great strength there can be no doubt. The immense masses of muscle around its jaws, shoulders, and forearms, proclaim tremendous force. They would seem, however, to be inferior in power to those of the Indian tiger.

Similarly, to talk of the majestic roar of the lion is mere majestic twaddle. On my mentioning this fact some years ago, the assertion was doubted, so I have been careful ever since to inquire the opinions of Europeans, who have heard both, if they could detect any difference between the roar of a lion and that of an ostrich; the invariable answer was – that they could not when the animal was at any distance. The natives assert that they can detect a variation between the commencement of the noise of each. There is, it must be admitted, considerable difference between the singing noise of a lion when full and his deep gruff growl when hungry. In general the lion's voice seems to come deeper from the chest than that of the ostrich; but to this day I can distinguish between them with certainty only by knowing that the ostrich roars by day and the lion by night.

In general the lion seizes the animal he is attacking by the flank near the hind leg, or by the throat below the jaw. It is questionable whether he ever attempts to seize an animal by the withers. The flank is the most common point of attack, and that is the part he begins to feast on first. The natives and lions are very similar in their tastes in the selection of tit-bits: an eland may be seen disembowelled by a lion, so completely, that he scarcely seems cut up at all. The bowels and fatty parts form a full meal for even the largest lion. The jackal comes sniffing about, and sometimes suffers for his temerity by a stroke from the lion's paw laying him dead. When gorged, the lion falls fast asleep and is then easily despatched. Hunting a lion with dogs involves very little danger as compared with hunting the Indian tiger; because the dogs bring him out of cover and make him stand at bay, giving the hunter plenty of time for a good deliberate shot.

Where game is abundant, there you may expect lions in proportionately large numbers. They are never seen in herds, but six or eight, probably one family, occasionally hunt together. One is in much more danger of being run over when walking in the streets of London, than he is of being devoured by lions in Africa, unless engaged in hunting the animal. Indeed, nothing that I have seen or heard about lions would constitute a barrier in the way of men or ordinary courage and enterprise.

MT 136

Elephant

The supreme quarry for profit and danger. In Botswana, in 1877 alone, the traders of Shoshong handled 75 tons of ivory (12 000 elephants). In the south-central Zambezi, between 1872 and 1874, 150 tons were taken. Livingstone estimates the annual *world* slaughter of elephants in his time as 30 000 (ZT 243). The inducement was guns. Muskets, war surplus from Waterloo days, I suppose, would fetch twenty times their European market value in ivory: one musket was worth a good tusk.

September–October 1861, in the gig on Lake Malawi/Nyasa.

One morning when sailing past a pretty-thickly inhabited part, we were surprised at seeing nine large bull-elephants standing near the beach quietly flapping their gigantic ears. Glad of an opportunity of getting some fresh meat, we landed and fired into one. They all retreated into a marshy piece of ground between two villages. Our men gave chase, and fired into the herd. Standing on a sand hummock, we could see the bleeding animals throwing showers of water with their trunks over their backs. The herd was soon driven back upon us, and a wounded one turned to bay. Yet neither this one, nor any of the others, ever attempted to charge. Having broken his legs with a rifle-ball, we fired into him at forty yards as rapidly as we could load and discharge the rifles. He simply shook his head at each shot, and received at least sixty Enfield balls before he fell. Our excellent sailor from the north of Ireland happened to fire the last, and, as soon as he saw the animal fall, he turned with an air of triumph to the Doctor and exclaimed, 'It was *my* shot that done it, sir!'

In a few minutes, upwards of a thousand natives were round the prostrate king of beasts; and, after our men had taken all they wanted, an invitation was given to the villagers to take the remainder. They rushed at it like hungry hyenas, and in an incredibly short time every inch of it was carried off. It was only by knowing that the meat would all be used, that we felt justified in the slaughter of this noble creature. The tusks weighed 62 lbs. each. A large amount of ivory might be obtained from the people of Nyassa, and we were frequently told of their having it in their huts.

ZT 388

Between Kariba and Chirundu, on the way down the Zambezi, December, 1855.

We entered a most beautiful valley, abounding in large game. Finding a buffalo lying down, I went to secure him for our food. Three bullets did not kill him, and, as he turned round as if for a charge, we ran for the shelter of some rocks. Before we gained them, we found that three elephants had cut off our retreat on that side: they, however, turned short off, and allowed us to gain the rocks. We then saw that the buffalo was moving off quite briskly, and in order not to be entirely balked, I tried a long shot at the last of the elephants, and, to the great joy of my people, broke his fore-leg. The young men soon brought him to a stand, and one shot in the brain despatched him.

On the following day, while my men were cutting up the elephant, great numbers of the villagers came to enjoy the feast. We were on the side of a fine green valley, studded here and there with trees, and cut by numerous rivulets. I had retired from the noise, to take an observation among some rocks of laminated grit, when I beheld an elephant and her calf at the end of the valley, about two miles distant. The calf was rolling in the mud, and the dam was standing fanning herself with her great ears. As I looked at them through my glass, I saw a long string of my own men appearing on the other side of them, and Sekwebu came and told me that these had gone off, saying, 'Our father will see today what sort of men he has got'. I then went higher up the side of the valley, in order to have a view of their mode of hunting. The goodly beast, totally unconscious of the approach of an enemy, stood for some time suckling her young one, which seemed about two years old; they then went into a pit containing mud, and smeared themselves all over with it, the little one frisking about his dam, flapping his ears and tossing his trunk incessantly, in elephantine fashion. She kept flapping her ears and wagging her tail, as if in the height of enjoyment. Then began the piping of her enemies, which was performed by blowing into a tube, or the hands closed together, as boys do into a key. They called out to attract the animal's attention –

'O chief! chief! we have come to kill you.
O chief! chief! many more will die besides you, &c.
The gods have said it,' &c. &c.

Both animals expanded their ears and listened, then left their bath as the crowd rushed towards them. The little one ran towards the end of the valley, but, seeing the men there, returned to his dam. She placed herself on the danger side of her calf, and passed her proboscis over it again and again, as if to assure it of safety. She frequently looked back to the men, who kept up an incessant shouting, singing, and piping; then looked at her young one and ran after it, sometimes sideways, as if her feelings were divided between anxiety to protect her offspring, and desire to revenge the temerity of her persecutors. The men kept about a hundred yards in her rear, until she was obliged to cross a rivulet. The time spent in descending and getting up the opposite bank, allowed of their coming up to the edge, and discharging their spears at about twenty yards distance. After the first discharge, she appeared with her sides red with blood, and, beginning to flee for her own life, seemed to think no more of her young. I had previously sent off

Sekwebu with orders to spare the calf. It ran very fast, but neither young nor old ever gallop; their quickest pace is only a sharp walk. Before Sekwebu could reach it, the calf had taken refuge in the water, and was killed. The pace of the dam gradually became slower. She turned with a shriek of rage, and made a furious charge back among the men. They vanished at right angles to her course and, as she ran straight on, she went through the whole party, but came near no one, except a man who wore a piece of cloth on his shoulders. Bright clothing is always dangerous in these cases. She charged three or four times, but, except in the first instance, never went farther than 100 yards. She often stood and faced the men, though she received fresh spears. It was by this process of spearing and loss of blood that she was killed, for at last, making a short charge, she staggered round and sank down dead in a kneeling posture. I turned from the spectacle of the destruction of noble animals, which might be made so useful in Africa, with a feeling of sickness, and it was not relieved by the recollection that the ivory was mine, though that was the case. I regretted to see them killed, and more especially the young one, the meat not being at all necessary at that time; but it is right to add, that I did not feel sick when my own blood was up the day before. We ought perhaps to judge those deeds more leniently in which we ourselves have no temptation to engage. Had I not been previously guilty of doing the very same thing, I might have prided myself on my superior humanity, when I experienced nausea in viewing my men kill these two.

MT 560

Upper Gwembe Valley (Lake Kariba), November, 1855.
Buffaloes abound, and we see large herds of them feeding in all directions by day. When much disturbed by man, they retire into the densest parts of the forest, and feed by night only. We secured a fine large bull by crawling close to a herd: when shot, he fell down, and the rest, not seeing their enemy, gazed about, wondering where the danger lay. The others came back to it, and, when we showed ourselves, much to the amusement of my companions, they lifted him up with their horns, and, half supporting him in the crowd, bore him away. All these wild animals usually gore a wounded companion and expel him from the herd; even zebras bite and kick an unfortunate or a diseased one. It is intended by this instinct, that none but the perfect and healthy ones should propagate the species. In this case they manifested their usual propensity to gore the wounded, but our appearance at that moment caused them to take flight, and this gave my men the impression that they were helping away their wounded companion. The herd ran away in the direction of our camp, and then came bounding past us again. We took refuge on a large ant-hill, and as they rushed by us at full gallop, I had a good opportunity of seeing that the leader of a herd of about sixty, was an old cow; all the others allowed her a full half-length in their front. On her withers sat about twenty buffalo-birds which act the part of guardian spirits to the animals. When the buffalo is quietly feeding, this bird may be seen hopping on the ground picking up food, or sitting on its back ridding it of the

ınsects with which their skins are sometimes infested. The sight of the bird
being much more acute than that of the buffalo, it is soon alarmed by the
approach of any danger, and, flying up, the buffaloes instantly raise their
heads to discover the cause, which has led to the sudden flight of their
guardian. They sometimes accompany the buffaloes in their flight on the
wing, at other times they sit as above described.

MT 545

South-west of Caborabasa, on the way down the Zambezi, February, 1856.

We observed the footprints of a black rhinoceros and her calf. We saw
other footprints among the hills of Semalembue, but the black rhinoceros is
remarkably scarce in all the country north of the Zambesi. The white
rhinoceros is quite extinct here, and will soon become unknown in the
country to the south. It feeds almost entirely on grasses, and is of a timid
unsuspecting disposition: this renders it an easy prey, and they are
slaughtered without mercy on the introduction of fire-arms. The black
possesses a more savage nature, and, like the ill-natured in general, is never
found with an ounce of fat in its body. From its greater fierceness and
wariness, it holds its place in a district much longer than its more timid and
better conditioned neighbour.

MT 611

Barotseland, on a trip with Sekeletu, July, 1853.

We shot a beautiful cow-eland, standing in the shade of a fine tree. It was
evident that she had lately had her calf killed by a lion, for there were five
long deep scratches on both sides of her hind-quarters, as if she had run to
the rescue of her calf, and the lion, leaving it, had attacked herself, but was
unable to pull her down. When lying on the ground, the milk flowing from
the large udder showed that she must have been seeking the shade, from the
distress its non-removal in the natural manner caused. She was a beautiful
creature, and Lebeóle, a Makololo gentleman who accompanied me,
speaking in reference to its size and beauty, said, 'Jesus ought to have given
us these instead of cattle'. It was a new undescribed variety of this splendid
antelope. It was marked with narrow white bands across the body, exactly
like those of the koodoo, and had a black patch of more than a hand-breadth
on the outer side of the forearm.

MT 210

Tsouga River, near Lake Ngami, August, 1849.

We discovered an entirely new species of antelope, called leché. It is a
beautiful water-antelope of a light brownish-yellow colour. Its horns —
exactly like those of the water-buck, rise from the head with a slight bend
backwards, then curve forwards at the points. The chest, belly, and orbits
are nearly white, the front of the legs and ankles deep brown. From the
horns, along the nape to the withers, the male has a small mane of the same
yellowish colour with the rest of the skin, and the tail has a tuft of black hair.

It is never found a mile from water; islets in marshes and rivers are its favourite haunts, and it is quite unknown except in the central humid basin of Africa. Having a good deal of curiosity, it presents a noble appearance as it stands gazing with head erect at the approaching stranger. When it resolves to decamp, it lowers its head, and lays its horns down to a level with the withers; it then begins with a waddling trot, which ends in its galloping and springing over bushes like the pallahs. It invariably runs to the water, and crosses it by a succession of bounds, each of which appears to be from the bottom. We thought the flesh good at first, but soon got tired of it.

MT 71

Near Serowe, Botswana, February, 1853.

Many of the plains here have large expanses of grass without trees, but you seldom see a treeless horizon. The ostrich is generally seen quietly feeding on some spot where no one can approach him without being detected by his wary eye. As the waggon moves along far to the windward, he thinks it is intending to circumvent him, so he rushes up a mile or so from the leeward, and so near to the front oxen that one sometimes gets a shot at the silly bird. When he begins to run, all the game in sight follow his example. He never swerves from the course he once adopts, but only increases his speed.

When the ostrich is feeding, his pace is from twenty to twenty-two inches; when walking, but not feeding, it is twenty-six inches; and when terrified, as in the case noticed, it is from eleven and a half to thirteen and even fourteen feet in length. Only in one case was I at all satisfied of being able to count the rate of speed by a stop watch, and, if I am not mistaken, there were thirty in ten seconds; generally one's eye can no more follow the legs than it can the spokes of a carriage-wheel in rapid motion. If we take the above number, and twelve feet stride as the average pace, we have a speed of twenty-six miles an hour. It cannot be very much above that, and is therefore slower than a railway locomotive. They are sometimes shot by the horseman making a cross cut to their undeviating course, but few Englishmen ever succeed in killing them.

The ostrich begins to lay her eggs before she has fixed on a spot for a nest, which is only a hollow a few inches deep in the sand, and about a yard in diameter. Both male and female assist in the incubation. Several eggs lie out of the nest, and are thought to be intended as food for the first of the newly-hatched brood till the rest come out and enable the whole to start in quest of food. I have several times seen newly-hatched young in charge of the cock, who made a very good attempt at appearing lame in the plover fashion, in order to draw off the attention of pursuers. The young squat down and remain immovable when too small to run far, but attain a wonderful degree of speed when about the size of common fowls.

The food of the ostrich consists of pods and seeds of different kinds of leguminous plants, with leaves of various plants; and, as these are often hard and dry, he picks up a great quantity of pebbles, many of which are as large as marbles. He picks up also some small bulbs, and occasionally a wild melon to afford moisture, for one was found with a melon which had choked him by sticking in his throat. It requires the utmost address of the Bushmen, crawling for miles on their stomachs, to stalk them successfully; yet the quantity of feathers collected annually shows that the numbers slain must be considerable, as each bird has only a few in the wings and tail. The male bird is of a jet black glossy colour, with the single exception of the white feathers, which are objects of trade. Nothing can be finer than the adaptation of these flossy feathers for the climate of the Kalahari, where these birds abound; for they afford a perfect shade to the body, with free ventilation beneath them. The hen ostrich is of a dark brownish-grey colour, and so are the half-grown cocks.

MT 153

On the Zambezi between Zumbo and Caborabasa on the way down, February, 1856.

The people here build their huts in gardens on high stages. This is necessary on account of danger from the spotted hyaena, which is said to be very fierce, and also as a protection against lions and elephants. The hyaena is a very cowardly animal, but frequently approaches persons lying asleep, and makes an ugly gash on the face. Mozinkwa had lost his upper lip in this way, and I have heard of men being killed by them; children too are sometimes carried off; for though he is so cowardly that the human voice will make him run away at once, yet, when his teeth are in the flesh, he holds on, and shows amazing power of jaw. Leg-bones of oxen, from which the natives have extracted the marrow and everything eatable, are by this animal crunched up with the greatest ease, which he apparently effects by turning them round in his teeth till they are in a suitable position for being split.

MT 600

Second trip to the Rovuma River, September, 1862.

Crocodiles in the Rovuma have a sorry time of it. Never before were reptiles so persecuted and snubbed. They are hunted with spears, and spring traps are set for them. If one of them enters an inviting pool after fish, he soon finds a fence thrown round it, and a spring trap set in the only path out of the enclosure. Their flesh is eaten, and relished. The banks, on which the female lays her eggs by night, are carefully searched by day, and all the eggs dug out and devoured. The fish-hawk makes havoc among the few young ones that escape their other enemies. Our men were constantly on the look-out for crocodiles' nests. One was found containing thirty-five newly-laid eggs, and they declared that the crocodile would lay as many more the second night in another place. The eggs were a foot deep in the sand on the top of a bank ten feet high. The animal digs a hole with its foot, covers the eggs, and leaves them till the river rises over the nest in about three months afterwards, when she comes back, and assists the young ones out. We once

saw opposite Tete young crocodiles in December, swimming beside an
island in company with an old one. The yolk of the egg is nearly as white as
the real white. In taste they resemble hen's eggs with perhaps a smack of
custard, and would be as highly relished by whites as by blacks, were it not
for their unsavoury origin in men-eaters.

ZT 443

Mabotsa and Kolobeng mission stations, late 1840s.
    Wherever mice abound, serpents may be expected, for the one preys on
the other. A cat in a house is, therefore, a good preventive against the
entrance of these noxious reptiles. Occasionally, however, notwithstanding
every precaution, they do find their way in, but even the most venomous
sorts bite only when put into bodily fear themselves, or when trodden upon,
or when the sexes come together. In making the door for our Mabotsa
house, I happened to leave a small hole at the corner below. Early one
morning a man came to call for some article I had promised. I at once went
to the door, and, it being dark, trod on a serpent. The moment I felt the cold
scaly skin twine round a part of my leg my latent instinct was roused, and I
jumped up higher than I ever did before, or hope to do again, shaking the
reptile off in the leap. I probably trod on it near the head, and so prevented it
biting me, but did not stop to examine.
    Some of the serpents are particularly venomous. One was killed at
Kolobeng of a dark brown, nearly black colour, 8 feet 3 inches long. This
species is so copiously supplied with poison, that, when a number of dogs
attack it, the first bitten dies almost instantaneously, the second in about five
minutes, the third in an hour or so, while the fourth may live several hours.
In a cattle-pen it produces great mischief in the same way. The one we killed
at Kolobeng continued to distil clear poison from the fangs for hours after
its head was cut off. This was probably that which passes by the name of the
'spitting serpent', which is believed to be able to eject its poison into the eyes.
They all required water, and come long distances to the Zouga, and other
rivers and pools, in search of it. We have another dangerous serpent – the
puff adder – and several vipers. One, named by the inhabitants 'Noga-
putsane', or serpent of a kid, utters a cry by night exactly like the bleating of
that animal. I heard one at a spot where no kid could possibly have been. It
is supposed by the natives to lure travellers to itself by this bleating. Several
varieties, when alarmed, emit a peculiar odour, by which the people become
aware of their presence in a house. We have also cobra of several colours or
varieties. When annoyed, they raise their heads up about a foot from the
ground, and flatten the neck in a threatening manner, darting out the tongue
and retracting it with great velocity, while their fixed glassy eyes glare as if in
anger. There are also various species of the green tree-climber. They climb
trees in search of birds and eggs, and are soon discovered by all the birds in
the neighbourhood collecting and sounding an alarm. Their fangs are
formed not so much for injecting poison on external objects as for keeping in
any animal or bird of which they have got hold. Other kinds appear to be

harmless, and even edible. Of the latter sort is the large python. The largest specimens of this are about 15 or 20 feet in length; they are perfectly harmless, and live on small animals; occasionally the steinbuck and pallah fall victims, and are sucked into its comparatively small mouth in boa-constrictor fashion. One we shot was 11 feet 10 inches long, and as thick as a man's leg. When shot through the spine, it was capable of lifting itself up about five feet high, and opened its mouth in a threatening manner, but the poor thing was more inclined to crawl away. The flesh is much relished by the Bakalahari and Bushmen: they carry away each his portion, like logs of wood, over their shoulders.

MT 143

Eastern Botswana, 1853.

Inquiries among the Bushmen and Bakalahari, who are intimately acquainted with the habits of the game, lead to the belief that many diseases prevail among wild animals. I have seen the kokong or gnu, káma or hartebeest, the tsessébe, kukama, and the giraffe, so mangy as to be uneatable even by the natives. Great numbers also of zebras are found dead with masses of foam at the nostrils, exactly as occurs in the common 'horse-sickness'. The production of the malignant carbuncle called *kuatsi*, or *selonda,* by the flesh when eaten, is another proof of the disease of the tame and wild being identical. I once found a buffalo blind from ophthalmia standing by the fountain Otse; when he attempted to run he lifted up his feet in the manner peculiar to blind animals. The rhinoceros has often worms on the conjunction of his eyes; but these are not the cause of the dimness of vision which will make him charge past a man who has wounded him, if he stands perfectly still, in the belief that his enemy is a tree. It probably arises from the horn being in the line of vision, for the variety which has a straight horn directed downwards away from that line, possesses acute eyesight, and is much more wary.

All the wild animals are subject to intestinal worms besides. I have observed bunches of tape-like thread and short worms of enlarged sizes in the rhinoceros. The zebras and elephants are seldom without them, and a thread-worm may often be seen under the peritoneum of these animals. Short red larvae, which convey a stinging sensation to the hand, are seen clustering round the orifice of the windpipe at the back of the throat; others are seen in the frontal sinus of antelopes; and curious flat leech-like worms with black eyes are found in the stomachs of leches. The zebra, giraffe, eland, and kukama, have been seen mere skeletons from decay of their teeth as well as from disease. The carnivora, too, become diseased and mangy. . . .

MT 136

In the Western Congo near Bambarre, roughly halfway along the line Kigoma–Kindu, 1870. The preliminary note is Waller's.

The subjoined account of the soko – which is in all probability an entirely new species of chimpanzee, and *not* the gorilla, is exceedingly interesting, and no doubt Livingstone had plenty of stories from which to select. Neither Susi nor Chuma can identify the soko of Manyuema with the gorilla, as we have it stuffed in the British Museum. They think, however, that the soko is quite as large and as strong as the gorilla, judging by the specimens shown to them, although they could have decided with greater certainty, if the natives had not invariably brought in the dead sokos disembowelled; as they point out, and as we imagine from Dr. Livingstone's description, the carcase would then appear much less bulky. Livingstone gives an animated sketch of a soko hunt.

24th August. – Four gorillas or sokos were killed yesterday: an extensive grass-burning forced them out of their usual haunt, and coming on the plain they were speared. They often go erect, but place the hand on the head, as if to steady the body. When seen thus, the soko is an ungainly beast who takes away my appetite by his disgusting bestiality of appearance. His light yellow face shows off his ugly whiskers, and faint apology for a beard; the forehead villainously low, with high ears, is well in the background of the great dog-mouth; the teeth are slightly human, but the canines show the beast by their large development. The hands, or rather the fingers, are like those of the natives. The flesh of the feet is yellow, and the eagerness with which the Manyuema devour it leaves the impression that eating sokos was the first stage by which they arrived at being cannibals; they say the flesh is delicious. Some Manyuema think that their buried dead rise as sokos, and one was killed with holes in his ears, as if he had been a man. He is very strong and fears guns but not spears: he never catches women. He sees women do him no harm, and never molests them; a man without a spear is nearly safe from him. They beat hollow trees as drums with hands, and then scream as music to it; when men hear them, they go to the sokos; but sokos never go to men with hostility. Manyuema say, 'Soko is a man, and nothing bad in him'.

They live in communities of about ten, each having his own female; an intruder from another camp is beaten off with their fists and loud yells. If one tries to seize the female of another, he is caught on the ground, and all unite in boxing and biting the offender. A male often carries a child, especially if they are passing from one patch of forest to another over a grassy space; he then gives it to the mother.

Katomba presented a young soko or gorilla that had been caught while its mother was killed; she sits eighteen inches high, has fine long black hair all over, which was pretty so long as it was kept in order by her dam. She is the least mischievous of all the monkey tribe I have seen, and seems to know that in me she has a friend, and sits quietly on the mat beside me. In walking, the first thing observed is that she does not tread on the palms of her hands, but on the backs of the second line of bones of the hands: in doing this the nails do not touch the ground, nor do the knuckles; she uses the arms thus supported crutch fashion, and hitches herself along between them; occasionally one hand is put down before the other, and alternates with the feet, or she walks upright and holds up a hand to any one to carry her. If refused, she turns her face down, and makes grimaces of the most bitter human weeping, wringing her hands, and sometimes adding a fourth hand or foot to make the appeal more touching. Grass or leaves she draws around her to make a nest, and resents anyone meddling with her property. She is a most friendly little beast, and came up to me at once, making her chirrup of welcome, smelled my clothing, and held out her hand to be shaken. I slapped her palm without offence, though she winced. She began to untie the cord with which she was afterwards bound, with fingers and thumbs, in quite a systematic way, and on being interfered with by a man looked daggers, and screaming tried to beat him with her hands: she was afraid of his stick, and faced him, putting her back to me as a friend. She holds out her hand for people to lift her up and carry her, quite like a spoiled child; then bursts into a passionate cry, somewhat like that of a kite, wringing her hands quite naturally, as if in despair. She eats everything, covers herself with a mat to sleep, and makes a nest of grass or leaves, and wipes her face with a leaf.

LJ 4 Aug 1870

Near Serowe, Botswana, February, 1853. Livingstone has been discussing the claims made, in particular, by Gordon Cumming in his 'warfare with wild animals' (Five years of a Hunter's South Africa, *New York, 1850*).

The numbers of animals said to have been met with and killed are by no means improbable, considering the amount of large game then in the country. Two other gentlemen hunting in the same region destroyed in one season no fewer than seventy-eight rhinoceroses alone. Sportsmen, however, would not now find an equal number, for as guns are introduced among the tribes all these fine animals melt away like snow in spring.

MT 152

Near Lake Dow, Botswana, February, 1853.

On these great flats all around we saw in the white sultry glare herds of zebras, gnus, and occasionally buffaloes, standing for days, looking wistfully towards the wells for a share of the nasty water. It is mere wanton cruelty to take advantage of the necessities of these poor animals, and shoot them down one after another, without intending to make the smallest use of either the flesh, skins, or horns.

I could not order my men to do what I would not do myself; but, though I tried to justify myself on the plea of necessity, I could not adopt this mode of hunting. If your object is to secure the best specimens for a museum it may be allowable, but if, as has been practised by some who come into the country and fire away indiscriminately, great numbers of animals are wounded and allowed to perish miserably, or are killed on the spot and left to be preyed on by vultures and hyaenas, and all for the sole purpose of making a 'bag', then I take it to be evident that such sportsmen are pretty far gone in the hunting form of insanity.

MT 161

The Botletle (or Tsouga) River, east of Lake Ngami, February, 1853.

Those among whom we now were, kill many elephants; and when the moon is full, choose that time for the chase on account of its coolness. Hunting this animal is the best test of courage this country affords. The Bushmen choose the moment succeeding a charge, when the elephant is out of breath, to run in and give him a stab with their long-bladed spears. In this case the uncivilized have the advantage over us, but I believe that with half their training Englishmen would beat the Bushmen. Our present form of civilization does not necessarily produce effeminacy, though it unquestionably increases the beauty, courage, and physical powers of the race. When at Kolobeng I took notes of the different numbers of elephants killed in the course of the season by the various parties which went past our dwelling, in order to form an idea of the probable annual destruction of this noble animal. There were parties of Griquas, Bechuanas, Boers, and Englishmen. All were eager to distinguish themselves, and success depended mainly on the courage which leads the huntsman to go close to the animal, and not waste the force of his shot on the air. It was noticeable that the average for the natives was under one per man, for the Griquas one per man, for the Boers two, and for the English officers twenty each. This was the more remarkable, as the Griquas, Boers, and Bechuanas employed both dogs and natives to assist them, while the English hunters generally had no assistance from either. They approached to within thirty yards of the animal, while the others stood at a distance of a hundred yards, or even more, and of course spent all the force of their bullets on the air. One elephant was found by Mr. Oswell with quite a crowd of bullets in his side, all evidently fired in this style, and they had not gone near the vital parts.   MT 166

North-west of the Victoria Falls, on the way back with the Makololo, August, 1860.

Seabenzo, the chief whom we found on the Tyotyo rivulet, had accompanied us some distance over the undulating highland plains; and as he and our own men needed meat, we killed an elephant. This, unless one really needs the meat, or is eager for the ivory, can scarcely be looked back on without regret. These noble beasts, capable of being so useful to man in the domestic state, are, we fear, destined, at no distant date, to disappear from the face of the earth. Yet, in the excitement, all this and more was at once forgotten, and we joined in the assault as eagerly as those who think only of the fat and savoury flesh.

The writings of Harris and Gordon Cumming contain such full and nauseating details of indiscriminate slaughter of the wild animals, that one wonders to see almost every African book since besmeared with feeble imitations of these great hunters' tales. Some tell of escapes from situations which, from our knowledge of the nature of the animals, it requires a painful stretch of charity to believe ever existed, even in dreams; and others of deeds which lead one to conclude that the proportion of born butchers, in the population, is as great as of public-house keepers to the people in Glasgow.   ZT 242

CHAPTER 5

Black Arcady

'What I want is Facts . . . Facts alone are wanted in life.' (Hard Times, *1854*)

Facts pour from Livingstone, as if the spirit of Positivism were behind him with a tawse. But he is akin to Dickens as well as to Gradgrind. Although maps, charts, sections, specimens, readings, tables, identifications, sketches, brought him all kinds of academic distinction, his books are not dull with them. Instead there is this virginal documentary of Africa, and the people of Africa who were first in all his considerations. He fixes their ways in sequence after sequence that owe their definition and colour to the transparency of his prose.

While he became a professional geographer, he remains an amateur anthropologist. His ethnography is pictorial, not statistical or analytic. I cannot evaluate it. One must remember that the sciences had not separated out a century ago and that even Darwin was still 'a prosperous amateur'. Livingstone's descriptions are attractive, and I credit them with the veracity and precision which are the twin habits of his mind and prose.

He discovers three Africas, the uncontaminated, the corrupted, and the enslaved. These few selections concentrate on the first and show the great respect and love he had for the people he slowly forgot were black. He cannot be blamed for not having left them alone, although sometimes the idyllic beauty of their lives make one wish he had. First, they in no way escape the failings of humanity, and he notes their propensities for unkindness as well as for goodness and content. Secondly, he sees so clearly in Botswana, on the Angola border, on the Shire, and in Zambia and the Congo that, if he leaves them alone, slavery will not: somehow he must recruit their best qualities to save them from their worst misfortunes.

His report on pristine Africa needs no interpretation, though I have ventured on a few sub-titles. It suggests certain limitations on his part, but sympathy and confidence shine through it. There is no attempt to be comprehensive here, of course, though I have tried to be representative. He describes several initiation ceremonies, for instance, but I have only given one. It is a kind of man, a kind of people, and a quality of prose that the extracts are trying to reveal.

The first few pieces are on the need for the intelligence of the rural African to be judged from his point of view and not ours. When Livingstone seems to say 'Good heavens, they're almost as intelligent as our own great-great-grandfathers', he is not actually condescending, but looking back to about 1700, when the scientific, financial and industrial revolutions were starting the technological transformation of the West.

It was long ago remarked, that in Africa everything was contrary; 'wool grows on the heads of men, and hair on the backs of sheep'. In feeble imitation of this dogma let us add, that the men often wear their hair long, the women scarcely ever. Where there are cattle, the women till the land, plant the corn, and build the huts. The men stay at home to sew, spin, weave, and talk, and milk the cows. The men seem to pay a dowry for their wives instead of getting one with them. Some Europeans aver that Africans and themselves are descended from monkeys. Some Africans believe that souls at death pass into the bodies of apes. Most writers believe the blacks to be savages, nearly all blacks believe the whites to be cannibals. The nursery hobgoblin of the one is black, of the other white. Without going further on with these unwise comparisons, we must smile at the heaps of nonsense which have been written about the negro intellect. When for greater effect we employ broken English, and use silly phrases as if translations of remarks, which, ten to one, were never made, we have unconsciously caricatured ourselves and not the negroes; for it is a curious fact that Europeans almost invariably begin to speak with natives by adding the letters *e* and *o* to their words 'Give*e* me corn*o*, me give*e* you biscuit*o*', or 'Look*o*, look*o*, me want*e* beer*o* muche'. Our sailors at Luanda began thus, though they had never seen blacks before. It seemed an innate idea that they could thus suit English to a people who all speak a beautiful language, and have no vulgar *patois*.

Quite as sensible if not more pertinent answers will usually be given by Africans to those who know their language, as are obtained from our own uneducated poor; and we should not forget that a couple of centuries back, the ancestors of common people in England – probably our own great-great-grandfathers – were as unenlightened as the Africans are now.

ZT 67

At Lotlakani we met an old Bushman who at first seemed to have no conception of morality whatever; when his heart was warmed by our presents of meat, he sat by the fire relating his early adventures: among these was killing five other Bushmen. 'Two', said he, counting on his fingers, 'were females, one a male, and the other two calves.' – 'What a villain you are to boast of killing women and children of your own nation! what will God say when you appear before him?' – 'He will say', replied he, 'that I was a very clever fellow.' This man now appeared to me as without any conscience, and, of course, responsibility, but, on trying to enlighten him by further conversation, I discovered that, though he was employing the word which is used among the Bakwains when speaking of the Deity, he had only the idea of a chief, and was all the while referring to Sekomi, while his victims were a party of rebel Bushmen against whom he had been sent. If I had known the name of God in the Bushman tongue the mistake could scarcely have occurred.

MT 159

The African form of government is patriarchal, and, according to the temperament of the Chief, despotic, or guided by the counsel of the elders of the tribe. Reverence for royalty sometimes leads the mass of the people to submit to great cruelty, and even murder, at the hands of a despot or madman; but on the whole the rule is mild, and the same remark applies in a degree to their religion. The races of this Continent seem to have advanced to a certain point and no further; their progress in the arts of working iron and copper, in pottery, basket-making, spinning, weaving, making nets, fish-hooks, spears, axes, knives, needles, and other things, whether originally invented by this people or communicated by another instructor, appears to have remained in the same state for a great number of centuries. This apparent stagnation of mind we cannot understand; but, since we have in the later ages of the world made what we consider great progress in the arts, we have unconsciously got into the way of speaking of some other races in much the same tone as that used by the Celestials in the Flowery Land. These same Chinese anticipated us in several most important discoveries by as many centuries as we may have preceded others. In the knowledge of the properties of the magnet, the composition of gunpowder, the invention of printing, the manufacture of porcelain, of silk, and in the progress of literature, they were before us. Had the power given by inventions to the nations of Christendom been awarded to the men who were first in the race, we see no earthly reason why the Buddhists and Mohammedans should not now have lorded it over us poor islanders with steamers, and artillery, or that the bonny lasses of Edinburgh should not have been exported regularly to the harems of the East.

ZT 598

When Mr. Oswell and I discovered the Zambesi in the centre of the continent in 1851, being unable to ascend it at the time ourselves, we employed the natives to draw a map embodying their ideas of that river. We then sent the native map home in order to be an aid to others in farther investigations. When I was able to ascend the Zambesi to 14° south, and subsequently descend it, I found, after all the care I could bestow, that the alterations I was able to make in the original native plan, were very trifling. The general idea their map gave was wonderfully accurate.

MT 529

Chinsamba gave us a great deal of his company during our visits. As we have often remarked in other cases, a Chief has a great deal to attend to in guiding the affairs of his people. He is consulted on all occasions, and gives his advice in a stream of words, which show a very intimate acquaintance with the topography of his district; he knows every rood cultivated, every weir put in the river, every hunting-net, loom, gorge, and every child of his tribe. Any addition made to the number of these latter is notified to him; and he sends thanks and compliments to the parents.

ZT 558

Mochokotsa then repeated our message twice, to be sure that he had it every word, and went back again. These Chiefs' messengers have most retentive memories; they carry messages of considerable length great distances, and deliver them almost word for word. Two or three usually go together, and when on the way, the message is rehearsed every night, in order that the exact words may be kept to. One of the native objections to learning to write is, that these men answer the purpose of transmitting intelligence to a distance as well as a letter would; and, if a person wishes to communicate with any one in the town, the best way to do so is either to go to or send for him. And as for corresponding with friends very far off, that is all very well for white people, but the blacks have no friends to whom to write.

ZT 267

We spent one night at Machambwe's village, and another at Chimbuzi's. It is seldom that we can find the headman on first entering a village. He gets out of the way till he has heard all about the strangers, or he is actually out in the fields looking after his farms. We once thought that when the headman came in from a visit of inspection, with his spear, bow and arrows, they had been all taken up for the occasion, but on listening to the details given by these men of the appearances of the crops at different parts, and the astonishing minuteness of the speakers' topography, we were persuaded we were wrong, and felt rather humiliated. Every knoll, hill, mountain, and every peak on a range has a name; and so has every watercourse, dell, and plain. It is not the want, but the super-abundance of names that misleads travellers, and though it is a little apart from the topic of the attention which the headmen pay to agriculture, yet it may be here mentioned, while speaking of the fulness of the language, that we have heard about a score of words to indicate different varieties of gait – one walks leaning forward, or backward, swaying from side to side, loungingly, or smartly, swaggeringly, swinging the arms, or only one arm, head down or up, or otherwise; each of these modes of walking was expressed by a particular verb; and more words were used to designate the different varieties of fools than we ever tried to count. Mr. Moffat has translated the whole Bible into the language of the Bechuana, and has studied this tongue for the last forty-four years; and, though knowing far more of the language than any of the natives who have been reared on the Mission-station of Kuruman, he does not pretend to have mastered it fully even yet.

ZT 537

Africa is a continent, and generalisations about its people are almost impossible. Livingstone is highly specific in referring to tribes by name and not to 'natives', 'blacks', 'negroes', 'Africans', 'Bantu', or what have you.

There is often a surprising contrast between neighbouring villages. One is well off and thriving, having good huts, plenty of food, and native cloth; and its people are frank, trusty, generous, and eager to sell provisions; while in the next the inhabitants may be ill-housed, disobliging, suspicious, ill fed, and scantily clad, and with nothing for sale, though the land around is as fertile as that of their wealthier neighbours.

ZT 366

We were received by the Bakóba, whose language clearly shows that they bear an affinity to the tribes in the north. They call themselves Bayeiye, *i.e.* men; but the Bechuanas call them Bakoba, which contains somewhat of the idea of slaves. They have never been known to fight, and, indeed, have a tradition that their forefathers, in their first essays at war, made their bows of the Palma-Christi; and, when these broke, they gave up fighting altogether. They have invariably submitted to the rule of every horde which has overrun the countries adjacent to the rivers on which they specially love to dwell. They are thus the Quakers of the body politic in Africa.

MT 64

The owners of huts lent to strangers have a great deal of toil in consequence; they have to clean them after the visitors have withdrawn; then, in addition to this, to clean themselves, all soiled by the dust left by the lodgers; their bodies and clothes have to be cleansed afterwards – they add food too in all cases of acquaintanceship, and then we have to remember the labour of preparing that food. My remaining here enables me to observe that both men and women are in almost constant employment. The men are making mats, or weaving, or spinning; no one could witness their assiduity in their little affairs and conclude that they were a lazy people. The only idle time I observe here is in the mornings about seven o'clock, when all come and sit to catch the first rays of the sun as he comes over our clump of trees, but even that time is often taken as an opportunity for stringing beads.

LJ 8 Jul 1867

We made a little détour to the southward, in order to get provisions in a cheaper market. This led us along the rivulet called Tamba, where we found the people, who had not been visited so frequently by the slave-traders as the rest, rather timid and very civil. It was agreeable to get again among the uncontaminated, and to see the natives look at us without that air of super-ciliousness, which is so unpleasant and common in the beaten track. The same olive colour prevailed. They file their teeth to a point, which makes the smile of the women frightful, as it reminds one of the grin of an alligator. The inhabitants throughout this country, exhibit as great a variety of taste, as appears on the surface of society amongst ourselves. Many of the men are dandies; their shoulders are always wet with the oil dropping from their lubricated hair, and everything about them is ornamented in one way or another. Some thrum a musical instrument the livelong day, and, when they wake at night, proceed at once to their musical performance. Others try to appear warlike by never going out of their huts, except with a load of bows and arrows, or a gun ornamented with a strip of hide for every animal they have shot; and others never go anywhere without a canary in a cage. Ladies may be seen carefully tending little lapdogs, which are intended to be eaten.

MT 452

A continuous tap-tapping in the villages shows that bark cloth is being made. The bark, on being removed from the tree, is steeped in water, or in a black muddy hole, till the outer of the two inner barks can be separated, then commences the tapping with a mallet to separate and soften the fibres. The head of this is often of ebony, with the face cut into small furrows, which, without breaking, separate and soften the fibres.

LJ 3 Dec 1866

My men were busy collecting a better breed of fowls and pigeons than those in their own country. Mr. Tell presented them with some large specimens from Rio Janeiro. Of these they were wonderfully proud, and bore the cock in triumph through the country of the Balonda, as evidence of having been to the sea. But at the village of Shinte, a hyaena came into our midst when we were all sound asleep, and picked him out in his basket from eighty-four others, and he was lost, to the great grief of my men. The anxiety these people have always shown to improve the breed of their domestic animals, is, I think, a favourable point in their character. They never ceased remarking on the fine ground for gardens over which we were passing; and when I happened to mention that most of the flour which the Portuguese consumed, came from another country, they exclaimed, 'Are they ignorant of tillage? They know nothing but buying and selling: they are not men!'

MT 439

After paying our Senna men, as they wished to go home, we landed them here. All were keen traders, and had invested largely in native iron-hoes, axes, and ornaments. Many of the hoes and spears had been taken from the slaving parties whose captives we liberated; for on these occasions our Senna friends were always uncommonly zealous and active. The remainder had been purchased with the old clothes we had given them, and their store of hippopotamus meat: they had no fears of losing them, or of being punished for aiding us. No white man on board could purchase so cheaply as these men could. Many a time had their eloquence persuaded a native trader to sell for a bit of dirty worn cloth things for which he had, but a little before, refused twice the amount of clean new calico. 'Scissors' being troubled with a cough at night, received a present of a quilted coverlet, which had seen a good deal of service. A few days afterwards, a good chance of investing in hoes offering itself, he ripped off both sides, tore them into a dozen pieces, and purchased about a dozen hoes with them.

ZT 404

With the game laws we move into a short section of comment on the socio-political tissue of tribal life. It will be seen shortly how Livingstone learns from Manenko to make haste slowly by scrupulously observing her practices. Among tribes uncorrupted by slaving such procedures are part of the system of good manners, of the civility (if not the civilization) he detects beneath outer forms that may shock him.

When we passed Mpende, we came into a country where the game-laws are strictly enforced. The lands of each chief are very well defined, the boundaries being usually marked by rivulets, great numbers of which flow into the Zambesi from both banks, and, if an elephant is wounded on one man's land and dies on that of another, the under half of the carcase is claimed by the lord of the soil; and so stringent is the law, that the hunter cannot begin at once to cut up his own elephant; but must send notice to the lord of the soil on which it lies, and wait until that personage sends one authorized to see a fair partition made. If the hunter should begin to cut up before the agent of the landowner arrives, he is liable to lose both the tusks and all the flesh. The hind leg of a buffalo must also be given to the man on whose land the animal was grazing, and a still larger quantity of the eland, which here and everywhere else in the country is esteemed right royal food. The only game-laws in the interior are, that the man who first wounds an animal, though he has inflicted but a mere scratch, is considered the killer of it, the second is entitled to a hind-quarter, and the third to a fore-leg. The chiefs are generally entitled to a share as tribute; in some parts it is the breast, in others the whole of the ribs and one fore-leg. I generally respected this law, although exceptions are sometimes made when animals are killed by guns. The knowledge that he who succeeds in reaching the wounded beast first, is entitled to a share, stimulates the whole party to greater exertions in despatching it.

MT 599

As we were now in the country of stringent game-laws, we were obliged to send all the way back to Nyampungo, to give information to the owner. The side upon which the elephant fell, had a short broken tusk; the upper one, which was ours, was large and thick. The Banyani remarked on our good luck. The men sent to give notice, came back late in the afternoon of the following day. They brought a basket of corn, a fowl, and a few strings of handsome beads, as a sort of thank-offering for our having killed it on their land, adding 'There it is; eat it and be glad'. Had we begun to cut it up before we got this permission, we should have lost the whole. They had brought a large party to eat their half, and they divided it with us in a friendly way. My men were delighted with the feast, though, by lying unopened a whole day, the carcase was pretty far gone. An astonishing number of hyaenas collected round, and kept up a loud laughter for two whole nights. Some of them do make a very good imitation of a laugh. I asked my men what the hyaenas were laughing at, as they usually give animals credit for a share of intelligence; they said, that they were laughing because we could not take the whole, and that they would have plenty to eat as well as we.

MT 607

When abreast of the high wooded island Kalabi we came in contact with one of the game-laws of the country, which has come down from the most ancient times. An old buffalo crossed the path a few yards in front of us; our guide threw his small spear at its hip, and it was going off scarcely hurt, when three rifle balls knocked it over. 'It is mine', said the guide. He had wounded it first, and the established native game-law is that the animal belongs to the man who first draws blood; the two legs on one side, by the same law, belonged to us for killing it.

ZT 220

As we were unable to march next morning, six of our young men, anxious to try their muskets, went off to hunt elephants. For several hours they saw nothing, and some of them, getting tired, proposed to go to a village and buy food. 'No!' said Mantlanyane, 'we came to hunt, so let us go on.' In a short time they fell in with a herd of cow elephants and calves. As soon as the first cow caught sight of the hunters on the rocks above her, she, with true motherly instinct, placed her young one between her fore-legs for protection. The men were for scattering, and firing into the herd indiscriminately. 'That won't do,' cried Mantlanyane, 'let us all fire at this one.' The poor beast received a volley, and ran down into the plain, where another shot killed her; the young one escaped with the herd. The men were wild with excitement, and danced round the fallen queen of the forest, with loud shouts and exultant songs. They returned, bearing as trophies, the tail and part of the trunk, and marched into camp as erect as soldiers, and evidently feeling that their stature had increased considerably since the morning.

The cutting up of an elephant is quite a unique spectacle. The men stand round the animal in dead silence, while the chief of the travelling party declares that, according to ancient law, the head and right hind-leg belong to him who killed the beast, that is, to him who inflicted the first wound; the left leg to him who delivered the second, or first touched the animal after it fell; the meat around the eye to the English, or chief of the travellers, and different parts to the headmen of the different fires, or groups, of which the camp is composed; not forgetting to enjoin the preservation of the fat and bowels for a second distribution. This oration finished, the natives soon become excited, and scream wildly as they cut away at the carcass with a score of spears, whose long handles quiver in the air above their heads. Their excitement becomes more and more intense, and reaches the culminating point when, as denoted by a roar of gas, the huge mass is laid fairly open. Some jump inside, and roll about there in their eagerness to seize the precious fat, while others run off, screaming, with pieces of the bloody meat, throw it on the grass, and run back for more: all keep talking and shouting at the utmost pitch of their voices. Sometimes two or three, regardless of all laws, seize the same piece of meat, and have a brief fight of words over it. Occasionally an agonized yell bursts forth, and a native emerges out of the moving mass of dead elephant and wriggling humanity, with his hand badly cut by the spear of his excited friend and neighbour: this requires a rag and some soothing words to prevent bad blood. In an incredibly short time tons of meat are cut up, and placed in separate heaps around.

ZT 164

Livingstone's knowledge of tribal procedures and his commonsense improvements on them, like his patience and consideration generally, show him exerting natural leadership with perfect acceptance. The second of these two extracts, by the way, devoid of emotion, wholly expository, and with its gleam of humour, seems to me of the highest quality as English prose.

The government of the Banyai is rather peculiar, being a sort of feudal republicanism. The chief is elected, and they choose the son of the deceased chief's sister in preference to his own offspring. When dissatisfied with one candidate, they even go to a distant tribe for a successor, who is usually of the family of the late chief, a brother, or a sister's son, but never his own son or daughter. When first spoken to on the subject, he answers as if he thought himself unequal to the task and unworthy of the honour, but, having accepted it, all the wives, goods, and children of his predecessor belong to him, and he takes care to keep them in a dependent position. The children of the chief have fewer privileges than common free men. They may not be sold, but, rather than choose any one of them for a chief, the free men would prefer to elect one of themselves who bore only a very distant relationship to the family. These free men are a distinct class who can never be sold; and under them there is a class of slaves whose appearance as well as position is very degraded. Monina had a great number of young men about him from twelve to fifteen years of age. These were all sons of free men, and bands of young lads like them in the different districts, leave their parents about the age of puberty, and live with such men as Monina for the sake of instruction. When I asked the nature of the instruction I was told 'Bonyái', which I suppose may be understood as indicating manhood, for it sounds as if we should say, 'to teach an American, Americanism', or 'an Englishman to be English'. While here they are kept in subjection to rather stringent regulations. They must salute carefully by clapping their hands on approaching a superior, and when any cooked food is brought, the young men may not approach the dish, but an elder divides a portion to each. They remain unmarried, until a fresh set of youths is ready to occupy their place under the same instruction. The parents send servants with their sons to cultivate gardens to supply them with food, and also tusks to Monina to purchase clothing for them. When the lads return to the village of their parents, a case is submitted to them for adjudication, and if they speak well on the point, the parents are highly gratified.

MT 617

The foregoing may be considered as a characteristic specimen of their mode of dealing with grave political offences. In common cases there is a greater show of deliberation. The complainant asks the man, against whom he means to lodge his complaint, to come with him to the chief. This is never refused. When both are in the *kotla*, the complainant stands up and states the whole case before the chief and the people usually assembled there. He stands a few seconds after he has done this, to recollect if he has forgotten anything. The witnesses to whom he has referred then rise up and tell all they themselves have seen or heard, but not anything that they have heard from others. The defendant, after allowing some minutes to elapse so that he may not interrupt any of the opposite party, slowly rises, folds his cloak around him, and, in the most quiet, deliberate way he can assume — yawning, blowing his nose, &c. — begins to explain the affair, denying the charge or admitting it, as the case may be. Sometimes, when galled by his remarks, the complainant utters a sentence of dissent; the accused turns quietly to him, and says, 'Be silent: I sat still while you were speaking; can't you do the same? Do you want to have it all to yourself?' And as the audience acquiesce in this bantering, and enforce silence, he goes on till he has finished all he wishes to say in his defence. If he has any witnesses to the truth of the facts of his defence, they give their evidence. No oath is administered; but occasionally, when a statement is questioned, a man will say, 'By my father', or 'By the chief, it is so'. Their truthfulness among each other is quite remarkable; but their system of government is such that Europeans are not in a position to realise it readily. A poor man will say, in defence against a rich one, 'I am astonished to hear a man so great as he make a false accusation'; as if the offence of falsehood were felt to be one against the society which the individual referred to had the greatest interest in upholding.

If the case is one of no importance, the chief decides it at once; if frivolous, he may give the complainant a scolding, and put a stop to the case in the middle of the complaint, or he may allow it to go on without paying any attention to it whatever. Family quarrels are often treated in this way, and then a man may be seen stating his case with great fluency, and not a soul listening to him. But if it is a case between influential men, or brought on by under-chiefs, then the greatest decorum prevails. If the chief does not see his way clearly to a decision, he remains silent; the elders then rise one by one and give their opinions, often in the way of advice rather than as decisions; and when the chief finds the general sentiment agreeing in one view, he delivers his judgment accordingly. He alone speaks sitting: all others stand.

No one refuses to acquiesce in the decision of the chief, as he has the power of life and death in his hands, and can enforce the law to that extent if he chooses; but grumbling is allowed, and, when marked favouritism is shown to any relative of the chief, the people generally are not so astonished at the partiality as we would be in England.

MT 183

African religious and moral sensibilities interest Livingstone greatly, of course, and deserve fuller treatment. He accentuates the positive, and seldom judges, although 'man's inhumanity to man' is his favourite quotation. The neurotic basis of tribal practices comes out in the picture of an initiation.

The primitive African faith seems to be that there is one Almighty Maker of heaven and earth; that he has given the various plants of earth to man to be employed as mediators between him and the spirit world, where all who have ever been born and died continue to live; that sin consists in offences against their fellow-men, either here or among the departed, and that death is often a punishment of guilt, such as witchcraft. Their idea of moral evil differs in no respect from ours, but they consider themselves amenable only to inferior beings, not to the Supreme. Evil speaking — lying — hatred — disobedience to parents — neglect of them — are said by the intelligent to have been all known to be sin, as well as theft, murder, or adultery, before they knew aught of Europeans or their teaching. The only new addition to their moral code is, that it is wrong to have more wives than one. This, until the arrival of Europeans, never entered into their minds even as a doubt.

ZT 521

Having taken lunar observations in the morning, I was waiting for a meridian altitude of the sun for the latitude; my chief boatman was sitting by, in order to pack up the instruments as soon as I had finished; there was a large halo, about 20° in diameter, round the sun; thinking that the humidity of the atmosphere, which this indicated, might betoken rain, I asked him if his experience did not lead him to the same view. 'O no,' replied he; 'it is the Barimo (gods, or departed spirits), who have called a *picho*; don't you see they have the Lord in the centre?'

MT 219

All the Bechuana and Caffre tribes south of the Zambesi practise circumcision *(boguera)*, but the rites observed are carefully concealed. The initiated alone can approach, but in this town I was once a spectator of the second part of the ceremony of the circumcision, called *sechu*. Just at dawn of day, a row of boys of nearly fourteen years of age stood naked in the *kotla*, each having a pair of sandals as a shield on his hands. Facing them stood the men of the town in a similar state of nudity, all armed with long thin wands, of a tough, strong, supple bush called *moretloa*, and engaged in a dance named 'koha', in which questions are put to the boys, as 'Will you guard the chief well?' 'Will you herd the cattle well?' and while the latter give an affirmative response, the men rush forward to them, and each aims a full-weight blow at the back of one of the boys; shielding himself with the sandals above his head, he causes the supple wand to descend and bend into his back, and every stroke inflicted thus makes the blood squirt out of a wound a foot or eighteen inches long. At the end of the dance, the boys' backs are seamed with wounds and weals, the scars of which remain through life. This is intended to harden the young soldiers, and prepare them for the rank of men. After this ceremony, and after killing a rhinoceros, they may marry a wife.

MT 146

Stopping one afternoon at Kebrabasa village, a man who pretended to be able to change himself into a lion came to salute us. Smelling the gunpowder from a gun which had been discharged, he went on one side to get out of the wind of the piece, trembling in a most artistic manner, but quite overacting his part. The Makololo explained to us that he was a Pondoro, or a man who can change his form at will, and added that he trembles when he smells gunpowder. 'Do you not see how he is trembling now?' We told them to ask him to change himself at once into a lion, and we would give him a cloth for the performance. 'Oh, no', replied they; 'if we tell him so, he may change himself and come when we are asleep and kill us.' Having similar superstitions at home, they readily became as firm believers in the Pondoro as the natives of the village. We were told that he assumes the form of a lion and remains in the woods for days, and is sometimes absent for a whole month. His considerate wife had built him a hut or den, in which she places food and beer for her transformed lord, whose metamorphosis does not impair his human appetite. No one ever enters this hut except the Pondoro and his wife, and no stranger is allowed even to rest his gun against the baobab-tree beside it: the Chief of another small village wished to fine our men for placing their muskets against it. At times the Pondoro employs his powers for the benefit of the village; and, after an absence of a day or two, his wife smells the lion, takes a certain medicine, places it in the forest, and there quickly leaves it, lest the lion should kill even her. This medicine enables the Pondoro to change himself back into a man, return to the village, and say 'Go and get the game that I have killed for you'. Advantage is of course taken of what a lion has actually done, and they go and bring home the buffalo or antelope killed when he was a lion, or rather found when he was pursuing his course of deception in the forest. We saw the Pondoro of another village dressed in a fantastic style, with numerous charms hung round him, and followed by a troop of boys who were honouring him with rounds of shrill cheering.

It is believed also that the souls of departed Chiefs enter into lions and render them sacred. On one occasion, when we had shot a buffalo in the path beyond the Kafue, a hungry lion, attracted probably by the smell of the meat, came close to our camp, and roused up all hands by his roaring. Tuba Mokoro, imbued with the popular belief that the beast was a Chief in disguise, scolded him roundly during his brief intervals of silence. 'You a Chief, eh? You call yourself a Chief, do you? What kind of Chief are you to come sneaking about in the dark, trying to steal our buffalo meat! Are you not ashamed of yourself? A pretty Chief truly; you are like the scavenger beetle, and think of yourself only. You have not the heart of a Chief; why don't you kill your own beef? You must have a stone in your chest, and no heart at all, indeed!' Tuba Mokoro producing no impression on the transformed Chief, one of the men, the most sedate of the party, who seldom spoke, took up the matter, and tried the lion in another strain. In his slow quiet way he expostulated with him on the impropriety of such conduct to strangers, who had never injured him. 'We were travelling peaceably through the country back to our own Chief. We never killed people, nor stole anything. The buffalo meat was ours, not his, and it did not become a great Chief like him to be prowling round in the dark, trying, like a hyena, to steal the meat of strangers. He might go and hunt for himself, as there was plenty of game in the forest.' The Pondoro, being deaf to reason, and only roaring the louder, the men became angry, and threatened to send a bullet through him if he did not go away. They snatched up their guns to shoot him, but he prudently kept in the dark, outside of the luminous circle made by our camp fires, and there they did not like to venture. A little strychnine was put into a piece of meat, and thrown to him, when he soon departed, and we heard no more of the majestic sneaker.

ZT 159

The technological gap between white and black in the nineteenth century was colossal yet the sheer possession of a white skin and straight hair was as great a wonder as any. Livingstone was himself a handyman, and an encyclopedia of African crafts could be made from his works: but relative to Europe, Asia and America, Africa was fast asleep.

Never before in Africa have we seen anything like the dense population on the shores of Lake Nyassa. In the southern part, there was an almost unbroken chain of villages. On the beach of wellnigh every little sandy bay, dark crowds were standing, gazing at the novel sight of a boat under sail; and wherever we landed we were surrounded in a few seconds by hundreds of men, women, and children, who hastened to have a stare at the 'chirombo' (wild animals). To see the animals feed was the greatest attraction; never did a Zoo's lions or monkeys draw more sightseers, than we did. Indeed, we equalled the hippopotamus on his first arrival on the banks of the Thames. The wondering multitude crowded round us at meal times and formed a thicket of dark bodies, all looking on, apparently, with the deepest interest; but they goodnaturedly kept each other to a line we made on the sand, and left us room to dine.

ZT 372

We met a venerable warrior, sole survivor, probably, of the Mantatee host which threatened to invade the colony in 1824. He retained a vivid recollection of their encounter with the Griquas: 'As we looked at the men and horses, puffs of smoke arose, and some of us dropped down dead! Never saw anything like it in my life, a man's brains lying in one place and his body in another!' They could not understand what was killing them; a ball struck a man's shield at an angle; knocked his arm out of joint at the shoulder; and leaving a mark, or burn as he said, on the shield, killed another man close by. We saw the man with his shoulder still dislocated. Sebituane was present at the fight, and had an exalted opinion of the power of white people ever afterwards.

ZT 292

I proposed to teach the Makololo to read, but, for the reasons mentioned, Sekeletu at first declined; after some weeks, however, his father-in-law, and some others determined to brave the mysterious book. To all who have not acquired it the knowledge of letters is quite unfathomable; there is nought like it within the compass of their observation; and we have no comparison with anything except pictures, to aid them in comprehending the idea of signs of words. It seems to them supernatural that we see in a book things taking place, or having occurred at a distance. No amount of explanation conveys the idea unless they learn to read. Machinery is equally inexplicable, and money nearly as much so until they see it in actual use. They are familiar with barter alone; and in the centre of the country, where gold is totally unknown, if a button and sovereign were left to their choice, they would prefer the former on account of its having an eye.

MT 188

Livingstone has a prospector's eye for coal, iron, gold and copper. He is in the neighbourhood of Katanga in 1868, and the extract dated 13th August may be the first European report of Katanga copper.

One of these plains, near the Kafue, is covered with the large stumps and trunks of a petrified forest. We halted a couple of days by the fine stream Sinjére, which comes from the Chiroby-roby hills, about eight miles to the north. Many lumps of coal, brought down by the rapid current, lie in its channel. The natives never seem to have discovered that coal would burn, and, when informed of the fact, shook their heads, smiled incredulously, and said 'Kodi' (really), evidently regarding it as a mere traveller's tale. They were astounded to see it burning freely on our fire of wood. They told us that plenty of it was seen among the hills; but, being long ago aware that we were now in an immense coalfield, we did not care to examine it further. Coal had been discovered to the south of this in 1856, and several seams were examined on the stream Revubue, a few miles distant from Tette. This was evidently an extension of the same field, but the mineral was more bituminous. In an open fire it bubbled up, and gave out gas like good domestic coal.

ZT 185

At every third or fourth village, we see a kiln-looking structure, about six feet high, by two-and-a-half or three feet in diameter. It is a clay, fire-hardened furnace, for smelting iron. No flux is used, whether the specular iron, the yellow haematite, or magnetic iron ore is fused, and yet capital metal is produced. Native manufactured iron is so good, that the natives declare English iron to be 'rotten' in comparison, and specimens of African hoes were pronounced at Birmingham to be nearly equal to the best Swedish iron. As we passed along, men sometimes ran from the fields they were working in, and offered for sale new hoes, axes, and spears of their own workmanship. It is certainly the iron age here; copper, according to the ideas of the natives who smelt it from malachite, is much more intractable than the metal from ironstone, which needs no flux; and as yet, so far as we can learn, neither tin nor zinc has ever been used to form an amalgam with copper in this country, so that we may expect the bronze age to come in an inverted order.

ZT 536

The fort of Tete has been the salvation of the Portuguese power in this quarter. It is a small square building, with a thatched apartment for the troops; and though there are but few guns, they are in a much better state than those of any fort in the interior of Angola. The cause of the decadence of the Portuguese power in this region is simply this. In former times considerable quantities of grain, as wheat, millet, and maize, were exported, also coffee, sugar, oil, and indigo, besides gold-dust and ivory. The cultivation of grain was carried on by means of slaves, of whom the Portuguese possessed a large number. The gold-dust was procured by washing at various points on the north, south, and west of Tete. A merchant took all his slaves with him to the washings, carrying as much calico and other goods as he could muster. On arriving at the washing-place he made a present to the chief, of the value of about a pound sterling. The slaves were then divided into parties, each headed by a confidential servant, who not only had the super-vision of his squad while the washing went on, but bought dust from the inhabitants, and made a weekly return to his master. When several masters united at one spot, it was called a 'Bara', and they then erected a temporary church, in which a priest from one of the missions performed mass. Both chiefs and people were favourable to these visits, because the traders purchased grain for the sustenance of the slaves with the goods they had brought. They continued at this labour until the whole of the goods were expended, and by this means about 130 lbs. of gold were annually produced. Probably more than this was actually obtained, but, as it was an article easily secreted, this alone was submitted to the authorities for taxation. At present the whole amount of gold obtained annually by the Portuguese is from 8 to 10 lbs. only. When the slave-trade itself began, it seemed to many of the merchants a more speedy mode of becoming rich than gold-washing and agriculture, and they continued to export them until they had neither hands to labour nor to fight for them. It was just the story of the goose and the golden egg. The coffee and sugar plantations and gold-washings were abandoned, because the labour had been exported to Brazil.

I examined what were formerly the gold-washings in the rivulet Mokoroze, which is nearly on the 16th parallel of latitude. The banks are covered with large groves of fine mango-trees, among which the Portuguese lived while superintending the washing for the precious metal. The process is very laborious. A quantity of sand is put into a wooden bowl with water; a half rotatory motion is given to the dish, which causes the coarser particles of sand to collect on one side of the bottom. These are carefully removed with the hand, and the process of rotation renewed until the whole of the sand is taken away, and the gold alone remains. It is found in very minute scales, and, unless I had been assured to the contrary, I should have taken it to be mica, for, knowing the gold to be of greater specific gravity than the sand, I imagined that a stream of water would remove the latter and leave the former; but here the practice is, to remove the whole of the sand by the hand. This process was, no doubt, a profitable one to the Portuguese, and it is probable that, with the improved plan by means of mercury, the sands would be lucrative. I had an opportunity of examining the gold-dust from different parts to the east and north-east of Tete: there are six well-known washing-places. From the description of the rock I received, I suppose gold is found both in clay-shale and quartz. At the range Mushinga to the N.N.W. the rock is said to be so soft, that the women pound it into powder in wooden mortars previous to washing.

Round towards the westward, the old Portuguese indicate a station which was near to Zumbo on the river Panyáme, near which much gold was found.

Further west, lay the now unknown kingdom of Abútua, which was formerly famous for the metal; and then, coming round towards the east, we have the gold-washings of the Mashóna, and further east, that of Manica, where gold is found much more abundantly than in any other part, and which has been supposed by some to be the Ophir of King Solomon. I saw the gold from this quarter as large as grains of wheat; that found in the rivers which run into the coalfield, being in very minute scales. If we place one leg of the compasses at Tete, and extend the other three and a half degrees, bringing it round from the north-east of Tete by west, and then to the south-east, we nearly touch or include all the known gold-producing country. As the gold on this circumference is found in coarser grains than in the streams running towards the centre, or Tete, I imagine that the real gold-field lies round about the coalfield; and, if I am right in the conjecture, then we have coal encircled by a gold-field, and abundance of wood, water, and provisions – a combination not often met with in the world. The inhabitants at present wash only when in want of a little calico. They know the value of gold perfectly well, for they bring it for sale in goose-quills, and demand 24 yards of calico for one penful. When the rivers in the district of Manica and other gold-washing places have been flooded, they leave a coating of mud on the banks. The natives observe the spots which dry soonest, and commence digging there, in firm belief that gold lies beneath. They are said not to dig deeper than their chins, believing that if they did so the ground would fall in and kill them. When they find a *piece* or flake of gold, they bury it again, from the superstitious idea that this is the seed of the gold, and, though they know the value of it well, they prefer losing it rather than the whole future crop. I doubted the authority of my informant; but I found the report verified by all the Portuguese who know the native language and mode of thinking, and give the statement for what it is worth. If it is really practised, the custom may have been introduced by some knowing one who wished to defraud the chiefs of their due; for we are informed in Portuguese history that in former times, these pieces or flakes of gold were considered the perquisites of the chiefs.

MT 630

13th August, 1968 – The Banyamwezi use a hammer shaped like a cone, without a handle. They have both kinds of bellows, one of goatskin the other of wood, with a skin over the mouth of a drum, and a handle tied to the middle of it; with these they smelt pieces of the large bars of copper into a pot, filled nearly full of wood ashes. The fire is surrounded by masses of anthills, and in these there are hollows made to receive the melted metal: the metal is poured while the pot is held with the hands, protected by wet rags.

LJ 13 Aug 1868

Livingstone appreciates African arts without being especially drawn to them. Their music is 'wild and not unpleasant' and he carefully describes and sketches the *marimba, sansa,* etc. 'I bought two finely-shaped earthen bottles' indicates a sensitivity that closer reading, however, shows to be the craftsman's rather than the artist's. His catholicity of taste cools to Calvinism in this account of a Makololo dance. The frost is very slight, however, and not overtly moral (as Moffat's would have been). The three passages on smoking pot are more clinically cool than articles I have read on the subject today.

   Men of remarkable ability have risen up among the Africans from time to time, as amongst other portions of the human family. Some have attracted the attention, and excited the admiration of large districts by their wisdom. Others, apparently by the powers of ventriloquism, or by peculiar dexterity in throwing the spear, or shooting with the bow, have been the wonder of their generation; but the total absence of literature leads to the loss of all former experience, and the wisdom of the wise has not been handed down. They have had their minstrels too, but mere tradition preserves not their effusions. One of these, and apparently a genuine poet, attached himself to our party for several days, and, whenever we halted, sang our praises to the villagers in smooth and harmonious numbers. It was a sort of blank verse, and each line consisted of five syllables. The song was short when it first began, but each day he picked up more information about us, and added to the poem until our praises became an ode of respectable length. When distance from home compelled his return, he expressed his regret at leaving us, and was, of course, paid for his useful and pleasant flatteries. Another, though a less gifted son of song, belonged to the Batoka of our own party. Every evening, while the others were cooking, talking, or sleeping, he rehearsed his songs, containing a history of everything he had seen in the land of the white men, and on the way back. In composing, extempore, any new piece, he was never at a loss; for if the right word did not come, he halted not, but eked out the measure with a peculiar musical sound meaning nothing at all. He accompanied his recitations on the *sansa,* an instrument the nine keys of which are played with the thumbs, while the fingers pass behind to hold it. The hollow end and ornaments face the breast of the player. Persons of a musical turn, if too poor to buy a *sansa,* may be seen playing vigorously on an instrument made with a number of thick corn-stalks sewn together, as a *sansa* frame, and keys of split bamboo, which, though making but little sound, seems to soothe the player himself. When the instrument is played with a calabash as a sounding-board, it emits a greater volume of sound. Pieces of shells and tin are added to make a jingling accompaniment, and the calabash is also ornamented.

                                                                         ZT 235

   As this was the first visit which Sekeletu had paid to this part of his dominions, it was to many a season of great joy. The head men of each village presented oxen, milk, and beer, more than the horde which accompanied him could devour, though their abilities in that line are something wonderful. The people usually show their joy and work off their excitement in dances and songs. The dance consists of the men standing nearly naked in a circle, with clubs or small battle-axes in their hands, and each roaring at the loudest pitch of his voice, while they simultaneously lift one leg, stamp heavily twice with it, then lift the other and give one stamp with that; this is the only movement in common. The arms and head are thrown about also in every direction; and all this time the roaring is kept up with the utmost possible vigour; the continued stamping makes a cloud of dust ascend, and they leave a deep ring in the ground where they have stood. If the scene were witnessed in a lunatic asylum it would be nothing out of the way, and quite appropriate even, as a means of letting off the excessive excitement of the brain; but here grey-headed men joined in the performance with as much zest as others whose youth might be an excuse for making the perspiration stream off their bodies with the exertion. Motibe asked what I thought of the Makololo dance. I replied, 'It is very hard work, and brings but small profit.' 'It is,' replied he, 'but it is very nice, and Sekeletu will give us an ox for dancing for him.' He usually does slaughter an ox for the dancers when the work is over.

The women stand by, clapping their hands, and occasionally one advances into the circle, composed of a hundred men, makes a few movements, and then retires. As I never tried it, and am unable to enter into the spirit of the thing, I cannot recommend the Makololo polka to the dancing world, but I have the authority of no less a person than Motibe, Sekeletu's father-in-law, for saying 'it is very nice'. They often asked if white people ever danced. I thought of the disease called St. Vitus's dance, but could not say that all our dancers were affected by it, and gave an answer which, I ought to be ashamed to own, did not raise some of our young country-women in the estimation of the Makololo.

MT 225

The Batoka of these parts are very degraded in their appearance, and are not likely to improve, either physically or mentally, while so much addicted to smoking the 'mutokwane' *(Cannabis sativa)*. They like its narcotic effects, though the violent fit of coughing, which follows a couple of puffs of smoke, appears distressing, and causes a feeling of disgust in the spectator. This is not diminished on seeing the usual practice of taking a mouthful of water, and squirting it out together with the smoke, then uttering a string of half-incoherent sentences, usually in self-praise. This weed is extensively used in all the tribes of the interior. It causes a species of frenzy, and Sebituane's soldiers, on coming in sight of their enemies, sat down and smoked it, in order that they might make an effective onslaught. I was unable to prevail on Sekeletu and the young Makololo to forego its use, although they cannot point to an old man in the tribe who has been addicted to this indulgence. I believe it was the proximate cause of Sebituane's last illness, for it sometimes occasions pneumonia. Never having tried it, I cannot describe the pleasurable effects it is said to produce, but the hachshish in use among the Turks is simply an extract of the same plant, and that, like opium, produces

different effects on different individuals. Some view everything as if looking
in through the wide end of a telescope, and others, in passing over a straw,
lift up their feet as if about to cross the trunk of a tree. The Portuguese in
Angola have such a belief in its effects that the use of it by a slave is
considered a crime.

MT 540

Sekeletu himself is a slave to the drug habit, and could hardly be induced
to give it up, even during the short time he was under medical treatment. We
had ample opportunities for observing the effects of this *matokwane* smoking
on our men. It makes them feel very strong in body, but it produces exactly
the opposite effect upon the mind. Two of our finest young men became
inveterate smokers, and partially idiotic. The performances of a group of
matokwane smokers are somewhat grotesque: they are provided with a
calabash of pure water, a split bamboo, five feet long, and the great pipe,
which has a large calabash or kudu's horn chamber to contain the water,
through which the smoke is drawn, Narghillé fashion, on its way to the
mouth. Each smoker takes a few whiffs, the last being an extra long one,
and hands the pipe to his neighbour. He seems to swallow the fumes; for,
striving against the convulsive action of the muscles of chest and throat, he
takes a mouthful of water from the calabash, waits a few seconds, and then
pours water and smoke from his mouth down the groove of the bamboo.
The smoke causes violent coughing in all, and in some a species of frenzy,
which passes away in a rapid stream of unmeaning words, or short sentences, as, 'the green grass grows', 'the fat cattle thrive', 'the fish swim'. No
one in the group pays the slightest attention to the oracle, who stops
abruptly, and, the instant common sense returns, looks rather foolish.

ZT 286

In making a detour one day in search of buffaloes or guinea-fowls, in
company with Masego, we came upon some women working in their maize-
gardens. They drew water for us, and spoke to us cheerily as we sat under a
tree. One of their husbands soon came running up in alarm, and made a
great demonstration of fighting. It was amusing to notice the effect of
Masego's quiet chaff on our pugnacious visitor. 'The women', said Masego
to him, 'had understood our civil petition for water perfectly; they showed
no fear of peaceable men; we asked water from them because we had no
vessel to draw with and they had; but if he insisted on fighting, he had better
call all his friends and come on; it was daylight, and all would see who was
the coward, and who was not.' The arrow was first taken from the bow-
string and put alongside the bow, then it was placed in the quiver, and,
though he continued talking and justifying his alarm, he listened, sat down,
followed us at a distance, and, uninvited, eventually proved himself very
useful as a guide. He afterwards explained that he had been smoking hemp,
and had been excited to this mad sort of conduct.

ZT 566

Liberality, rated very highly as a virtue and having almost ritual significance (as well as its human temptations): this, and punctilious manners (however curious), are the prevailing impressions of unspoiled African society.

We had now come among people who had plenty, and were really very liberal. My men never returned from a village without some corn or maize in their hands. The real politeness with which food is given by nearly all the interior tribes, who have not had much intercourse with Europeans, makes it a pleasure to accept. Again and again I have heard an apology made for the smallness of the present, or regret expressed that they had not received notice of my approach in time to grind more, and generally they readily accepted our excuse at having nothing to give in return, by saying that they were quite aware that there are no white men's goods in the interior. When I had it in my power, I always gave something really useful. To Katema, Shinte, and others I gave presents which cost me about 2*l.* each, and I could return to them at any time without having a character for stinginess. How some men can offer three buttons, or some other equally contemptible gift, while they have abundance in their possession, is to me unaccountable. The people receive the offering with a degree of shame, and ladies may be seen to hand it quickly to the attendants, and, when they retire, laugh until the tears stand in their eyes, saying to those about them, 'Is that a white man? then there are niggards among them too. Some of them are born without hearts!' When these tricks are repeated, the natives come to the conclusion that people who show such a want of sense must be told their duty; they therefore let them know what they ought to give, and travellers then complain of being pestered with their 'shameless begging'. I was troubled by importunity on the confines of civilization only.

MT 601

Three of Ma-mburuma's men brought us a present of meal and fowls, as we rested on the 28th on an island near Podebode. Their mode of salutation, intended to show good manners and respectful etiquette, was to clap the thigh with one hand while approaching with the present in the other; and, on sitting down before us, to clap the hands together, then to continue clapping on the thigh when they handed the present to our men, and with both hands when they received one in return, and also on their departure. This ceremonious procedure is gone through with grave composure, and mothers may be observed enjoining on their children the proper clapping of the hands, as good manners are taught among ourselves.

ZT 329

Clapping the hands in various ways is the polite way of saying 'Allow me', 'I beg pardon', 'Permit me to pass', 'Thanks', it is resorted to in respectful introduction and leave-taking, and also is equivalent to 'Hear hear'. When inferiors are called they respond by two brisk claps of the hands, meaning 'I am coming'. They are very punctilious amongst each other. A

large ivory bracelet marks the headman of a village; there is nothing else to
show differences of rank.

LJ 26 Oct 1866

Livingstone, who (as Kirk says) 'did not know what fear was', admires
courage and fortitude, and scoffs (as he had equal right to) at invalidism. He
records a callousness in the best tribes that darkened in the broken areas to
depravity and horror. At Nyangwe, as will be seen in a later section, he
experiences a Victorian My Lai, and his gentle spirit took what was perhaps its
mortal wound.

After three hours' sail, on the morning of the 29th, the river was narrowed
again by the mountains of Mburuma, into one channel, and another rapid
dimly appeared. It was formed by two currents guided by rocks to the
centre. In going down it, the men sent by Sekeletu behaved very nobly. The
canoes entered without previous survey, and the huge jobbling waves of mid-
current began at once to fill them. With great presence of mind, and without
a moment's hesitation, two men lightened each by jumping overboard; they
then ordered a Batoka man to do the same, as 'the white men must be
saved'. 'I cannot swim', said the Batoka. 'Jump out, then, and hold on to the
canoe,' which he instantly did. Swimming alongside, they guided the
swamping canoes down the swift current to the foot of the rapid, and then
ran them ashore to bale them out. A boat could have passed down safely,
but our canoes were not a foot above the water at the gunwales.

Thanks to the bravery of these poor fellows, nothing was lost, although
everything was well soaked. As the men were bringing the last canoe down
close to the shore, the stern swung round into the current, and all except one
man let go, rather than be dragged off. He clung to the bow, and was swept
out into the middle of the stream. Having held on when he ought to have let
go, he next put his life in jeopardy by letting go when he ought to have held
on; and was in a few seconds swallowed up by a fearful whirlpool. His
comrades launched out a canoe below, and caught him as he rose the third
time to the surface, and saved him, though much exhausted and very cold.

ZT 329

Both men and women submit to an operation without wincing, or any of
that shouting which caused young students to faint in the operating theatre
before the introduction of chloroform. The women pride themselves on their
ability to bear pain. A mother will address her little girl, from whose foot a
thorn is to be extracted, with 'Now, Ma, you are a woman; a woman does
not cry'. A man scorns to shed tears. When we were passing one of the deep
wells in the Kalahari, a boy, the son of an aged father, had been drowned in
it while playing on its brink. When all hope was gone, the father uttered an
exceedingly great and bitter cry. It was sorrow without hope. This was the
only instance I ever met with of a man weeping in this country.

The Bechuanas will keep on the sick-list as long as they feel any weakness. We had to nurse the sick like children; and, like children recovering from illness, the better they became the more impudent they grew. This was seen in the peremptory orders they would give with their now piping voices. Nothing that we did pleased them; and the laughter with which I received their ebullitions, though it was only the real expression of gladness at their recovery, and amusement at the ridiculous part they acted, only increased their chagrin.

MT 131 and 169

The father of Moyara was a powerful chief, but the son now sits among the ruins of the town, with four or five wives and very few people. At his hamlet a number of stakes are planted in the ground, and I counted fifty-four human skulls hung on their points. These were Matebele, who, unable to approach Sebituane on the island of Loyéla, had returned sick and famishing. Moyara's father took advantage of their reduced condition, and, after putting them to death, mounted their heads in the Batoka fashion. The old man who perpetrated this deed now lies in the middle of his son's huts, with a lot of rotten ivory over his grave. One cannot help feeling thankful that the reign of such wretches is over. They inhabited the whole of this side of the country, and were probably the barrier to the extension of the Portuguese commerce in this direction. When looking at these skulls, I remarked to Moyara, that many of them were those of mere boys. He assented readily and pointed them out as such. I asked why his father had killed boys. 'To show his fierceness', was the answer. 'Is it fierceness to kill boys?' 'Yes, they had no business here.' When I told him that this probably would ensure his own death if the Matebele came again, he replied, 'When I hear of their coming I shall hide the bones'. He was evidently proud of these trophies of his father's ferocity, and I was assured by other Batoka, that few strangers ever returned from a visit to this quarter. If a man wished to curry favour with a Batoka chief, he ascertained when a stranger was about to leave, and waylaid him at a distance from the town, and when he brought the head back to the chief, it was mounted as a trophy; the different chiefs vieing with each other as to which should mount the greatest number of skulls in his village.

MT 531

22nd November. – This evening the Babemba, came at dusk, and killed a Wanyamwezi woman on one side of the village, and a woman and child on the other side of it. I took this to be the result of the warlike demonstration mentioned above; but one of Mohamad Bogharib's people, named Bin Juma, had gone to a village on the north of this and seized two women and two girls, in lieu of four slaves who had run away. The headman, resenting this, shot an arrow into one of Bin Juma's party, and Bin Juma shot a woman with his gun.

This, it turned out, had roused the whole country, and next morning we were assailed by a crowd of Babemba on three sides: we had no stockade, but the men built one as fast as the enemy allowed, cutting down trees and carrying them to the line of defence, while others kept the assailants at bay with their guns. Had it not been for the crowd of Banyamwezi which we have, who shot vigorously with their arrows, and occasionally chased the Imbozhwa, we should have been routed. I did not go near the fighting, but remained in my house to defend my luggage if necessary. The women went up and down the village with sieves, as if winnowing, and singing songs, and lullilooing, to encourage their husbands and friends who were fighting: each had a branch of the fig tree in her hand, which she waved, I suppose as a charm. About ten of the Imbozhwa are said to have been killed, but dead and wounded were at once carried off by their countrymen. They continued the assault from early dawn till 1 p.m., and showed great bravery, but they wounded only two with their arrows. Their care to secure the wounded was admirable: two or three at once seized the fallen man, and ran off with him, though pursued by a great crowd of Banyamwezi with spears, and fired at by the Swahili — Victoria-cross fellows truly many of them were! Those who had a bunch of animals' tails, with medicine, tied to their waists, came sidling and ambling up to near the unfinished stockade, and shot their arrows high up into the air, to fall among the Wanyamwezi, then picked up any arrows on the field, ran back, and returned again. They thought that by the ambling gait they avoided the bullets, and when these whistled past them they put down their heads, as if to allow them to pass over; they had never encountered guns before.

24th November. – The Babemba came early this morning, and called on Mohamad to come out of his stockade if he were a man who could fight, but the fence is now finished, and no one seems willing to obey the taunting call: I have nothing to do with it, but feel thankful that I was detained, and did not, with my few attendants, fall into the hands of the justly infuriated Babemba. They kept up the attack today, and some went out to them, fighting till noon: when a man was killed and not carried off, the Wanyamwezi brought his head and put it on a pole on the stockade — six heads were thus placed. A fine young man was caught and brought in by the Wanyamwezi, one stabbed him behind, another cut his forehead with an axe. I called in vain to them not to kill him. As a last appeal, he said to the crowd that surrounded him, 'Don't kill me, and I shall take you to where the women are'. 'You lie,' said his enemies; 'you intend to take us where we may be shot by your friends;' and they killed him. It was horrible.

LJ 1868

Chapter 6

Chiefs and Commoners

The double hope of this book is to make Livingstone known as his prose deserves and to bring to bear on our own problems his genius for race relations. I had thought of substantiating his tact and judgment among whites, and then trying to show how he simply transferred these qualities to the blacks and succeeded with them on the basis of common humanity rather than by any special treatment. The principle, which is an important one, is I think true of Livingstone, but it is made difficult to demonstrate, particularly in South Africa, by his two obvious failures. With the Portuguese his contacts (as he presents them) seem to vindicate the courtesy and candour of his mind, both in the fairness of his praise and the fearlessness of his blame. But the Boers couldn't stand him; and on the Shiré he seemed completely at a loss with his own countrymen.

The Shiré I shall ignore. It was a small affair of white-white fractiousness and might be explained away as the product of exceptionally trying circumstances and personnel. The quarrel with the Boers is different. It was over white-black relationships; and it was with a race whose intransigence has changed very little from that day to this and whose leadership in South Africa has given the Republic its present notoriety in the world. The problem of apartheid is not my concern here; but since I do contend that Livingstone has something to teach the world about race relations, his one clash with those who held the very opposite views to his own has more than local significance.

The story is as short as the controversy over it has been long. A commando of 400 men under Pieter Scholtz was sent by Commandant-General Pretorius from the Transvaal against the Bakwena, whose conduct they regarded as unsatisfactory. Believing Livingstone to have been supplying arms to the tribe, a patrol from the commando, under Theunis Pretorius, wrecked his house on 1st November, 1852, while he was in Cape Town seeing his family off to England. The grievance held by the Boers does not really stand up to examination. Jan Smuts[1] said of it in Edinburgh in 1929 'I once took the opportunity to discuss the matter with President Kruger, and his explanation ... was that Gordon Cumming – another of your errant countrymen – had supplied the border tribes with rifles and ammunition in exchange for ivory; and the Boers, finding the natives armed, concluded erroneously that Livingstone had done so, and treated him accordingly.' The circumstances of the raid throw enough light on Livingstone, however, to be worth reporting in a little more detail.

Livingstone made a long trip through the Transvaal in the 1840s. He came in via Rustenburg (which is marked on his map in the *Missionary Travels*), striking what is now the line of the Johannesburg–Pretoria road at about Irene. He went north through Pretoria and then in a loop, roughly Settlers–Nylstroom–Warmbad, and back towards Rustenberg and then west again. He came, he says, to visit 'the poor enslaved tribes', and he gives a critical account of how these had been taken over by the Boers following the latter's defeat of their overlord, Mizilikazi. 'I never avoided the whites', Livingstone continues, 'but tried hard to cure and administer remedies to their sick without money ... I was invariably treated with respect.' He is 'sensible of no mental bias towards or against' them. However, as I have stressed, he certainly contrasts the Transvalers with the Afrikaners he had met elsewhere:

> While in Cape Colony, we passed through districts inhabited by the descendants of Dutch and French refugees who had fled from religious persecution. Those living near the capital differ but little from the middle classes in English counties, and are distinguished by public spirit and general intelligence; while those situated far from the centres of civilization are less informed, but are a body of frugal, industrious, and hospitable peasantry ... The population here described ought not to be confounded with some Boers

who fled from British rule on account of the emancipation of their Hottentot slaves.

MT 97

Nonetheless, Livingstone understood the philosophy of the Transvalers and appeals to Commandant Krieger if he does not reflect it in 'a fair and impartial statement'. Obviously what he does not share with Commandant Krieger *et al* is the deep sympathy on his own part with the blacks, or the belief of the Boers that their Africans, being a liberated, were thus a subject race.

In the light of this difference of opinion, which I shall not pursue, the second chapter of *Missionary Travels* opens uncompromisingly and even tactlessly:

Another adverse influence with which the mission had to contend was the vicinity of the Boers of the Magaliesberg. These are not to be confounded with the Cape colonists, who sometimes pass by the name. Those who have fled from English law on various pretexts, and have been joined by English deserters and every other variety of bad character in their distant localities, are unfortunately of a very different stamp. The great objection many of the Boers had, and still have, to English law is that it makes no distinction between black men and white. They felt aggrieved by their supposed losses in the emancipation of their Hottentot slaves, and determined to erect themselves into a republic, in which they might pursue without molestation the 'proper treatment of the blacks'. It is almost needless to add that the 'proper treatment' has always contained in it the essential element of slavery, namely, compulsory unpaid labour.

More than the charge of slavery, which Livingstone wields like a whip in this chapter, it could be argued that what was bugging him was the matter he quickly comes to, the destruction of his family home at Kolobeng. He says, however, 'Though I do feel sorry for the loss ... the plundering set me entirely free for my expedition to the north and I have never since had a moment's concern for anything I left behind. The Boers resolved to shut up the interior and I determined to open the country; and we shall see who have been most successful in resolution – they or I.'

Coupland quotes Stanley's remark that Livingstone's 'strong nature was opposed to forgiveness'. There must be some truth in this, though *(a)* we have to reconcile it with the generally mild temper of his books and *(b)* Coupland himself correlates it with Stanley's 'technique of disparagement and detraction'.[2]

The truth about Kolobeng will never be known. The most thoroughly documented account of it I have read is in Edward C. Tabler's *The Far Interior*, which is sympathetic to the Boers. Tabler complains that people are inclined to believe missionaries rather than Transvalers but, as he fails to bring (let alone prove) a single charge of gun-running against the missions, on this score, at least, it is commonsense and not sanctimoniousness that must acquit them. The critical issue is what guns were found in the mission. All the parties' language on this point is suspiciously vague, excepting only Scholtz's report –

in which, however, as will be seen, the mountain labours to bring forth a
mouse. Paul Kruger says[3] 'Theunis Pretorius found a complete workshop for
repairing guns, and a quantity of materials of war which Livingstone was
storing for Sechele [sic] ... Scholtz accordingly confiscated the missionary's
arsenal'. Livingstone's chapter is full of talk about guns; but, when it comes to
what was in the house, he writes: 'English gentlemen who had come ... to hunt
in the country beyond had deposited large quantities of stores'.[4] We know the
big-game rush had been intensified by the discovery of Lake Ngami. Hunters
do not leave their rifles to rust in the off-season but they might well store cases
of ammunition: that is all Kruger's wording requires, and it is innocent.
Scholtz's mouse was '2 percussion rifles, some muskets and the missionary's
smithing and gun-making tools'.[5] This is incriminating, though hardly an
arsenal. Livingstone was a hunter and explorer, he was used to big safaris, and
it *was* his house! Scholtz's remark[6] that the mission looked more like a
smuggler's and gunmaker's shop shows zero comprehension of the human
dynamo he was speaking of:

> My views of what is missionary duty are not so contracted as those whose
> ideal is a dumpy sort of man with a Bible under his arm. I have laboured in
> bricks and mortar, at the forge and carpenter's bench as well as in preaching
> and medical practice. I feel that ... I am serving Christ when shooting a
> buffalo for my men or taking an astronomic observation or ... after having
> got information which will I hope lead to more abundant blessing being
> bestowed on Africa.[7]

Scholtz's judgement on Livingstone is as tendentious, perhaps, as the £100-a-
year Scotsman's is on the Boers:

> A fountain is bought, and the lands which it can water parcelled out and
> let to villagers. As they increase in numbers the rents rise and the church
> becomes rich. With £200 per annum in addition, from government, the
> salary amounts to £400–£500 a year. The clergymen then preach
> abstinence from politics as a Christian duty. It is quite clear that with £400 a
> year, little else except pure spirituality is required.[8]

Livingstone adds that traders (among them Boers) were selling guns on the
frontier and growing rich from it, but missionaries were not, and remained
poor. He is also tart about the Boers' use of forced labour: 'We make the
people work for us in consideration of allowing them to live in our country', he
quotes Commandant Krieger as saying.[9] One contrasts this with the Bakwena
chief Sechele's spirited even noble retort to Commandant-General Pretorius, on
receiving an invitation to accept the same status:

> 'I was made an independent chief and placed here by God and not by
> you. I was never conquered by Msilikatzi, as those tribes whom you rule

over [which was true]; and the English are my friends. I get everything I wish from them. I cannot hinder them from going where they like.'[10]

Hard-hitting, even bitter as these pages of Livingstone are, I seldom find rancour in them. He was a matter-of-fact man, and his condemnations are as precise (within the limits of ascertainable fact) as they are impartial and, indeed, sorrowful. He not only says the commandos carried off '200 of our schoolchildren into slavery', he gives (in a letter[11]) 124 of these children's names. He thus joins the long tradition of documented protest against executive high-handedness which is (and needs to be) as lively in South Africa today as anywhere in the world.

Chapter II of *Missionary Travels*, in reflecting the eternal yesterday of South African politics, is, alas, as familiar as today's paper. But there are signs that the Livingstone touch is beginning to percolate. 'Fantastic, Say Guests at Pretoria All-Race Party'; so ran a 5-column headline in the *Cape Argus* of 8th July, 1972.[12] Readers who do not live in South Africa may smile at the following account and wonder at its excitement but those of us who do will recognise in it a growing tendency, and a hopeful preface to the second part of this book:

The Argus Correspondent – Pretoria, Saturday, 8th July

Malawi's multiracial party in the heart of Pretoria this week was 'fantastic' and 'very good for the South Africans of all colours who attended', according to some of the guests. White Government officials and Mr. Blaar Coetzee, Minister of Community Development, and Mrs. Coetzee, were among those who were there.

The party, which took the form of a buffet lunch with liquor being served freely to Black and White alike, took place at the large home of the Malawi Ambassador, Mr. Joe Kachingwe, in the exclusive suburb of Waterkloof.

Hobnobbing with the White guests were Black socialites from Soweto and other non-White areas. According to an African reporter who was there, 'it was a pleasure to see Blacks and Whites intermingling easily and without any friction – a thing that would have appeared impossible a few years back'.

Livingstone was received at the courts of many chiefs, some of such stature that they have a part in African history. I am indebted to *The Far Interior* for a description of the political world through which Livingstone was moving between 1842 and 1864. Tabler's account explains the widespread power of the Zulus and their appearances (so confusing to the reader of Livingstone), in unconnected places and under unrecognisable names. His 'Mazitu' in Malawi are here recognised as the Angoni, his 'Landeens' in the Zambezi delta, as the Shangana from Mashonaland. I have not included Tabler's account of Mzilikazi, as this was Moffat's friend and Livingstone never met him. But his Matabele also broke away from Tshaka, settling first near Pretoria but withdrawing before the Trekkers (after the Battle of Vegkop in 1836), to establish an empire in Rhodesia as far around Bulawayo as his impis could keep in awe.

Between 1820 and 1836 there occurred among the Bantu of the south-eastern coastlands a series of events that resulted in the displacement of several formidable and warlike hordes ... that roamed over wide areas of South Africa and spread havoc and destruction. These events and their after-math were aptly named the *Mfecane*, 'the Crushing', by the Bantu them-selves. The prime mover in the migrations was the formation of the Zulu power in north-eastern Natal, where closely related tribes were forcibly united into a military state by Tshaka, the first great Zulu king. Groups that would not submit to Tshaka fled ... and slaughtered and looted as they travelled slowly onwards. One was a group of Swazi that invaded the high plateau of Mashonaland, proceeded northward over the Zambezi and found a home near Lake Malawi, where they became known as the Angoni. Close behind them came the Shangana, who established themselves east of the Sabi River in the Melsetter district of Rhodesia ... and raided from the Zambezi to the Limpopo and between the Portuguese fortifications on the coast and Mashonaland.

The Zulus set a great mob in motion about 1821 and in a short while the Bantu of the densely inhabited country between the Orange and the Vaal were dislodged. This half-starved rabble ... was called the 'Mantati Horde' after one of its leaders, a woman Mantatise; it was compelled by hunger to keep moving in search of food ... Whatever cattle and grain were taken it was consumed at once, and, the locality being devastated, there was no choice but to go on ... Luckily the migrants were barred from the Cape Colony by high water in the Orange River, so they turned back and pro-ceeded to lay waste the northern Free State, driving the inhabitants to the north and west. Increased by fresh adherents, the Horde crossed the Vaal into Botswana where Robert Moffat, who presided over the London Mission-ary Society's station at Kuruman ... asked the half-civilised Griquas for help and received it ... An estimated 15 000 Mantati were soundly and decisively beaten ... [in 1823]. The Horde broke up after the battle ... One section, of southern Sotho origin, a few hundred in number and led by Sebituane, kept together and hacked a path through Botswana to the Zambezi, gaining strength as they went. Sebituane was born a commoner near the sources of the Vaal River, but he was a born leader ... His mixed tribe, the Makololo, travelled north on what was to be the Missionaries' Road. During this part of their anabasis they were twice attacked by the Matabele but Sebituane managed to hold his followers together and to steal more cattle. On the way they overcame the Tswana near Lake Ngami. This was circa 1825. The Makololo did not like the country and decided to move, so Sebituane, hearing of the presence on the west coast of white men, whom he strongly wished to see, started his people towards Damaraland; however, they were turned back by thirst and again lost all their cattle in the desert. Sebituane then marched north and reached the Zambezi. His general, Bololo, decisively defeated the army of the souther Barotse at the Chobe River ... A Batonga force was beaten near the Falls by the Makololo, who then subdued the Kafue Highlands, which were suitable for cattle-raising, and settled there. These were profitable wars, but the peace obtained by the conquerors was not to last long. . . .

Msilikazi could not forget his ambition to conquer the Makololo, perhaps because he knew they were the owners of a country fit for cattle raising that was even farther from his white enemies, whom he really feared. He sent an army of 2 000 men to attack them soon after he settled on the Rhodesian plateau. Part of the Matabele were ferried to an island in midstream, and, while the detachment was camped there for the night, its boatmen stole away and marooned it. Some of its members starved to death, and Sebituane, when the rest were sufficiently weak, rescued them and accepted them as recruits. . . . Even though he was victorious in the first encounter, Sebituane thought that the Kafue Highlands were no longer safe so . . . he resettled his subjects around the town of Linyanti in the Chobe Swamp, a move that insured future safety by putting more rivers and marshes between him and his rowdy new neighbours. . . .[13]

Livingstone meets Sebituane through another famous chief, Sechele, who owed his power to the former, and whose tribe, the Bawena, occupied territory between Sebituane's kraal and Kuruman. The story of Sechele's conversion is a comedy, in which his will-power is as amusing as Livingstone's tact. Sillery has a good paragraph on it:

Sechele's state of grace did not last very long. The following year it was found that one of his former wives . . . whom he had not been able to send away because she had a young child and no parents, was going to have a child by him, begotten after his baptism. Sechele at once confessed and added as an excuse that having been accustomed to her he had not at the time felt as if he was sinning . . . For this enormity he was cut off from the fellowship, but Livingstone allowed him to attend services as a spectator, not wishing to have him as an enemy. Sechele apparently bore no grudge for this humiliation and relations between the two men seem to have continued as good as ever.[14]

This is a very early incident but it already contains the blend of qualities that is beginning to declare itself as the Livingstone Touch:

I attached myself to the tribe called Bakuena, or Bakwains, the chief of which, named Sechele, was then living with his people at a place called Shokuane. I was from the first struck by his intelligence, and by the marked manner in which we both felt drawn to each other. As this remarkable man has not only embraced Christianity, but expounds its doctrines to his people, I will here give a brief sketch of his career.

When Sechele was still a boy, his father, also called Mochoasele, was murdered by his own people for taking to himself the wives of his rich under-chiefs. The children being spared, their friends invited Sebituáne, the chief of the Makolólo, who was then in those parts, to reinstate them in the chief-

tainship. Sebituane surrounded the town of the Bakwains by night; and just
as it began to dawn his herald proclaimed in a loud voice that he had come
to revenge the death of Mochoasele. This was followed by Sebituane's
people beating loudly on their shields all round the town. The panic was
tremendous, and the rush like that from a theatre on fire, while the Makololo
used their javelins on the terrified Bakwains with a dexterity which they
alone can employ. Sebituane had given orders to his men to spare the sons
of the chief; and one of them, meeting Sechele, put him in ward by giving
him such a blow on the head with a club as to render him insensible. The
usurper was put to death; and Sechele, reinstated in his chieftainship, felt
much attached to Sebituane. The circumstances here noticed ultimately led
me, as will be seen by and by, into the new, well-watered country to which
this same Sebituane had preceded me by many years.

Sechele married the daughters of three of his underchiefs, who had, on
account of their blood relationship, stood by him in his adversity. This is one
of the modes adopted for cementing the allegiance of a tribe. The government is patriarchal, each man being by virtue of paternity, chief of his own
children. They build their huts around his, and the greater the number of
children the more his importance increases. Hence children are esteemed one
of the greatest blessings, and are always treated kindly. Near the centre of
each circle of huts there is a spot called a 'kotla', with a fireplace; here they
work, eat, or sit and gossip over the news of the day. A poor man attaches
himself to the *kotla* of a rich one, and is considered a child of the latter. An
underchief has a number of these circles around his; and the collection of
kotlas around the great one in the middle of the whole, that of the principal
chief, constitutes the town. The circle of huts immediately around the *kotla*
of the chief is composed of the huts of his wives, and those of his blood
relations. He attaches the underchiefs to himself and his government
by marrying, as Sechele did, their daughters, or inducing his brothers to
do so. They are fond of the relationship to great families. If you meet a party
of strangers, and the head man's relationship to some uncle of a certain chief
is not at once proclaimed by his attendants, you may hear him whispering,
'Tell him who I am'. This usually involves a counting on the fingers of
a part of his genealogical tree; and ends in the important announcement
that the head of the party is half-cousin to some well-known ruler.

Sechele was thus seated in his chieftainship when I made his acquaintance. On the first occasion in which I ever attempted to hold a public
religious service, he remarked that it was the custom of his nation, when any
new subject was brought before them, to put questions on it; and he begged
me to allow him to do the same in this case. On expressing my entire
willingness to answer his questions, he said, 'You startle me – these words
make all my bones to shake – I have no more strength in me: but my forefathers were living at the same time yours were, and how is it that they did
not send them word about these terrible things sooner? They all passed
away into darkness without knowing whither they were going.' I got out of
the difficulty by explaining the geographical barriers in the North, and the

gradual spread of knowledge from the South, to which we first had access by means of ships; and I expressed my belief that, as Christ had said, the whole world would yet be enlightened by the Gospel. Pointing to the great Kalahári desert, he said, 'You never can cross that country to the tribes beyond; it is utterly impossible even for us black men, except in certain seasons, when more than the usual supply of rain falls, and an extraordinary growth of water-melons follows. Even we who know the country would certainly perish without them.' Re-asserting my belief in the words of Christ, we parted; and it will be seen further on that Sechele himself assisted me in crossing that desert which had previously proved an insurmountable barrier to so many adventurers.

As soon as he had an opportunity of learning, he set himself to read with such close application that, from being comparatively thin, the effect of having been fond of the chase, he became quite corpulent from want of exercise. He was by no means an ordinary specimen of the people, for I never went into the town but I was pressed to hear him read some chapters of the Bible. Isaiah was a great favourite with him; and he was wont to use the same phrase nearly which the professor of Greek at Glasgow, Sir D. K. Sandford, once used respecting the Apostle Paul, when reading his speeches in the Acts: 'He was a fine fellow, that Paul!' 'He was a fine man, that Isaiah; he knew how to speak.' Sechele invariably offered me something to eat on every occasion of my visiting him.

Seeing me anxious that his people should believe the words of Christ, he once said, 'Do you imagine these people will ever believe by your merely talking to them? I can make them do nothing except by thrashing them; and if you like, I shall call my head men, and with our *litupa* (whips of rhinoceros-hide) we will soon make them all believe together.' The idea of using entreaty and persuasion to subjects to become Christians – whose opinion on no other matter would he condescend to ask – was especially surprising to him. He considered that they ought only to be too happy to embrace Christianity at his command. During the space of two years and a half he continued to profess to his people his full conviction of the truth of Christianity; and in all discussions on the subject he took that side, acting at the same time in an upright manner in all the relations of life. He felt the difficulties of his situation long before I did, and often said, 'O, I wish you had come to this country before I became entangled in the meshes of our customs!' In fact, he could not get rid of his superfluous wives, without appearing to be ungrateful to their parents, who had done so much for him in his adversity.

In the hope that others would be induced to join him in his attachment to Christianity, he asked me to begin family worship with him in his house. I did so; and by-and-by was surprised to hear how well he conducted the prayer in his own simple and beautiful style, for he was quite a master of his own language. At this time we were suffering from the effects of a drought, which will be described further on, and none except his family, whom he ordered to attend, came near his meeting. 'In former times,' said he, 'when a chief was fond of hunting, all his people got dogs and became fond of hunting too. If he was fond of dancing or music, all showed a liking to these amusements too. If the chief loved beer, they all rejoiced in strong drink. But in this case it is different. I love the Word of God, and not one of my brethren will join me.'

Sechele continued to make a consistent profession for about three years; and perceiving at last some of the difficulties of his case, and also feeling compassion for the poor women, who were by far the best of our scholars, I had no desire that he should be in any hurry to make a full profession by baptism, and putting away all his wives but one. His principal wife, too, was about the most unlikely subject in the tribe ever to become anything else than an out-and-out greasy disciple of the old school. She has since become greatly altered, I hear, for the better; but again and again have I seen Sechele send her out of church to put her gown on, and away she would go with her lips shot out, the very picture of unutterable disgust at his new-fangled notions.

When he at last applied for baptism, I simply asked him how he, having the Bible in his hand, and able to read it, thought he ought to act. He went home, gave each of his superfluous wives new clothing, and all his own goods which they had been accustomed to keep in their huts for him, and sent them to their parents with an intimation that he had no fault to find with them, but that in parting with them he wished to follow the will of God. On the day on which he and his children were baptized, great numbers came to see the ceremony. Some thought, from a stupid calumny circulated by enemies to Christianity in the south, that the converts would be made to drink an infusion of 'dead men's brains', and were astonished to find that water only was used at baptism. Seeing several of the old men actually in tears during the service, I asked them afterwards the cause of their weeping; they were crying to see their father, as the Scotch remark over a case of suicide, 'so far left to himself'. They seemed to think that I had thrown the glamour over him and that he had become mine. Here commenced an opposition which we had not previously experienced. All the friends of the divorced wives became the opponents of our religion. The attendance at school and church diminished to very few besides the chief's own family. They all treated us still with respectful kindness, but to Sechele himself they said things which, as he often remarked, had they ventured on in former times, would have cost them their lives. It was trying, after all we had done, to see our labours so little appreciated; but we had sown the good seed, and have no doubt but it will yet spring up, though we may not live to see the fruits.

MT 14–19

Sechele lived till 1892. He thus saw Bechuanaland declared a Protectorate in 1885, when, as Sillery writes, 'it must have seemed that he had escaped the Boers only to be swallowed by the British'.[15]

The Sebituane sequence that now follows moves to the extreme north of Botswana, and to present-day Zambia and Rhodesia.

The Makololo whom we met on the Chobe were delighted to see us; and as their chief Sebituane was about twenty miles down the river, Mr. Oswell and I proceeded in canoes to his temporary residence. He was about forty-five years of age; of a tall and wiry form, an olive or coffee-and-milk colour, and slightly bald; in manner cool and collected, and more frank in his answers than any other chief I ever met. He was the greatest warrior ever heard of beyond the colony, for, unlike Mosilikatse, Dingaan, and others, he always led his men into battle himself. When he saw the enemy he felt the edge of his battle-axe and said, 'Aha! it is sharp, and whoever turns his back on the enemy will feel its edge'. So fleet of foot was he, that all his people knew there was no escape for the coward, as any such would be cut down without mercy. In some instances of skulking, he allowed the individual to return home; then calling him, he would say, 'Ah, you prefer dying at home to dying in the field, do you? You shall have your desire.' This was the signal for his immediate execution.

Sebituane was one in that immense horde of savages driven back by the Griquas from Kuruman in 1824. He then fled to the north with an insignificant party of men and cattle. A great variety of fortune followed him in the northern part of the Bechuana country; twice he lost all his cattle by the attacks of the Matebele, but always kept his people together, and retook more than he lost. He then crossed the Desert by nearly the same path that we did. He had captured a guide; and, as it was necessary to travel by night in order to reach water, the guide took advantage of this and gave him the slip. After marching till morning, and going as they thought right, they found themselves on the trail of the day before. Many of his cattle burst away from him in the frenzy of thirst. He stocked himself again among the Batletli, on Lake Kumadau, whose herds were of the large-horned species of cattle. Conquering all around the lake, he heard of white men living at the west coast; and haunted by what seems to have been the dream of his whole life, a desire to have intercourse with the white man, he passed away to the south-west, into the parts opened up lately by Messrs. Galton and Andersson. There, suffering intensely from thirst, he and his party came to a small well. He decided that the men, not the cattle, should drink it, the former being of most value, as they could fight for more, should these be lost. In the morning they found the cattle had escaped to the Damarás.

Returning to the north poorer than he started, he ascended the Teoughe to the hill Sorila, and crossed over a swampy country to the eastwards. Pursuing his course onwards to the low-lying basin of the Zambezi, he saw that it presented no attraction to a pastoral tribe like his, so he moved down that river among the Bashubía and Batoka, who were then living in all their glory. His narrative resembled closely the 'Commentaries of Caesar', and the history of the British in India. He was always forced to attack the different tribes, and to this day his men justify every step he took as perfectly just and right. The Batoka lived on large islands in the Zambesi; and, feeling perfectly secure in their fastnesses, often allured fugitive or wandering tribes on to uninhabited islets on pretence of ferrying them across and there left them to perish for the sake of their goods. The river is so large, that the sharpest eye cannot tell the difference between an island and the bend of the opposite bank; but Sebituane, with his usual foresight, requested the island chief who ferried him across to take his seat in the canoe with him, and detained him by his side till all his people and cattle were safely landed. The whole Batoka country was then densely peopled and they had a curious taste for ornamenting their villages with the skulls of strangers. When Sebituane appeared near the great falls, an immense army collected to make trophies of the Makololo skulls; but instead of succeeding in this they gave him a good excuse for conquering them, and capturing so many cattle that his people were quite incapable of taking any note of the sheep and goats. He overran all the high lands towards the Kafue, and settled in what is called a pastoral country, of gently undulating plains, covered with short grass and but little forest. The Makololo have never lost their love for this fine healthy region.

But the Matabele, a Caffre or Zulu tribe, under Mosilikatse crossed the Zambesi; and, attacking Sebituane in this choice spot, captured his cattle and women. Rallying his men, he followed and recaptured the whole. A fresh attack was also repulsed, and Sebituane thought of going further down the Zambesi, to the country of the white men. He had an idea, whence imbibed I never could learn, that if he had a cannon he might live in peace. He had led a life of war, yet no one apparently desired peace more than he did. A prophet induced him to turn his face again to the westward. This man, by name Tlapáne, was called a *senoga* – one who holds intercourse with the gods. He probably had a touch of insanity, for he was in the habit of retiring no one knew whither, but perhaps into some cave, to remain in a hypnotic or mesmeric state until the moon was full. Then, returning to the tribe quite emaciated, he excited himself, until he was in a state of ecstasy. These pretended prophets commence their operations by violent action. Stamping, leaping, and shouting in a peculiarly violent manner, or beating the ground with a club, they induce a kind of fit, and while in it pretend that their utterances are unknown to themselves. Tlapane, pointing eastwards, said, 'There, Sebituane, I behold a fire: shun it; it is a fire which may scorch thee. The gods say, go not thither.' Then, turning to the west, he said, 'I see a city and a nation of black men – men of the water; their cattle are red; thine own tribe, Sebituane, is perishing, and will be all consumed; thou wilt govern black men, and, when thy warriors have captured red cattle, let not the owners be killed; they are thy future tribe – they are thy city; let them be spared.' This vaticination, which loses much in the translation, I have given rather fully, as it shows an observant mind. The fire pointed to was evidently the Portuguese fire-arms, of which he must have heard. The black men referred to were the Barotse; and Sebituane spared their chiefs, even though they attacked him first. He had ascended the Barotse valley, but was pursued by the Matabele, as Mosilikatse never could forgive his former defeats. They came up the river in a very large body. Sebituane placed some goats on one of the large islands of the Zambezi, as a bait to the warriors, and some men in canoes to co-operate in the manoeuvre. When they were all ferried over to the island, the canoes were removed, and the Matabele found themselves completely in a trap, being perfectly unable to swim. They subsisted for some time on the roots of grass after the goats were eaten, but gradually became so emaciated, that, when the Makololo landed, they had only to perform the part of executioners on the adults, and to adopt the rest into their own tribe. Afterwards Mosilikatse was goaded on by his warriors to revenge this loss; so he sent an immense army, carrying canoes with them, in order that no such mishap might occur again. Sebituane had by this time incorporated the Barotse, and taught his young men to manage canoes; so he went from island to island, and watched the Matabele on the mainland so closely that they could not use their canoes to cross the river anywhere without parting their forces. At last all the Makololo and their cattle were collected on the island of Loyélo; and lay all around, keeping watch night and day over the enemy. After some time spent in this way, Sebituane went in a canoe towards them, and, addressing them by an interpreter, asked why they wished to kill him; he had never attacked them, never harmed their chief: 'Au!' he continued, 'the guilt is on your side.' The Matabele made no reply; but the Makololo next day saw the canoes they had carried so far, lying smashed, and the owners gone. They returned towards their own country, and fever, famine, and the Batoka completed their destruction; only five men returned to Mosilikatse.

Sebituane had now not only conquered all the black tribes over an immense tract of country, but had made himself dreaded even by the terrible Mosilikatse. He never could trust this ferocious chief, however; and, as the Batoka on the islands had been guilty of ferrying his enemies across the Zambezi, he made a rapid descent upon them, and swept them all out of their island fastnesses. He thus unwittingly performed a good service to the country, by completely breaking down the old system which prevented trade from penetrating into the great central valley. Of the chiefs who escaped, he said, 'They love Mosilikatse, let them live with him: the Zambezi is my line of defence'; and men were placed all along it as sentinels.

Sebituane knew everything that happened in the country, for he had the art of gaining the affections both of his own people and of strangers. When a party of poor men came to his town to sell their hoes or skins, no matter how ungainly they might be, he soon knew them all. A company of these indigent strangers, sitting far apart from the Makololo gentlemen around the chief, would be surprised to see him come alone to them, and, sitting down, inquire if they were hungry. He would order an attendant to bring meal, milk, and honey, and, mixing them in their sight in order to remove any suspicion from their minds, make them feast, perhaps for the first time in their lives, on a lordly dish. Delighted beyond measure with his affability and liberality, they felt their hearts warm towards him, and gave him all the information in their power; and as he never allowed a party of strangers to go away without giving every one of them, servants and all, a present, his praises were sounded far and wide. 'He has a heart! he is wise!' were the usual expressions we heard before we saw him.

He was much pleased with the proof of confidence we had shown in bringing our children, and promised to take us to see his country, so that we might choose a part in which to locate ourselves. Our plan was, that I should remain in the pursuit of my objects as a missionary, while Mr. Oswell explored the Zambezi to the east. Poor Sebituane, however, just after realising what he had so long ardently desired, fell sick of inflammation of the lungs, which originated in and extended from an old wound, got at Melita. I saw his danger, but, being a stranger, I feared to treat him medically, lest, in the event of his death, I should be blamed by his people. I mentioned this to one of his doctors, who said, 'Your fear is prudent and wise; this people would blame you.' On the Sunday afternoon in which he died, when our usual religious service was over, I visited him with my little boy Robert. 'Come near', said Sebituane, 'and see if I am any longer a man; I am done.' He was thus sensible of the nature of his disease, so I ventured to assent, and added a single sentence regarding hope after death. 'Why do you speak of death?' said one of a relay of fresh doctors; 'Sebituane will never die'. If I had persisted, the impression would have been produced that by speaking about it I wished him to die. After sitting with him some time, and commending him to the mercy of God, I rose to depart, when the dying chieftain, raising himself up a little called a servant, and said, 'Take Robert to Maunku (one of his wives), and tell her to give him some milk'. These were the last words of Sebituane.

MT 83

When Livingstone arrived at Linyanti (north-west of the Chobe National Park) on 23 May, 1853, 'the population ... turned out en masse to see the wagons in motion'. Sebituane's son, Sekeletu, was now in power. The liquidation of his rival, Mpepe, is a bit of African power politics that would have pleased Machiavelli:

I found Sekeletu a young man of eighteen years of age, of that dark-yellow or coffee-and-milk colour, of which the Makololo are so proud, because it distinguishes them considerably from the black tribes on the rivers. He is about five feet seven in height, and neither so goodlooking, nor of so much ability, as his father was, but is equally friendly to the English.

My object being first of all to examine the country for a healthy locality, before attempting to make a path to either the east or west coast, I proposed to Sekeletu the plan of ascending the great river which we had discovered in 1851. He volunteered to accompany me; and when we got about sixty miles away, on the road to Sesheke, we encountered Mpepe. Sekeletu and his companions were mounted on oxen, though, having neither saddle nor bridle, they were perpetually falling off. Mpepe, armed with his little axe, came along a path parallel to, but a quarter of a mile distant from, that of our party; and when he saw Sekeletu he ran with all his might towards us; but Sekeletu, being on his guard, galloped off to an adjacent village. He then withdrew somewhere till all our party came up. Mpepe had given his own party to understand that he would cut down Sekeletu, either on their first meeting, or at the breaking up of their first conference. I happened to sit down between the two in the hut where they met: being tired with riding all day in the sun, I soon asked Sekeletu where I should sleep, and he replied, 'Come, I will show you'. As we rose together, I unconsciously covered Sekeletu's body with mine, and saved him from the blow of the assassin. I knew nothing of the plot, but remarked that all Mpepe's men kept hold of their arms, even after we had sat down – a thing quite unusual in the presence of a chief; and when Sekeletu showed me the hut in which I was to spent the night, he said to me, 'That man wishes to kill me'. I afterwards learnt that some of Mpepe's attendants had divulged the secret; and, bearing in mind his father's instructions, Sekeletu put Mpepe to death that night. It was managed so quietly, that, although I was sleeping within a few yards of the scene, I knew nothing of it till the next day. Nokuáne went to the fire at which Mpepe sat, with a handful of snuff, as if he were about to sit down and regale himself therewith. Mpepe said to him, 'Nsepísa' (cause me to take a pinch); and, as he held out his hand, Nokuane caught hold of it, while another man seized the other hand, and, leading him out a mile, speared him. This is the common mode of executing criminals. They are not allowed to speak; though on one occasion a man, feeling his wrist held too tightly, said, 'Hold me gently, can't you? you will soon be led out in the same way yourselves'.

Soon after our arrival at Linyanti, Sekeletu took me aside, and pressed me to mention those things I liked best and hoped to get from him. Anything, either in or out of his town, should be freely given if I would only mention it. I explained to him that my object was to elevate him and his people to be Christians; but he replied he did not wish to learn to read the Book, for he was afraid 'it might change his heart, and make him content with only one wife, like Sechele'. I assured him that nothing was expected but by his own voluntary decision. 'No, no; he wanted always to have five wives at least.' I liked the frankness of Sekeletu, for nothing is so wearying to the spirit as talking to those who agree with everything advanced.

MT 178

The charming Sekeletu proved a weaker chief than his great father, and, when Livingstone returned with the Makololo from Tete, in 1860, he found him with leprosy. The missionary's intimacy with the tribe affords a perspicuous account of its decay. He adds the following footnote recording the end, not only of Sekeletu, but of his admired Makololo:

Sekeletu died in the beginning of 1864. A civil war broke out about the succession to the chieftainship; a large body of those opposed to the late Chief's uncle, Impololo, being regent, departed with their cattle to Lake

Ngami; an insurrection by the black tribes followed; Impololo was slain, and the kingdom, of which, under an able sagacious mission, a vast deal might have been made, has suffered the usual fate of African conquests. That fate we deeply deplore; for, whatever other faults the Makololo might justly be charged with, they did not belong to the class who buy and sell each other, and the tribes who have succeeded them do.

Livingstone provides many other full length and thumb-nail portraits of Africans, chiefs and commoners. Each – friendly, kind, proud, dull, eccentric, maddening or dangerous – is a person. There are no stereotypes: everyone is met with respect and humour. By virtue of this gallery the travels take on the interest of a picaresque novel. The psychology Livingstone displays has a connoisseurship quite novelistic and, although he never sustains descriptions for their own sakes, he often reveals the talent of a novelist. Especially memorable are the self-important Pangola near Zumbo, the sinister Masho-tlane on the upper Zambezi, the merry Monga from Kariba, the loyal Sekwebu and his pathetic death at sea, and the wily Zambians, Chitapangwa and Matipa. The substantial length of some of these accounts permits me to include very few but one that cannot be omitted is the encounter with the redoubtable but charming Manenko and her entourage, whom Livingstone met in Barotse-land, on the way to Luanda:

Manenko was a tall strapping woman about twenty, distinguished by a profusion of ornaments and medicines hung round her person; the latter are supposed to act as charms. Her body was smeared all over with a mixture of fat and red ochre, as a protection against the weather; a necessary pre-caution, for, like most of the Balonda ladies, she was otherwise in a state of frightful nudity. This was not from want of clothing, for, being a chief, she might have been as well clad as any of her subjects, but from her peculiar ideas of elegance in dress. When she arrived with her husband, Sambánza, they listened for some time to the statements I was making to the people of Nyamoana, after which the husband, acting as spokesman, commenced an oration, stating the reasons for their coming, and, during every two or three seconds of the delivery, he picked up a little sand, and rubbed it on the upper part of his arms and chest. This is a common mode of salutation in Londa. When Sambanza had finished his oration, he rose up, and showed his ankles ornamented with a bundle of copper rings; had they been very heavy, they would have made him adopt a straggling walk. Some chiefs have really so many, as to be forced, by the weight and size, to keep one foot apart from the other; the weight being a serious inconvenience in walking. The gentle-men like Sambanza, who wish to imitate their betters, do so in their walk; so you see men, with only a few ounces of ornament on their legs, strutting along as if they had double the number of pounds. When I smiled at Sambanza's walk, the people remarked, 'That is the way in which they show off their lordship in these parts'. The same thing is thought pretty by our own dragoons in walking jauntingly.

When erecting our sheds at the village, Manenko fell upon our friends from Masiko in a way that left no doubt on our minds that she is a most accomplished scold. Masiko had, on a former occasion, sent to Samoána for a cloth and, after receiving it, sent it back, because it had the appearance of having had 'witchcraft medicine' on it; this was a grave offence, and now Manenko had a good excuse for venting her spleen, the ambassadors having called at her village, and slept in one of the huts without leave. If her family was to be suspected of dealing in evil charms, why were Masiko's people not to be thought guilty of leaving the same in her hut? She advanced and receded in true oratorical style, belabouring her own servants as well for allowing the offence, and, as usual in more civilized feminine lectures, she leaned over the objects of her ire, and screamed forth all their faults and failings ever since they were born, and her despair of ever seeing them become better, until they were all 'killed by alligators'. Masiko's people followed the plan of receiving this torrent of abuse in silence, and, as neither we nor they had anything to eat, we parted next morning.

Manenko gave us some manioc-roots in the morning, and had determined to carry our baggage to her uncle's, Kabompo or Shinte. We had heard a sample of what she could do with her tongue; and as neither my men nor myself had much inclination to encounter a scolding from this black Mrs. Caudle, we made ready the packages; but she came and said the men whom she had ordered for the service had not yet come; they would arrive tomorrow. Being on low and disagreeable diet, I felt annoyed at this further delay, and ordered the packages to be put into the canoes to proceed up the river without her servants; but Manenko was not to be circumvented in this way; she came forward with her people, and said her uncle would be angry if she did not carry forward the tusks and goods of Sekeletu, seized the luggage, and declared that she would carry it in spite of me. My men succumbed sooner to this petticoat government than I felt inclined to do, and left me no power; and, being unwilling to encounter her tongue, I was moving off to the canoes, when she gave me a kind explanation, and, with her hand on my shoulder, put on a motherly look, saying, 'Now, my little man, just do as the rest have done'. My feelings of annoyance of course vanished, and I went out to try and get some meat.

On starting one morning, we had to cross, in a canoe, a stream which flows past the village of Nyamoana. Manenko's doctor waved some charms over her, and she took some in her hand and on her body before she ventured upon the water. She was accompanied by her husband and her drummer; the latter continued to thump most vigorously, until a heavy drizzling mist set in and compelled him to desist. Her husband used various incantations and vociferations to drive away the rain, but down it poured incessantly, and on our Amazon went, in the very lightest marching order, and at a pace that few of the men could keep up with. Being on ox-back, I kept pretty close to our leader, and asked her why she did not clothe herself during the rain, and learned that it is not considered proper for a chief to appear effeminate. He or she must always wear the appearance of robust youth, and bear vicissitudes without wincing. My men, in admiration of her pedestrian powers, every now and then remarked, 'Manenko is a soldier'; and thoroughly wet and cold, we were all glad when she proposed a halt to prepare our night's lodging on the banks of a stream.

The number of little villages seemed about equal to the number of valleys. At some we stopped and rested, the people becoming more liberal as we advanced. Others we found deserted, a sudden panic having seized the inhabitants, though the drum of Manenko was kept beaten pretty constantly, in order to give notice of the approach of great people. When we had decided to remain for the night at any village, the inhabitants lent us the roofs of their huts, which in form resemble those of the Makololo, or a Chinaman's hat, and can be taken off the walls at pleasure. They lifted them off, and brought them to the spot we had selected as our lodging, and, when my men had propped them up with stakes, they were then safely housed for the night. Every one who comes to salute either Manenko or ourselves, rubs the upper parts of the arms and chest with ashes; those who wish to show profounder reverence, put some also on the face.

Manenko having brought us to a stand, on account of slight indisposition and a desire to send forward notice of our approach to her uncle, I asked why it was necessary to send forward information of our movements if Shinte had idols who could tell him everything? 'She just did it' was the reply. I was labouring under fever, and did not find it very difficult to exercise patience with her whims; but it being Saturday, I thought we might as well go to the town for Sunday. 'No; her messenger must return from her uncle first.' Being sure that the answer of the uncle would be favourable, I thought we might go on at once, and not lose two days in the same spot. 'No, it is our custom'; and everything else I could urge was answered in the genuine pertinacious lady style. She ground some meal for me with her own hands, and, when she brought it, told me she had actually gone to a village and begged corn for the purpose. She said this with an air as if the inference must be drawn by even a stupid white man: 'I know how to manage, don't I?'

During the night we were all awakened by a terrific shriek from one of Manenko's ladies. She piped out so loud and long that we all imagined she had been seized by a lion, and my men snatched up their arms, which they always place so as to be ready at a moment's notice, and ran to the rescue; but we found the alarm had been caused by one of the oxen thrusting his head into her hut, and smelling her: she had put her hand on his cold wet nose, and thought it was all over with her.

On Sunday afternoon messengers arrived from Shinte, expressing his approbation of the objects we had in view in our journey through his country, and that he was glad of the prospect of a way being opened by which white men might visit him, and allow him to purchase ornaments at pleasure. Manenko now threatened in sport to go on, and I soon afterwards perceived that what now seemed to me the dilly-dallying way of this lady, was the proper mode of making acquaintance with the Balonda; and much of the favour with which I was received in different places was owing to my sending forward messengers, to state the object of our coming, before entering each town and village. When we came in sight of a village, we sat down under the shade of a tree, and sent forward a man to give notice who we were, and what were our objects. The head man of the village then sent out his principal men, as Shinte now did, to bid us welcome, and show us a tree under which we might sleep. Before I had profited by the rather tedious teaching of Manenko, I sometimes entered a village, and created unintentional alarm.

On the 17th, Tuesday, we were honoured with a grand reception by Shinte about eleven o'clock. Sambanza claimed the honour of presenting us, Manenko being slightly indisposed. The *kotla*, or place of audience, was about a hundred yards square, and two graceful specimens of a species of banian stood near one end; under one of these sat Shinte, on a sort of throne covered with a leopard's skin. He had on a checked jacket, and a kilt of scarlet baize edged with green; many strings of large beads hung from his neck, and his limbs were covered with iron and copper armlets and bracelets; on his head he wore a helmet made of beads woven neatly together, and crowned with a great bunch of goose-feathers. Close to him sat three lads with large sheaves of arrows over their shoulders.

When we entered the *kotla*, the whole of Manenko's party saluted Shinte by clapping their hands; and Sambanza did obeisance by rubbing his chest and arms with ashes. One of the trees being unoccupied, I retreated to it for the sake of the shade, and my whole party did the same. We were now about forty yards from the chief, and could see the whole ceremony. The different sections of the tribe came forward in the same way that we did, the head man of each making obeisance with ashes which he carried with him for the purpose; then came the soldiers, all armed to the teeth, running and shouting towards us, with their swords drawn, and their faces screwed up so as to appear as savage as possible, for the purpose, I thought, of trying whether they could not make us take to our heels. As we did not, they turned round towards Shinte, and saluted him; then retired. When all had come, and were seated, then began the curious capering usually seen in *pichos*. A man starts up, and imitates the most approved attitudes observed in actual fight, — as if throwing one javelin, receiving another on the shield, springing to one side to avoid a third, running backwards or forwards, leaping &c. This over, Sambanza, and the spokesman of Nyamoana, stalked backwards and forwards in front of Shinte, and gave forth, in a loud voice, all they had been able to learn, either from myself or people, of my past history and connection with the Makololo; the return of the captives; the wish to open the country to trade; the Bible as a word from heaven; the white man's desire for the tribes to live in peace: he ought to have taught the Makololo that first, for the Balonda never attacked them, yet they had assailed the Balonda: perhaps he is fibbing, perhaps not; they rather thought he was; but as the Balonda had good hearts, and Shinte had never done harm to any one, he had better receive the white man well, and send him on his way. Sambanza was gaily attired, and, besides a profusion of beads, had a cloth so long that a boy carried it after him as a train.

Behind Shinte sat about a hundred women, clothed in their best, which happened to be a profusion of red baize. The chief wife of Shinte, one of the Matebele or Zulus, sat in front with a curious red cap on her head. During the intervals between the speeches, these ladies burst forth into a sort of plaintive ditty; but it was impossible for any of us to catch whether it was in praise of the speaker, of Shinte, or of themselves. This was the first time I had ever seen females present in a public assembly. In the south the women are not permitted to enter the *kotla*; and even when invited to come to a religious service there, would not enter until ordered to do so by the chief; but here they expressed approbation by clapping their hands, and laughing at different speakers; and Shinte frequently turned round and spoke to them.

A party of musicians, consisting of three drummers and four performers on the piano, went round the *kotla* several times, regaling us with their music. The drums are neatly carved from the trunk of a tree, and have a small hole in the side covered with a bit of spider's web: the ends are covered with the skin of an antelope pegged on; and when they wish to tighten it they hold it to the fire to make it contract: the instruments are beaten with the hands.

The piano, named *marimba*, consists of two bars of wood placed side by side, here quite straight, but, farther north, bent round so as to resemble half the tire of a carriage-wheel; across these are placed about fifteen wooden keys, each of which is two or three inches broad, and fifteen or eighteen inches long; their thickness is regulated according to the deepness of the note required: each of the keys has a calabash beneath it; from the upper part of each, a portion is cut off to enable them to embrace the bars, and form hollow sounding-boards to the keys, which also are of different sizes, according to the note required; and little drumsticks elicit the music. Rapidity of execution seems much admired among them, and the music is pleasant to the ear.

When nine speakers had concluded their orations, Shinte stood up, and so did all the people. He had maintained true African dignity of manner all the while, but my people remarked that he scarcely ever took his eyes off me for a moment. He seemed in good humour, and said he had expected 'that a man who came from the gods, would have approached and talked to him'. That had been my own intention in going to the reception, but when we came and saw the formidable preparations, and all his own men keeping at least forty yards off from him, I yielded to the solicitations of my men, and remained by the tree opposite to that under which he sat. His remark confirmed my previous belief that a frank, open, fearless manner is the most winning with all these Africans. I stated the object of my journey and mission, and to all I advanced the old gentleman clapped his hands in appro-bation. He replied through a spokesman; then all the company joined in the response by clapping of hands too.

After the more serious business was over, I asked if he had ever seen a white man before. He replied, 'Never; you are the very first I have seen with a white skin and straight hair; your clothing too is different from any we have ever seen'. They had been visited by native Portuguese and Mambari only.

On learning from some of the people that 'Shinte's mouth was bitter for want of tasting ox-flesh', I presented him with an ox, to his great delight; and as his country is so well adapted for cattle, I advised him to begin a trade in cows with the Makololo. He was pleased with the idea; and when we returned from Loanda, we found that he had profited by the hint, for he had got three, and one of them justified my opinion of the country, for it was more like a prize heifer for fatness than any we had seen in Africa. He soon afterwards sent us a basket of green maize boiled, another of manioc-meal, and a small fowl.

During this time Manenko had been extremely busy with all her people in getting up a very pretty hut and court-yard, to be, as she said, her residence always when white men were brought by her along the same path. When she heard that we had given an ox to her uncle, she came forward to us with the air of one wronged, and explained that 'This white man belonged to her; she had brought him here, and therefore the ox was hers, not Shinte's.' She ordered her men to bring it, got it slaughtered by them, and presented her uncle with a leg only. Shinte did not seem at all annoyed at the occurrence.

Shinte was most anxious to see the pictures of the magic lantern, but fever had so weakening an effect, and I had such violent action of the heart, with buzzing in the ears, that I could not go for several days; when I did go for the purpose, he had his principal men and the same crowd of court beauties near him as at the reception. The first picture exhibited was Abraham about to slaughter his son Isaac; it was shown as large as life, and the uplifted knife was in the act of striking the lad; the Balonda men remarked that the picture was much more like a god than the things of wood or clay they worshipped. I explained that this man was the first of a race to whom God had given the Bible we now held, and that among his children our Saviour appeared. The ladies listened with silent awe; but, when I moved the slide, the uplifted dagger moving towards them, they thought it was to be sheathed in their bodies instead of Isaac's. 'Mother! mother!' all shouted at once, and off they rushed helter-skelter, tumbling pell-mell over each other, and over the little idol-huts and tobacco-bushes: we could not get one of them back again. Shinte, however, sat bravely through the whole, and afterwards examined the instrument with interest. An explanation was always added after each time of showing its powers, so that no one should imagine there was aught supernatural in it. It was the only mode of instruction I was ever pressed to repeat. The people came long distances, for the express purpose of seeing the .objects and hearing the explanations.

On the 24th we expected to have started but Sambanza, who had been sent off early in the morning for guides, returned at midday without them, and drunk. This was the first case of real babbling intoxication we had seen in this region. As far as we could collect from his incoherent sentences, Shinte had said the rain was too heavy for our departure, and the guides still required time for preparation. As it rained nearly all day, it was no sacrifice to submit to his advice and remain. Sambanza staggered to Manenko's hut; she, however, who had never promised 'to love, honour, and obey him', coolly bundled him into the hut, and put him to bed.

As the last proof of friendship, Shinte came into my tent, though it could scarcely contain more than one person, looked at all the curiosities, the quicksilver, the looking-glass, books, hair-brushes, comb, watch, &c. &c., with the greatest interest; then closing the tent, so that none of his own people might see the extravagance of which he was about to be guilty, he drew out from his clothing a string of beads, and the end of a conical shell, which is considered, in regions far from the sea, of as great value as the Lord Mayor's badge is in London. He hung it round my neck, and said, 'There, now you have a proof of *my* friendship'.

MT 273 . . .

Pangola (whom Livingstone meets on the middle Zambezi, near Zumbo).

On the 23rd of June we entered Pangola's principal village, which is upwards of a mile from the river. We established ourselves under a wild fig-tree, round whose trunk witchcraft medicine had been tied, to protect from thieves the honey of the wild bees, which had their hive in one of the limbs.

Pangola arrived, tipsy and talkative. 'We are friends, we are great friends; I have brought you a basket of green maize – here it is!' We thanked him, and handed him two fathoms of cotton cloth, four times the market-value of his present. No, he would not take so small a present; he wanted a double-barrelled rifle – one of Dixon's best. 'We are friends, you know; we are all friends together.' But although we were willing to admit that, we could not give him our best rifle, so he went off in high dudgeon. Early next morning, as we were commencing Divine service, Pangola returned, sober. We explained to him that we wished to worship God, and invited him to remain; he seemed frightened and retired: but after service he again importuned us for the rifle. It was of no use telling him that we had a long journey before us, and needed it to kill game for ourselves. – 'He too must obtain meat for himself and people, for they sometimes suffered from hunger.' He then got sulky, and his people refused to sell food except at extravagant prices. Knowing that we had nothing to eat, they felt sure of starving us into compliance. But two of our young men, having gone off at sunrise, shot a fine waterbuck, and down came the provision market to the lowest figure; they even became eager to sell, but our men were angry with them for trying compulsion, and would not buy. Black greed had outwitted itself, as happens often with white cupidity; and not only here did the traits of Africans remind us of Anglo-Saxons elsewhere: the notoriously ready disposition to take an unfair advantage of a man's necessities shows that the same mean motives are pretty widely diffused among all races. It may not be granted that the same blood flows in all veins, or that all have descended from the same stock; but the traveller has no doubt that the white rogue and black are men and brothers.

Next morning, as we went on our way, we saw the rifle-loving Chief approaching with some armed men. Before meeting us, he left the path and drew up his 'following' under a tree, expecting us to halt, and give him a chance of bothering us again; but, having already had enough of that, we held right on: he seemed dumb-foundered, and could hardly believe his own eyes. For a few seconds he was speechless, but at last recovered so far as to be able to say, 'You are passing Pangola. Do you not see Pangola?' Mbia was just going by at the time with the donkey, and, proud of every opportunity of airing his small stock of English, shouted in reply, 'All right! then get on. Click, click, click.' This fellow, Pangola, would have annoyed and harassed a trader until his unreasonable demands were complied with.

                                                                                            ZT 197

Chitapangwa (Central Zambia). This encounter brings out a feature of Livingstone's travels kindly explained to me by Professor Ernst Westphal, Head of the Department of African Languages at the University of Cape Town. Livingstone's own skill was in Tswana, a language closely related to that of the Barotse, and which he had mastered at Kuruman. He always had Barotse canoemen in his company and, certainly as far down as Sebituane's empire extended, they made the Zambezi and its tributaries a linguistic freeway for him. In his last safari his approach was from the Rovuma, and difficulties with interpreters lost him the sure touch he had enjoyed before:

Chitapangwa sent to inquire if we wanted an audience. 'We must take something in our hands the first time we came before so great a man.' Being tired from marching, I replied, 'Not till the evening', and sent notice at 5 p.m. of my coming. We passed through the inner stockade, and then on to an enormous hut, where sat Chitapangwa, with three drummers and ten or more men, two with rattles in their hands. The drummers beat furiously, and the rattlers kept time to the drums, two of them advancing and receding in a stooping posture, with rattles near the ground, as if doing the chief obeisance, but still keeping time with the others. I declined to sit on the ground, and an enormous tusk was brought for me. The chief saluted courteously. He has a fat jolly face, and legs loaded with brass and copper leglets. I mentioned our losses by desertion but his power is merely nominal, and he could do nothing. After talking awhile he came along with us to a group of cows, and pointed out one. 'That is yours', said he. The tusk on which I sat was sent after me too as being mine, because I had sat upon it. He put on my cloth as token of acceptance, and sent two large baskets of sorghum to the hut afterwards, and then sent for one of the boys to pump him after dark.

1st February, 1867. — We found a small party of black Arab slave-traders here from Bagamoio on the coast, and as the chief had behaved handsomely, as I thought, I went this morning and gave him one of our best cloths; but when we were about to kill the cow, a man interfered and pointed out a smaller one. I asked if this was by the orders of the chief. The chief said that the man had lied, but I declined to take any cow at all if he did not give it willingly.

I proposed to go but Chitapangwa got very angry, saying, I came only to show my things, and would buy nothing: he then altered his tone, and requested me to take the cow first presented and eat it, and as we were all much in need I took it. We were to give only what we liked in addition; but this was a snare, and when I gave two more cloths he sent them back, and demanded a blanket. The boys alone have blankets; so I told him these were not slaves, and I could not take from them what I had once given. Though it is disagreeable to be thus victimized, it is the first time we have tasted fat for six weeks and more.

6th February. – Chitapangwa came with his wife to see the instruments which I explained to them as well as I could.

13th February. – I gave one of the boxes at last, Chitapangwa offering a heavy Arab wooden one to preserve our things, which I declined to take, as I had parted with our own partly to lighten a load. Abraham unwittingly told me that he had not given me the chief's statement in full when he pressed me to take his cow. It was, 'Take and eat the one you like, and give me a blanket'. Abraham said 'He has no blanket', and then 'Take it and eat it, and give him any pretty thing you like'. I was thus led to mistake the chief, and he, believing that he had said explicitly he wanted a blanket for it, naturally held out. It is difficult to get these lads to say what one wants uttered: either with enormous self-conceit, they give different, and, as they think, better statements, suppress them altogether, or return false answers: this is the great and crowning difficulty of my intercourse.

I got ready to go, but the chief was very angry, and came with all his force, exclaiming that I wanted to leave against his will and power, though he wished to adjust matters, and send me away nicely. He does not believe that we have no blankets. It is hard to be kept waiting here, but all may be for the best: it has always turned out so, and I trust in Him on whom I can cast all my cares. The Lord look on this and help me. Though I have these nine boys, I feel quite alone. The chief is not so bad, as the boys are so cowardly. They assume a chirping, piping tone of voice in speaking to him, and do not say what at last has to be said, because in their cringing souls they believe they know what should be said better than I do. It does not strike them in the least that I have grown grey amongst these people; and it is immense conceit in mere boys to equal themselves to me. The difficulty is greater, because when I do ask their opinions I only receive the reply, 'It is as you please, sir'.

14th February. – I showed the chief one of the boys' blankets, which he is willing to part with for two of our cloths, each of which is larger than it, but he declines to receive it, because we have new ones. I invited him, since he disbelieved my assertions, to look in our bales, and if he saw none, to pay us a fine for the insult: he consented in a laughing way to give us an ox. All our personal intercourse has been of the good-natured sort. It is the communications to the boys, by three of the Chief's men who are our protectors, or rather spies, that is disagreeable; I won't let them bring these fellows near me.

15th February. – He came early in the morning, and I showed that I had no blanket, and he took the old one, and said that the affair was ended. A long misunderstanding would have been avoided, had Abraham told me fully what the chief said at first.

20th February, 1867. – I told the chief before starting that my heart was sore, because he was not sending me away so cordially as I liked. He at once ordered men to start with us, and gave me a brass knife with ivory sheath, which he had long worn, as a memorial. He explained that we ought to go north as, if we made easting, we should ultimately be obliged to turn west, and all our cloth would be expended ere we reached the Lake Tanganyika; he took a piece of clay off the ground and rubbed it on his tongue as an oath that what he said was true, and came along with us to see that all was right; and so we parted.

LJ 1867

Sekwebu.
Sekwebu and one attendant alone remained with me now. He was very intelligent, and had been of the greatest service to me; indeed, but for his good sense, tact, and command of the language of the tribes through which we passed, I believe we should scarcely have succeeded in reaching the coast. I naturally felt grateful to him; and as his chief wished *all* my companions to go to England with me, and would probably be disappointed if none went, I thought it would be beneficial for him to see the effects of civilization, and report them to his countrymen; I wished also to make some return for his very important services. Others had petitioned to come, but I explained the danger of a change of climate and food, and with difficulty restrained them. The only one who now remained begged so hard to come on board ship, that I greatly regretted that the expense prevented my acceding to his wish to visit England. I said to him, 'You will die if you go to such a cold country as mine'. 'That is nothing', he reiterated; 'let me die at your feet'.

When we parted from our friends at Kilimane, the sea on the bar was frightful even to the seamen. This was the first time Sekwebu had seen the sea. Captain Peyton had sent two boats in case of accident. The waves were so high that, when the cutter was in one trough, and we in the pinnace in another, her mast was hid. We then mounted to the crest of the wave, rushed down the slope, and struck the water again with a blow which felt as if she had struck the bottom. Poor Sekwebu looked at me when these terrible seas broke over, and said, 'Is this the way you go? Is this the way you go?' I smiled, and said, 'Yes; don't you see it is?' and tried to encourage him. He was well acquainted with canoes, but never had seen aught like this. When we reached the ship – a fine, large brig of sixteen guns and a crew of one hundred and thirty – she was rolling so, that we could see a part of her bottom. It was quite impossible for landsmen to catch the ropes and climb up, so a chair was sent down, and we were hoisted in as ladies usually are, and received so hearty an English welcome from Captain Peyton and all on board, that I felt myself at once at home in everything, except my own mother-tongue. I seemed to know the language perfectly, but the words I wanted, would not come at my call. When I left England I had no intention of returning, and directed my attention earnestly to the languages of Africa, paying none to English composition. With the exception of a short interval in Angola, I had been three and a half years without speaking English, and this, with thirteen years of previous partial disuse of my native tongue, made me feel sadly at a loss on board the 'Frolic'.

We left Kilimane on the 12th of July, and reached Mauritius on the 12th of August, 1856. Sekwebu was picking up English, and becoming a favourite with both men and officers. He seemed a little bewildered, everything on board a man-of-war being so new and strange; but he remarked to me several times, 'Your countrymen are very agreeable', and 'What a strange country this is — all water together'. He also said, that he now understood why I used the sextant. When we reached Mauritius a steamer came out to tow us into the harbour. The constant strain on his untutored mind seemed now to reach a climax, for during the night he became insane. I thought at first that he was intoxicated. He had descended into a boat, and, when I attempted to go down and bring him into the ship, he ran to the stern, and said, 'No! no! it is enough that I die alone. You must not perish; if you come I shall throw myself into the water.' Perceiving that his mind was affected, I said, 'Now, Sekwebu, we are going to Ma Robert'. This struck a chord in his bosom, and he said, 'O yes; where is she, and where is Robert?' and he seemed to recover. The officers proposed to secure him by putting him in irons, but, being a gentleman in his own country, I objected, knowing that the insane often retain an impression of ill-treatment, and I could not bear to have it said in Sekeletu's country that I had chained one of his principal men, as they had seen slaves treated. I tried to get him on shore by day, but he refused. In the evening a fresh accession of insanity occurred — he tried to spear one of the crew, then leaped overboard, and, though he could swim well, pulled himself down hand under hand, by the chain cable. We never found the body of poor Sekwebu.

MT 681

1   Macnair, p. 409.
2   Coupland, p. 183–184.
3   Sillery, p. 114, quoting from the *Memoirs* of President Kruger (London, 1902).
4   MT 39.
5   Tabler, p. 205.
6   Tabler, p. 211.
7   Fletcher, p. 17.
8   MT 34.
9   MT 30.
10 MT 37.
11 Schapera, p. 88.
12 One turns the page to find similar headlines reporting the appointment of Mr. J. Baker, 'the first black American official to serve in the American Embassy in Pretoria'.
13 Tabler, pp. 184–196.
14 Sillery, p. 95.
15 Sillery, p. 209.

Chapter 7

The Open Sore

Human bodies being the most admirable things, there is a certain attraction in the idea of being able to buy one. There they would be, in the market place for inspection, men, women and children, body and will, for purchase and absolute possession: *'non Angli sed sunt angeli'*.

If today people find this idea disgusting, they owe their reactions to nothing instinctive but to the energy of a few individuals who, applying their vehemence to the fulcrum of a good cause, moved the world's conscience.

Slavery was accepted until the eighteenth century. The highest civilizations used it without question. The Bible condones it. As I say, it is quite an idea, and one would suspect the sanity of anyone unable to contemplate its advantages.

Many accepted practices require something in the nature of a moral mutation before they are abandoned. A mutation is a quality which, after generations of pressure from the environment, suddenly switches, so that what was first a random modification starts to breed as normal. Hence our horror at slavery: what was natural has become abnormal to us.

The abolition of slavery took generations. The Quakers were probing the moral issue in 1672. In 1772, in Lord Mansfield's famous words, 'tracing the subject to natural principles, the claim of slavery can never be supported'. Wesley[1] took his church into the movement, and Wilberforce snowballed it into abolition and emancipation in 1807 and 1834. In the year of Livingstone's death, 1873, 'The great slave market of Zanzibar was closed for ever'[2] (we had hoped). In 1973, slavery is an effort to imagine.

Apartheid, the heir of slavery, is similarly plausible, attractive and inhumane. The proof of this is in our own hearts and in the alacrity with which it has been adopted by some who have suffered most from it. It is as old a growth as slavery, and its roots are as deep, hard and crooked. But in the global village it is coming to be seen as a weed, an abnormality. In due course and with due patience it should go, so that in 2073, our great-great-grandchildren will say 'Apartheid? what on earth was that?'

What was the environment that turned people's minds, hearts and, at length, instincts against slavery? First a troubled conscience, created throughout the eighteenth and nineteenth centuries by preaching, principle and law: second, the appalling facts and figures researched by the Abolitionists. Feeling culminating in fact: and the feeling was ripe in 1834, the year of Wilberforce's death and the passing of what Coupland calls 'the noblest measure in the history of the House of Commons'.[3] Livingstone was not a sentimentalist; ironically, his last beating at his father's hands was for refusing to read a pious work of Wilberforce's. He was a facts man, as I have tried to stress. If a thing worked, and with tolerable hardships only, he was realist enough to put up with it. He saw no objection to the Tswana leaving their homelands near Kuruman to sell their labour in the Cape, for instance,[4] (although this could have been simply because the Transvalers were trying to corner it for their own farms). He neither sought trouble nor shrank from it: there is a surprising residue of sympathy for what one might call (by a stretch of imagination) 'decent' slavery and slave-trading. Nothing could really exonerate them in his eyes, but his emotions did not simply rush ahead of the evidence but rather accompanied it, finding the whole business at first distressing and in the end, diabolic.

When Wilberforce died in 1834, half his work, although he did not know it, was unfinished. Thanks to the power of the Royal Navy, the slave trade in the North Atlantic was stopped and the West Coast of Africa was clean. Nobody bothered about the East Coast. Arabs had slaved there for over 1 000 years and, jointly with Indian-Pakistani finance, were still shipping 20 000 men, women and children a year from Zanzibar, mostly to Persia and Arabia. The Portuguese had joined Britain in 1836 in the suppression of the West Coast Trade, but on the East it continued to various outlets, Cuba, for instance, with the connivance of the Portuguese Government, if not in Lisbon, certainly in Mozambique. It was in Central and East Africa that Livingstone found what he called the 'open sore of the world', draining into the Indian Ocean.

Is it sadism that produces so many extracts of those 'old, unhappy, far-off things'? Possibly. Possibly that Livingstone without the slave trade is the beef without the mustard. The best excuse is that the high qualities of the man and his prose continue unchanged through his Inferno:

> When endeavouring to give some account of the slave-trade of East Africa, it was necessary to keep far within the truth, in order not to be thought guilty of exaggeration; but in sober seriousness the subject does not admit of exaggeration. To overdraw its evils is a simple impossibility. The sights I have seen, though common incidents of the traffic, are so nauseous that I always strive to drive them from memory. In the case of most disagreeable recollections I can succeed, in time, in consigning them to oblivion, but the slaving scenes come back unbidden, and make me start up at dead of night horrified by their vividness.
>
> LJ 12 Jul 1872

Of the following general statements on the slave trade, the first describes the vicious spiral of slaving, the second contains some prophetic remarks on the American Civil War then raging, and the third is an indictment of British hypocrisy that has lost little of its force:

> We have been careful to mention in the text the different ways in which the slave-trade is carried on, because we believe that our Expedition is the first that ever saw slavery at its fountain-head, and in all its phases. The assertion has been made that the slave-trade was like any other branch of commerce, subject to the law of supply and demand, and that therefore it ought to be free. From what we have seen, it involves so much of murder in it, as an essential element, that it can scarcely be allowed to remain in the catalogue of commerce.
>
> We have the system nearest to that of justice, indeed the only one that approaches it, when the criminal is sold for his crimes. Next, on the plea of witchcraft, a child is taken from the poorer classes of parents as a fine, or to pay a debt, and sold to a travelling native slave-trader. Then children kidnapped by a single robber, or by a gang going from their own village to the next to steal the children who are out drawing water or gathering wood. We have seen places where every house was a stockade, and yet the people were not safe. Next comes the system of retaliation of one hamlet against another to make reprisals, and the same thing on a larger scale between tribes; the portion of the tribe which flees becomes vagrant, and eventually armed with muskets, the produce of previous slaving, attacks peaceful tribes, and depopulates the country for the supply of the ocean slave-trade. Again, we have the slave-traders from the Coast, who may be either Arabs or half-caste Portuguese. For them slaves are collected, by the natives of a commercial turn, along the most frequented routes: in this branch the Ajawa and Babisa are conspicuous.
>
> And lastly, we have still another and more ample source of supply for the ocean slave-trade, and we regret to say the means for its success are drawn

directly from Europeans. Trading parties are sent out from Portuguese and Arab coast towns with large quantities of muskets, ammunition, cloth, and beads. The two last articles are used for paying their way during the earlier part of the journey and for the purchase of ivory. These parties usually settle down with some chieftain and cultivate the soil; but we know of no instance in which they have not, at one part of their journey, joined one tribe in attacking another for the sake of the captives they could take. The system causes a frightful loss of life. The bow cannot stand for a moment against the musket. Flight, starvation, and death ensue; and we must again record our conviction that the mortality after these slave wars, in addition to the losses on the journey to the Coast and during the sea passage, makes it certain that not more than one in five ever reach the 'kind masters' in Cuba and elsewhere, whom, according to slave-owners' interpretation of Scripture, Providence intended for them.

ZT 592 . . .

The result of our observation of the actual working of the slave-trade at its source is, that it must prove an insurmountable barrier to all moral and commercial progress. It perpetuates barbarism in the country from which the slaves are drawn, and it has a most injurious influence on the land to which they are taken. The introduction of African labourers to compete with Europeans renders labour unpopular among the latter, and throws an obstacle in the way of the progress of society; because nothing tends more to elevate a people than that the best minds should be bent to, and delight in, labour dignified by being undertaken for the general improvement.

We would speak tenderly of the terrible revolution now going on in America. The war is entirely due to the presence in one section of that great country of a slave population, whose number does not form more than one-sixth part of the entire American community. The introduction of a race from a barbarous country was a great mistake. To degrade and deny that race the rights of manhood, a still greater blunder; for the debasement was sure to react on the master and on his children. In fact, the degradation of the slave must not only demoralize the master, but probably the master is the greater loser of the two. Then the presence of *millions* of a degraded race makes amalgamation or transportation impossible; there they must remain; if they cannot be elevated, they must prove a severe retribution on the descendants of those who were goaded on by our own forefathers in the slave-trade. But we do not believe in any incapacity of the African in either mind or heart; and our American brethren deserve our warmest sympathy in the gigantic task before them. From the evils connected with the slave-trade our statesmen have nobly striven to rescue and defend us; and no reasonable expense, that preserves us from contamination, should be esteemed a sacrifice: if we escape, it is not because, as a nation, we are innocent.

ZT 595

19th May. – The emancipation of our West-Indian slaves was the work of but a small number of the people of England – the philanthropists and all the more advanced thinkers. Numerically they were a very small minority, and powerful only from the superior abilities of the leading men, and from having the right, the true, and just on their side. Of the rest of the population an immense number had no sympathies to spare for any beyond their own fireside circles. We must never lose sight of the fact that though the majority perhaps are on the side of freedom, large numbers of Englishmen are not slaveholders only because the law forbids the practice. In this we see a great part of the reason of the frantic sympathy with the rebels in the great Black war in America. It is true that we do sympathize with brave men, though we may not approve of the objects for which they fight. We admired Stonewall Jackson and we praised Lee, but, unquestionably, there existed besides an eager desire that slaveocracy might prosper, and the Negro go to the wall.

LJ 1869

Livingstone finds slavery part of the African 'way of life' and defended as such. As 'serfdom', the result of conquest, it is practised by his favourite tribes. He seems very soft on the Makololo, and on the Zulu tribes who harvested slaves every autumn and whose terror tactics he must have known all about. I think he is more pragmatic than disingenuous here. He levels his serious criticism against the use of human beings as commodities and currency, a practice he does not find among his favourites but, 'if we exclude the Arabs, among two families of Africans alone on the east side of the continent'. (LJ 27 Nov 66) Even here the documentary coolness of his records and his sympathy with the temptation to which the tribes were exposed are remarkable. His concern does not spring from meddlesome idealism but from a horror at death and indignity which his own men share in part and which undercuts his natural conservatism:

The whole country, though so very rugged, had all been cultivated, and densely peopled. Many banana-trees, uncared for patches of corn, and congo-bean bushes attested former cultivation. The population had all been swept away; ruined villages, broken utensils, and human skeletons, told a sad tale of 'man's inhumanity to man'. So numerous were the slain, that it was thought the inhabitants had been slaughtered in consequence of having made raids on the Zulus for cattle.

We conjectured this to be the cause of the wholesale butchery, because Zulus do not usually destroy any save the old, and able-bodied men. The object of their raids in general is that the captured women and children may be embodied into the tribe, and become Zulus. The masters of the captives are kind to them, and the children are put on the same level as those of any ordinary man. In their usual plan, we seem to have the condition so bepraised by some advocates for slavery. The members of small disunited communities are taken under a powerful government – obtain kind masters, whom they are allowed to exchange for any one else within the tribe, and their children become freemen. It is, as our eyes and nostrils often found by the putrid bodies of the slain, a sad system nevertheless – yet by no means so bad as that which, causing a still greater waste of human life, consigns the surviving victims to perpetual slavery. The Zulus are said never to sell their captives.

ZT 385

The Makololo women work but little. Indeed the families of that nation are spread over the country, one or two only in each village, as the lords of the land. They all have lordship over great numbers of subjected tribes, who pass by the general name Makalaka, and who are forced to render certain services, and to aid in tilling the soil; but each has his own land under cultivation, and otherwise lives nearly independent. This species of servitude may be termed serfdom, as it has to be rendered in consequence of subjection by force of arms, but it is necessarily very mild. It is so easy for any one who is unkindly treated to make his escape to other tribes, that the Makololo are compelled to treat them, to a great extent, rather as children than slaves. Some masters who fail to secure the affections of the conquered people frequently find themselves left without a single servant, in consequence of the impossibility of enforcing a fugitive slave law, and the readiness with which those who are themselves subjected assist the fugitives across the rivers in canoes.

MT 186

When crossing at the confluence of the Leeba and Makondo, one of my men picked up a bit of a steel watch-chain of English manufacture, and we were informed that this was the spot where the Mambari cross in coming to Masiko. These Mambari are very enterprising merchants: when they mean to trade with a town, they deliberately begin the affair by building huts, as if they knew that little business could be transacted without a liberal allowance of time for palaver. They bring Manchester goods into the heart of Africa; these cotton prints look so wonderful that the Makololo could not believe them to be the work of mortal hands. On questioning the Mambari they were answered that English manufactures came out of the sea, and beads were gathered on its shore. To Africans our cotton-mills are fairy dreams. 'How can the irons spin, weave, and print so beautifully?' Our country is like what Taprobane was to our ancestors: a strange realm of light, whence came the diamond, muslin, and peacocks; an attempt at explanation of our manufactures usually elicits the expression, 'Truly! ye are gods!'

MT 271

The Manganja Chiefs sell their own people, for we met slave-dealers in several highland villages, who had certainly been encouraged to come among them for slaves. The Chiefs always seemed ashamed of the traffic, and tried to excuse themselves. 'We do not sell many, and only those who have committed crimes.' As a rule the regular trade is supplied from the low and criminal classes, and hence the ugliness of slaves. Others are probably sold on the accusation of witchcraft. Friendless orphans also sometimes disappear suddenly, and no one inquires what has become of them. The temptation to sell their people is peculiarly great, as there is but little ivory on the hills, and often the Chief has nothing but human flesh with which to buy foreign goods. The Ajawa offer cloth, brass rings, pottery, and sometimes handsome young women, and agree to take the trouble of carrying off by night all those whom the Chief may point out to them. They give four yards of cotton cloth for a man, three for a woman, and two for a boy or girl.

ZT 127

Livingstone often moved into territory untouched but surrounded by the slave-trade. One of his bitter regrets was that his journeys opened such territories to exploitation. In between areas of ruinous full slavery (Zambia and the Congo) and non-(or only African) slavery (the middle and upper Zambezi), were grey zones of cupidity and insolence, which he and his men contrasted with the patriarchal dignity of unspoiled tribal life:

After we had passed up the Zambezi, however, a party of slaves, belonging to the two native Portuguese who assassinated the Chief, Mpangwe, and took possession of his lands at Zumbo, followed on our footsteps, and, representing themselves to be our 'children', bought great quantities of ivory, from the Bawe, for a few coarse beads a tusk. They also purchased ten large new canoes to carry it, at the rate of six strings of red or white beads, or two fathoms of grey calico, for each canoe, and, at the same cheap rate, a number of good-looking girls.

ZT 240

Barotseland, January, 1854.
    I suspect that offences of the slightest character among the poor, are made the pretext for selling them or their children to the Mambari. A young man of Lobale had fled into the country of Shinte, and located himself without showing himself to the chief. This was considered an offence sufficient to warrant his being seized and offered for sale while we were there. He had not reported himself, so they did not know the reason of his running away from his own chief, and that chief might accuse them of receiving a criminal. It was curious to notice the effect of the slave-trade in blunting the moral susceptibility: no chief in the south would treat a fugitive in this way. My men were horrified at the act.
    Another incident, which occurred while were were here, may be mentioned, as of a character totally unknown in the south. Two children, of seven and eight years old, went out to collect firewood a short distance from their parents' home, and were kidnapped; the distracted parents could not find a trace of them. This happened so close to the town, where there are no beasts of prey, that we suspect some of the high men of Shinte's court were the guilty parties; they can sell them by night. The Mambari erect large huts of a square shape to stow these stolen ones in; they are well fed, but aired by night only. The frequent kidnapping from outlying hamlets explains the

stockades we saw around them; the parents have no redress, for even Shinte himself seems fond of working in the dark. One night he sent for me, though I always stated I liked all my dealings to be aboveboard. When I came he presented me with a slave-girl of about ten years old; he said he had always been in the habit of presenting his visitors with a child. On my thanking him, and saying that I thought it wrong to take away children from their parents, that I wished him to give up this system altogether, and trade in cattle, ivory, and bees'-wax, he urged that she was 'to be a child' to bring me water, and that a great man ought to have a child for the purpose, yet I had none. As I replied that I had four children, and should be very sorry if my chief were to take my little girl and give her away, and that I would prefer this child to remain and carry water for her own mother, he thought I was dissatisfied with her size, and sent for one a head taller; after many explanations of our abhorrence of slavery, and how displeasing it must be to God to see his children selling one another, and giving each other so much grief as this child's mother must feel, I declined her also. If I could have taken her into my family and then returned her as a free woman, according to a promise I should have made to the parents, I might have done so; but to take her away, and probably never be able to secure her return, would have produced no good effect on the minds of the Balonda; they would not then have seen evidence of our hatred to slavery, and the kind attentions of my friends would, as it almost always does in similar cases, have turned the poor thing's head. The difference in position between them and us is as great as between the lowest and highest in England, and we know the effects of sudden elevation on wiser heads than hers, whose owners have not been born to it.

MT 296

Approaching Lake Mweru, 2 November, 1867.

These valleys along which we travel are beautiful. Green is the prevailing colour; but the clumps of trees assume a great variety of forms, and often remind one of English park scenery. The long line of slaves and carriers, brought up by their Arab employers, adds life to the scene: they are in three bodies, and number 450 in all. Each party has a guide with a flag, and when that is planted all that company stops till it is lifted, and a drum is beaten, and a kudu's horn sounded. One party is headed by about a dozen leaders, dressed with fantastic head-gear of feathers and beads, red cloth on the bodies, and skins cut into strips and twisted: they take their places in line, the drum beats, the horn sounds harshly, and all fall in.

The Africans cannot stand sneers. When any mishap occurs in the march (as when a branch tilts a load off a man's shoulder) all who see it set up a yell of derision; if anything is accidentally spilled, or if one is tired and sits down, the same yell greets him, and all are excited thereby to exert themselves. They hasten on with their loads, and hurry with the sheds they build, the masters only bringing up the rear, and helping anyone who may be sick. The distances travelled were quite as much as the masters or we could bear. Had frequent halts been made — as, for instance, a half or a quarter of an hour at the end of every hour or two — but little distress would have been felt; but five hours at a stretch is more than men can bear in a hot climate. The female slaves held on bravely; nearly all carried loads on their heads; the head, or lady of the party, who is also the wife of the Arab, was the only exception. She had a fine white shawl, with ornaments of gold and silver on her head. These ladies had a jaunty walk, and never gave in on the longest march; many pounds' weight of fine copper leglets above the ankles seemed only to help the sway of their walk: as soon as they arrive at the sleeping-place they begin to cook, and in this art they show a good deal of expertness, making savoury dishes for their masters out of wild fruits and other not very likely materials.

LJ 2 Nov 1867

On the abortive trip towards Lake Bangweulu, September, 1863.

The slave-traders carry matters with a high hand; and no wonder, for the possession of gunpowder gives them almost absolute power. The mode by which tribes armed with bows and arrows carry on warfare, or defend themselves, is by ambuscade. They never come out in open fight, but wait for the enemy behind trees, or in the long grass of the country, and shoot at him unawares. If men come against them with firearms, when the long grass is all burned off, the tribe attacked are as helpless as a wooden ship would be before an iron-clad steamer. The time of year selected for this kind of warfare is nearly always that in which the grass is actually burnt off, or is so dry as readily to take fire. The dry grass in Africa looks more like ripe English wheat late in the autumn, than anything else we can compare it to. Let us imagine an English village standing in a field of this sort, bounded only by the horizon, and enemies setting fire to a line of a mile or two, by running along with bunches of burning straw in their hands, touching here and there the inflammable material, . . . the wind blowing towards the doomed village . . . the inhabitants with only one or two old muskets, but ten to one no powder, . . . the long line of flames, leaping thirty feet into the air with dense masses of black smoke . . . and pieces of charred grass falling down in showers. Would not the stoutest English villager, armed only with the bow and arrow against the enemy's musket, quail at the idea of breaking through that wall of fire? When at a distance, we once saw a scene like this, and had the charred grass, literally as thick as flakes of black snow, falling around us, there was no difficulty in understanding the secret of the slave-trader's power.

ZT 525

Rounding the south of Lake Malawi, 19th September, 1863.

We found an Arab slave-party here, and went to look at the slaves; seeing this, Mponda was alarmed lest we should proceed to violence in his town, but I said to him that we went to look only. Eighty-five slaves were in a pen. The majority were boys of about eight or ten years of age; others were grown men and women. Nearly all were in the taming-stick; a few of the younger ones were in thongs, the thong passing round the neck of each. Several pots were on the fires cooking *dura* and beans. A crowd went with us, expecting a scene, but I sat down, and asked a few questions about the journey, in front. The slave-party consisted of five or six half-caste coast Arabs, who said that they came from Zanzibar; but the crowd made such a noise that we could not hear ourselves speak. I asked if they had any objections to my looking at the slaves. The owners pointed out the different slaves, and said that after feeding them, and accounting for the losses in the way to the coast, they made little by the trip. I suspect that the gain is made by those who ship them to the ports of Arabia, for at Zanzibar most of the younger slaves we saw went at about seven dollars a head. I said to them it was a bad business altogether.   LJ 19 Sep 1866

Near the south shore of Lake Malawi, October, 1863.
   While sitting at Nkwinda's, a man behind the court hedge-wall said, with great apparent glee, that an Arab slaving party on the other side of the confluence of the Shire and Lake were 'giving readily two fathoms of calico for a boy, and two and a half for a girl; never saw trade so brisk, no haggling at all'.
   We arrived at Katosa's village on the 15th October, and found about thirty young men and boys in slave-sticks. They had been bought by other agents of the Arab slavers, still on the east side of the Shire. They were resting in the village, and their owners soon removed them. The weight of the goree seemed very annoying when they tried to sleep. This taming instrument is kept on, until the party has crossed several rivers and all hope of escape has vanished from the captive's mind.   ZT 560

On the Rovuma.
   19th June, 1866. – We passed a woman tied by the neck to a tree and dead, others tied up in a similar manner, and one lying in the path shot or stabbed, for she was in a pool of blood. The explanation we got invariably was that the Arab who owned these victims was enraged at losing his money by the slaves becoming unable to march, and vented his spleen by murdering them; but I have nothing more than common report in support of attributing this enormity to the Arabs.
   25th June. – On leaving Chirikaloma we came on to Namalo, whose village that morning had been deserted, the people moving off in a body towards the Mtambwé country, where food is more abundant. A poor little girl was left in one of the huts from being too weak to walk, probably an orphan.
   26th June. – We passed a slave woman shot or stabbed through the body and lying on the path: a group of men stood about a hundred yards off on one side, and another of women on the other side, looking on; they said an Arab who passed early that morning had done it in anger at losing the price he had given her, because she was unable to walk any longer.
                                    LJ 1866

The quick of Livingstone's pity seems to have been for children, perhaps in compensation for the sacrifice he had made of his own. This is in the Congo:

28th July. – Slavery is a great evil wherever I have seen it. A poor old woman and child are among the captives, the boy, about three years old seems a mother's pet. His feet are sore from walking in the sun. He was offered for two fathoms, and his mother for one fathom; he understood it all and cried bitterly, clinging to his mother. She had, of course, no power to help him; they were separated at Karungu afterwards.

LJ 1867

Angola, near the Congo border, May, 1855.
   While on the way to Cabango, we saw fresh tracks of elands, the first we had observed in this country. A poor little slave-girl, being ill, turned aside in the path, and, though we waited all the next day making search for her, she was lost. She was tall and slender for her age, as if of too quick growth, and probably, unable to bear the fatigue of the march, lay down and slept in the forest, then, waking in the dark, went farther and farther astray. The treatment of the slaves witnessed by my men, certainly did not raise slave-holders in their estimation. Their usual exclamation was, 'They have no hearts'; and they added, with reference to the slaves, 'Why do they let them?' as if they thought that the slaves had the natural right to rid the world of such heartless creatures, and ought to do it.

MT 455

Near Nkhotakota, Lake Malawi, October, 1863.
   Our new companions were trading in tobacco, and had collected quantities of the round balls, about the size of nine-pounder shot, into which it is formed. One of them owned a woman, whose child had been sold that morning for tobacco. The mother followed him, weeping silently, for hours along the way we went; she seemed to be well known, for, at several hamlets, the women spoke to her with evident sympathy; we could do nothing to alleviate her sorrow – the child would be kept until some slave-trader passed, and then sold for calico. The different cases of slave-trading observed by us are mentioned, in order to give a fair idea of its details.

ZT 548

The sexual side of the slave trade are sometimes visible through Livingstone's massive Victorian discretion:

Lake Malombe, just south of Lake Malawi, October, 1861.
   As we were resting for a few minutes a young effeminate-looking man from some sea-coast tribe came in great state to have a look at us. He walked under a large umbrella, and was followed by five handsome girls gaily dressed and adorned with a view to attract purchasers. One was carrying his pipe for smoking bang, another his bow and arrows; a third his battle-axe; a fourth one of his robes; while the last was ready to take his

umbrella when he felt tired. This show of his merchandise was to excite the cupidity of any Chief who had ivory, and may be called the lawful way of carrying on the slave-trade. He sat and looked at us a few minutes, the young ladies kneeling behind him; and, having satisfied himself that we were not likely to be customers, he departed.

ZT 393

Nyangwe, 1872.

28th April. – Abed sent over Manyuema to buy slaves for him and got a pretty woman for 300 cowries and a hundred strings of beads; she can be sold again to an Arab for much more in ivory.

LJ 1872

Top of Lake Mweru, waiting to start for Kigoma/Ujiji, 1868.

18th November. – A pretty little woman ran away from her husband and came to Mpamari. Her husband brought three hoes, a checked cloth and two strings of beads to redeem her; but this old fellow wants her for himself, and by native law he can keep her as his slave-wife. Slave-owners make a bad neighbourhood, for the slaves are always running away and the headmen are expected to restore the fugitives for a bit of cloth. An old woman of Mpamari fled three times; she was caught yesterday, and tied to a post for the young slaves to plague her. Her daughter burst into an agony of tears on seeing them tying her mother, and Mpamari ordered her to be tied to the mother's back for crying; I interceded for her, and she was let go. He said, 'You don't care, though Sayed Majid loses his money'. I replied, 'Let the old woman go, she will be off again tomorrow'. But they cannot bear to let a slave have freedom. I don't understand what effect his long prayers and prostrations towards Mecca have on his own mind, they cannot affect the minds of his slaves favourably, nor do they mine, though I am as charitable as most people.

The tiresome tale of slaves running away was repeated during the night by two of Mpamari's making off, though in the yoke, and they had been with him from boyhood. Not one good-looking woman is now left of his fresh slaves; all the pretty ones obtain favour by their address, beg to be unyoked, and then escape. A Mobemba man wanted a woman who was in the chain, so he loosed five out, and took her off; the others made clear heels of it, and now that the grass is long and green, no one can trace their course.

LJ 1868

If not quite humour, there is variety and sometimes a dour satisfaction in Livingstone's record of the slave trade:

Tete, 1858.

A rather singular case of voluntary slavery came to our knowledge: a free black, an intelligent active young fellow, called Chibanti, who had been our pilot on the river, told us that he had sold himself into slavery. On asking why he had done this, he replied that he was all alone in the world, had neither father nor mother, nor any one else to give him water when sick, or food when hungry; so he sold himself to Major Sicard, a notoriously kind master, whose slaves had little to do, and plenty to eat. 'And how much did you get for yourself?' we asked. 'Three thirty-yard pieces of cotton cloth', he replied; 'and I forthwith bought a man, a woman, and child, who cost me two of the pieces, and I had one piece left.' This, at all events, showed a cool and calculating spirit; he afterwards bought more slaves, and in two years owned a sufficient number to man one of the large canoes. His master subsequently employed him in carrying ivory to Quillimane, and gave him cloth to hire mariners for the voyage; he took his own slaves, of course, and thus drove a thriving business; and was fully convinced that he had made a good speculation by the sale of himself, for had he been sick his master must have supported him.

ZT 49

Tete, Christmas, 1860.

A large party of slaves, belonging to the Commandant, after having been away the greater part of a year, had just returned from a trading expedition to Moselekatse's country. They had taken inland a thousand muskets and a large quantity of gunpowder; these being, they said, the only articles Moselekatse cares to purchase. They started on their journey back, with ivory, ostrich feathers, a thousand sheep and goats, and thirty head of fine cattle. Moselekatse sent, in addition, as a token that the traders and he had parted good friends, a splendid white bull to the Commandant. The ostrich feathers had been packed in reeds, a fire broke out in the camp one night, and most of them were burned. On their way the cattle had to pass through a tsetse country, and they all died from the effects of the bite. The white bull perished within two days of Senna; six hundred of the sheep and goats had been eaten, either because they became lame, or because the drivers were hungry. The Commandant having an attack of fever was unable to calculate his losses, but intended to imprison the slaves who, as usual, thought more of their own comfort than of their master's gain. Slave labour is certainly very dear.

ZT 338

Chupanga, New Year, 1860.

A worn out slave-trader, sadly diseased, and nearly blind, used to relate to us in a frank and open manner the moving incidents of his past career. It was evident that he did not see slavery in the same light as we did. On expressing our surprise that so humane a man could have been guilty of so much cruelty, as the exportation of slaves entailed, he indignantly denied that he had ever torn slaves away from their homes. He had exported 'brutos do mato', beasts of the field, alone, that is, natives still wild, or lately caught in forays. This way of viewing the matter made him gravely tell us, that when his wife died, to dull the edge of his grief he made a foray amongst the

tribes near the mouth of the Shire, and took many captives. He had commenced slave-trading at Angola and made several fortunes; but somehow
managed to dissipate them all in riotous living in a short time at Rio de
Janeiro, — 'The money a man makes in the slave-trade', said he, 'is all bad,
and soon goes back to the devil.'

ZT 138

The most telling indictment of slavery is in the two pictures Livingstone
gives of the Shire Valley when he first explored it in 1859 and two years later
when he went up it again with Bishop Mackenzie to help establish the
Universities Mission at Magomero. In the brief interval slavery had come down
from the Lake and the valley was in chaos. This sequence has been much con-
densed so as to concentrate on the lives of the Africans: in full it is a gem of
ecological beauty:

About the middle of August, 1859, after cutting wood at Shamoara, we
again steamed up the Shire, with the intention of becoming better acquainted
with the people. The Shire is much narrower than the Zambesi, but deeper,
and more easily navigated. It drains a low, and exceedingly fertile valley of
from fifteen to twenty miles in breadth. Ranges of wooded hills bound this
valley on both sides. For the first twenty miles the hills on the left bank are
close to the river; then comes Morambala, whose name means 'the lofty
watch-tower', a detached mountain 500 yards from the river's brink, which
rises, with steep sides on the west, to 4 000 feet in height, and is about seven
miles in length. It is wooded up to the very top, and very beautiful. A small
village peeps out about halfway up the mountain; it has a pure and bracing
atmosphere; and is perched above mosquito range. The people on the
summit have a very different climate and vegetation from those of the
plains; but they have to spend a great portion of their existence amidst white
fleecy clouds, which, in the rainy season, rest daily on the top of their
favourite mountain. We were kindly treated by these mountaineers on our
first ascent; before our second they were nearly all swept away by Mariano.
Beyond Morambala the Shire comes winding through an extensive marsh.
For many miles to the north a broad sea of fresh green grass extends, and is
so level, that it might be used for taking the meridian altitude of the sun.
After steaming through a portion of this marsh, we came to a broad belt of
palm, and other trees, crossing the fine plain on the right bank. Marks of
large game were abundant. Many gardens of maize, pumpkins, and tobacco,
fringed the marshy banks as we went on. They belong to natives of the hills,
who come down in the dry season, and raise a crop on parts at other times
flooded. While the crops are growing, large quantities of fish are caught;
they are dried for sale or for future consumption.
Beyond the marsh the country is higher, and has a much larger
population. We passed a long line of temporary huts, on a plain on the right
bank, with crowds of men and women hard at work making salt. They
obtain it by mixing the earth, which is here highly saline, with water, in a pot

with a small hole in it, and then evaporating the liquid, which runs through, in the sun. From the number of women we saw carrying it off in bags, we concluded that vast quantites must be made at these works.

Above the palm-trees, a succession of rich low islands stud the river. Many of them are cultivated and grow maize at all times of the year, for we saw it in different stages of growth; some patches ripe, and others half-grown, or just sprouting out of the ground. The shores are adorned with rows of banana-trees, and the fruit is abundant and cheap. Many of the reedy banks are so intertwined with convolvulus, and other creepers, as to be absolutely impenetrable. They are beautiful to the eye, a smooth wall of living green rising out of the crystal water, and adorned with lovely flowers; but so dense, that, if capsized in the water, one could scarcely pass through to land.

On the 25th August we reached Dakanamoio Island, opposite the perpendicular bluff on which Chibisa's village stands; he had gone, with most of his people, to live near the Zambesi, but his headman was civil, and promised us guides and whatever else we needed. A few of the men were busy cleaning, sorting, spinning, and weaving cotton. This is a common sight in nearly every village, and each family appears to have its patch of cotton, as our own ancestors in Scotland had each his patch of flax.

Chibisa and his wife, with a natural show of parental feeling, had told the Doctor, on his previous visit, that a few years before some men had kidnapped and sold their little daughter, and that she was now a slave to the padrè at Tette. On his return to Tette, the Doctor tried hard to ransom and restore the girl to her parents, and offered twice the value of a slave; the padrè seemed willing, but she could not be found; she had been sold, it might be, to the distant tribe Bazizulu, or he could not tell where. Custom had rendered his feelings callous, and Chibisa had to be told that his child would never return.

Late in the afternoon of the first day's steaming, after we left the wooding-place, we called at the village of Chikanda-Kadze, a female Chief, to purchase rice for our men; but we were now in the blissful region where time is absolutely of no account, and where men may sit down and rest themselves when tired; so they requested us to wait till next day, and they would then sell us some food. As our forty black men, however, had nothing to cook for supper, we were obliged to steam on to reach a village a few miles above. When we meet those who care not whether we purchase or let it alone, or who think men ought only to be in a hurry when fleeing from an enemy, our ideas about time being money, and the power of the purse, receive a shock. The state of eager competition, which in England wears out both mind and body, and makes life bitter, is here happily unknown.

Next day we arrived at the village of Mbame, where the people raised large quantities of rice, and were eager traders; the rice was sold at wonderfully low rates, and we could not purchase a tithe of the food brought for sale.

A native minstrel serenaded us in the evening, playing several quaint tunes on a species of one-stringed fiddle, accompanied by wild, but not unmusical songs. He told the Makololo that he intended to play all night to induce us to give him a present. The nights being cold, the thermometer falling to 47°, with occasional fogs, he was asked if he was not afraid of perishing from cold; but, with the genuine spirit of an Italian organ-grinder, he replied, 'Oh, no; I shall spend the night with my white comrades in the big canoe; I have often heard of the white men, but have never seen them till now, and I must sing and play well to them.' A small piece of cloth, however, bought him off, and he moved away in good humour.

The Manganja country is delightfully well watered. The clear, cool, gushing streams are very numerous. Once we passed seven fine brooks and a spring in a single hour, and this, too, near the close of the dry season. Mount Zomba, which is twenty miles long, and from 7 000 to 8 000 feet high, has a beautiful stream flowing through a verdant valley on its summit, and running away down into Lake Shirwa. The highlands are well wooded, and many trees, admirable for their height and timber, grow on the various watercourses. 'Is this country good for cattle?' we inquired of a Makololo herdsman, whose occupation had given him skill in pasturage. 'Truly,' he replied, 'do you not see abundance of those grasses which the cattle love, and get fat upon?'

The Manganja are an industrious race; and in addition to working in iron, cotton, and basket-making, they cultivate the soil extensively. All the people of a village turn out to labour in the fields. It is no uncommon thing to see men, women, and children hard at work, with the baby lying close by beneath a shady bush. When a new piece of woodland is to be cleared, they proceed exactly as farmers do in America. The trees are cut down with their little axes of soft native iron; trunks and branches are piled up and burnt, and the ashes spread on the soil. The corn is planted among the standing stumps which are left to rot. If grass land is to be brought under cultivation, as much tall grass as the labourer can conveniently lay hold of is collected together and tied into a knot. He then strikes his hoe round the tufts to sever the roots, and leaving all standing, proceeds until the whole ground assumes the appearance of a field covered with little shocks of corn in harvest. A short time before the rains begin, these grass shocks are collected in small heaps, covered with earth, and burnt, the ashes and burnt soil being used to fertilize the ground. Large crops of the *mapira* are raised, with millet, beans, and ground-nuts; also patches of yams, rice, pumpkins, cucumbers, cassava, sweet potatoes, tobacco, and hemp, or bang *(Cannabis sativa)*. Maize is grown all the year round. Every family of any importance owns a cotton patch which, from the entire absence of weeds, seemed to be carefully cultivated. Most were small, none seen on this journey exceeding half an acre; but on the former trip some were observed of more than twice that size.

Iron ore is dug out of the hills, and its manufacture is the staple trade of the southern highlands. Each village has its smelting-house, its charcoal-burners, and blacksmiths. They make good axes, spears, needles, arrow-heads, bracelets and anklets, which, considering the entire absence of machinery, are sold at surprisingly low rates; a hoe over two pounds in weight is exchanged for calico of about the value of fourpence. In villages near Lake Shirwa and elsewhere, the inhabitants enter pretty largely into the manufacture of crockery, or pottery, making by hand all sorts of cooking, water, and grain pots, which they ornament with plumbago found in the hills. Some find employment in weaving neat baskets from split bamboos, and others collect the fibre of the *buaze*, which grows abundantly on the hills, and make it into fish-nets. These they either use themselves, or exchange with the fishermen on the river or lakes for dried fish and salt. A great deal of native trade is carried on between the villages, by means of barter in tobacco, salt, dried fish, skins, and iron. Many of the men are intelligent-looking, with well-shaped heads, agreeable faces, and high fore-heads. We soon learned to forget colour, and we frequently saw coun-tenances resembling those of white people we had known in England, which brought back the looks of forgotten ones vividly before the mind. But the most wonderful of ornaments, if such it may be called, is the pelele, or upper-lip ring of the women. The middle of the upper lip of the girls is pierced close to the septum of the nose, and a small pin inserted to prevent the puncture closing up. After it has healed, the pin is taken out and a larger one is pressed into its place, and so on successively for weeks, and months, and years. The process of increasing the size of the lip goes on till its capacity becomes so great that a ring of two inches diameter can be introduced with ease. All the highland women wear the pelele, and it is common on the Upper and Lower Shire. The poorer classes make them of hollow, or of solid bamboo, but the wealthier of ivory, or tin. The tin pelele is often made in the form of a small dish. The ivory one is not unlike a napkin-ring. No woman ever appears in public without the pelele, except in times of mourning for the dead. It is frightfully ugly to see the upper lip projecting two inches beyond the tip of the nose. When an old wearer of a hollow bamboo ring smiles, by the action of the muscles of the cheeks, the ring and lip outside it, are dragged back and thrown above the eyebrows. 'Why do the women wear these things?' we inquired of the old Chief, Chinsunse. Evidently surprised at such a stupid question, he replied, 'For beauty, to be sure! Men have beards and whiskers; women have none; and what kind of creature would a woman be without whiskers, and without the pelele? She would have a mouth like a man, and no beard; ha! ha! ha!'

The Manganja are not a sober people: they brew large quantities of beer, and like it well. Having no hops, or other means of checking fermentation, they are obliged to drink the whole brew in a few days, or it becomes unfit for use. Great merry-makings take place on these occasions, and drinking, drumming, and dancing continue day and night, till the beer is gone. As we entered a village one afternoon, not a man was to be seen; but some women were drinking beer under a tree. In a few moments the native doctor, staggered out of a hut, with his cupping-horn dangling from his neck, and began to scold us for a breach of etiquette. 'Is this the way to come into a man's village, without sending him word that you are coming?' Our men soon pacified the fuddled but good-humoured medico, who, entering his beer-cellar, called on two of them to help him to carry out a huge pot of beer, which he presented to us. While he was thus hospitably employed, the Chief awoke in a fright, and shouted to the women to run away, or they would all be killed. The ladies laughed at the idea of their being able to run away, and remained beside the beer-pots. We selected a spot for our camp, our men cooked the dinner as usual, and we were quietly eating it, when scores of armed men, streaming with perspiration, came pouring into the village. They looked at us, then at each other, and turning to the Chief upbraided him for so needlessly sending for them. 'These people are peaceable; they do not hurt you; you are killed with beer:' so saying, they returned to their homes.

The aged Chief, Muata Manga, could hardly have been less than ninety years of age; his venerable appearance struck the Makololo. 'He is an old man,' said they, 'a very old man; his skin hangs in wrinkles, just like that on elephants' hips.' 'Did you never', he was asked, 'have a fit of travelling come over you; a desire to see other lands and people?' No, he had never felt that, and had never been far from home in his life. For long life they are not indebted to frequent ablutions. An old man told us that he remembered to have washed once in his life, but it was so long since that he had forgotten how it felt. 'Why do you wash?' asked Chinsunse's women of the Makololo; 'our men never do.'

On the Upper Shire Valley, a man, after favouring us with some queer geographical remarks, followed us for several days. The Makololo became very much annoyed with him, for he proclaimed in every village we entered – 'These people have wandered; they do not know where they are going.' In vain did they scold and order him away. As soon as we started, he appeared again in the line of march, with his little bag over his shoulder, containing all his worldly gear, and as ready with his uncalled-for remarks as before. Every effort failed to drive him away, until at length the happy expedient was hit on, of threatening to take him down to the river and wash him; he at once made off, and we saw him no more. Much skin disease is seen among the Manganja. We noticed some men marked with smallpox, and asked the Chief, Mongazi, if he knew whether it had come to them from the coast, or from the interior. Being, as usual, amiably tipsy and anxious to pay us a compliment, he graciously replied he did not know, but thought it must have come to them from the English.

We discovered Lake Nyassa a little before noon on the 16th September, 1859. The Chief of the village near the confluence of the Lake and River, an old man, called Mosauká, hearing that we were sitting under a tree, came and kindly invited us to his village. He took us to a magnificent banyan-tree, of which he seemed proud. The roots had been trained down to the ground into the form of a gigantic arm-chair, without the seat. Mosauká brought us a present of a goat and basket of meal 'to comfort our hearts'. He told us that a large slave-party, led by Arabs, were encamped close by. They had been up-country the past year, and were on their way back, with plenty of slaves, ivory, and malachite. In a few minutes half a dozen of the leaders came over to see us. They were armed with long muskets, and, to our mind, were a villainous-looking lot. They evidently thought the same of us, for they offered several young children for sale, but, when told that we were English, showed signs of fear, and decamped during the night.

This is one of the great slave-paths from the interior: the track crosses Nyassa and the Shire, on its way to the Arab port, Kilwa, and the Portuguese ports of Iboe and Mosambique. At present, slaves, ivory, malachite, and copper ornaments, are the only articles of commerce. By means of a small steamer, purchasing the ivory of the Lake and River above the cataracts, the slave-trade in this quarter would be rendered unprofitable, – for it is only by the ivory being carried by the slaves, that the latter do not eat up all the profits of a trip.

On the 31st January, 1861, our new ship, *The Pioneer*, arrived from England, and anchored outside the bar; but the weather was stormy, and she did not venture in till the 4th of February.

The Expedition had been up to this point eminently successful. We had opened a cotton-field, which, taking in the Shire and Lake Nyassa, was 400 miles in length. We had gained the confidence of the people wherever we had gone; and as all we had previously known of the desire of the natives to trade had been amply confirmed, a perfectly new era had commenced in a region much larger than the cotton-fields of the Southern States of America.

We had, however, as will afterwards be seen, arrived at the turning-point of our career, and soon came into contact with the Portuguese slave-trade. . . .

Next forenoon we halted at the village of our old friend Mbame, to obtain new carriers. After resting a little, Mbame told us that a slave party on its way to Tette would presently pass through his village. 'Shall we interfere?' we inquired of each other. We remembered that all our private baggage was in Tette, which, if we freed the slaves, might, together with some Government property, be destroyed in retaliation; but this system of slave-hunters dogging us where previously they durst not venture, and, on pretence of being 'our children', setting one tribe against another, to furnish themselves with slaves, would so inevitably thwart all our efforts, that we resolved to run all risks, and put a stop, if possible, to the slave-trade, which now followed on the footsteps of our discoveries . . .

On the morning of the 22nd we were informed that the Ajawa were near, and were burning a village a few miles off. Leaving the rescued slaves, we moved off to seek an interview with these scourges of the country. On our way we met crowds of Manganja fleeing from the war in front. These poor fugitives from the slave hunt had, as usual, to leave all the food they possessed, except the little they could carry on their heads. We passed field after field of Indian corn or beans, standing ripe for harvesting, but the owners were away. The villages were all deserted: one where we breakfasted two years before, and saw a number of men peacefully weaving cloth, and,

among ourselves, called it the 'Paisley of the hills', was burnt; the stores of
corn were poured out in cartloads, and scattered all over the plain. About
two o'clock we saw the smoke of burning villages, and heard triumphant
shouts, mingled with the wail of the Manganja women, lamenting over their
slain. The Bishop then engaged us in fervent prayer; and, on rising from our
knees, we saw a long line of Ajawa warriors, with their captives, coming
round the hill-side. The first of the returning conquerors were entering their
own village below, and we heard women welcoming them back with 'lilliloo-
ings'. The Ajawa headman left the path on seeing us, and stood on an anthill
to obtain a complete view of our party; and in a few seconds they were all
around us, though mostly concealed by the projecting rocks and long grass.
In vain we protested that we had not come to fight, but to talk with them.
Flushed with recent victory over three villages, and confident of an easy
triumph over a mere handful of men, they began to shoot their poisoned
arrows, sending them with great force upwards of a hundred yards, and
wounding one of our followers through the arm. Our retiring slowly up the
ascent from the village only made them more eager to prevent our escape;
and, in the belief that this retreat was evidence of fear, they closed upon us in
bloodthirsty fury. Some came within fifty yards, dancing hideously; others
having quite surrounded us, and availing themselves of the rocks and long
grass hard by, were intent on cutting us off, while others made off with their
women and a large body of slaves. Four were armed with muskets, and we
were obliged in self-defence to return their fire and drive them off. When
they saw the range of the rifles, they very soon desisted, and ran away; but
some shouted to us from the hills the consoling intimation, that they would
follow, and kill us where we slept. Only two of the captives escaped to us,
but probably most of those made prisoners that day fled elsewhere in the
confusion. We returned to the village which we had left in the morning, after
a hungry, fatiguing, and most unpleasant day.

The Bishop, feeling as most Englishmen would at the prospect of the
people now in his charge being swept off into slavery, proposed to go at once
to the rescue of the captive Manganja, and drive the marauding Ajawa out
of the country. All were warmly in favour of this, save Dr. Livingstone, who
opposed it on the ground that it would be better to wait, and see the effect of
the check the slave-hunters had just experienced. The Ajawa were goaded
on by Portuguese agents from Tette, and there was no bond of union among
the Manganja on which to work. It was possible that the Ajawa might be
persuaded to something better, though, from having long been in the habit of
slaving for the Quillimane market, it was not very probable. But the
Manganja could easily be overcome piecemeal by any enemy; old feuds
made them glad to see calamities befall their next neighbours. We could
only counsel them to unite against the common enemies of their country,
and added distinctly that we English would on no account enter into their
quarrels. On the Bishop inquiring whether, in the event of the Manganja
again asking aid against the Ajawa, it would be his duty to accede to their
request, – 'No,' replied Dr. Livingstone, 'do not interfere in native quarrels.'

The good Bishop was as intensely averse to using arms, before he met the slave-hunters, as any man in England. In the course he pursued he may have made a mistake, but it is a mistake which very few Englishmen on meeting bands of helpless captives, or members of his family in bonds, would have failed to commit likewise.

ZT 348–416

Livingstone took his first look at Lake Malawi from a little dinghy in which he sailed its full length:

'How far is it to the end of the lake?' we enquired of an intelligent-looking native at the south part. 'The other end of the lake!' he exclaimed in real or well-feigned astonishment, 'whoever heard of such a thing? Why if one started when a mere boy to walk to the other end of the lake, he would be an old grey-headed man before he got there. I never heard of such a thing being attempted.'

On the Lake the slave-trade was going on at a terrible rate. Would that we could give a comprehensive account of the horrors of the slave-trade, with an approximation to the number of lives it yearly destroys; but neither we, nor any one else, have the statistics necessary for a work of this kind. We were informed by Colonel Rigby, late H.M. Political Agent, and Consul at Zanzibar, that 19 000 slaves from this Nyassa country alone pass annually through the Custom-house of that island. This is exclusive, of course, of those sent to Portuguese slave-ports. Let it not be supposed for an instant that this number, 19 000, represents all the victims. Besides those actually captured, thousands are killed and die of their wounds and famine, driven from their villages by the slave raid proper. Thousands perish in internecine war waged for slaves with their own clansmen and neighbours, slain by the lust of gain, which is stimulated, be it remembered always, by the slave purchasers of Cuba and elsewhere. The many skeletons we have seen, amongst rocks and woods, by the little pools, and along the paths of the wilderness, attest the awful sacrifice of human life, which must be attributed, directly or indirectly, to this trade of hell. It is our deliberate opinion from what we know and have seen, that not one-fifth of the victims of the slave-trade ever become slaves. Taking the Shire Valley as an average, we should say not even one-tenth arrive at their destination. As the system, therefore, involves such an awful waste of human life, – or shall we say of human labour? – and moreover tends directly to perpetuate the barbarism of those who remain in the country, the argument for the continuance of this course because a fraction of the enslaved may find good masters, seems of no great value. This reasoning, if not the result of ignorance, may be of maudlin philanthropy. A small armed steamer on Lake Nyassa could easily, by exercising a control, and furnishing goods in exchange for ivory and other products, break the neck of this infamous traffic in that quarter; for nearly all must cross the Lake or the Upper Shire.

ZT 390–392

The massacre at Nyangwe in 1870 was Livingstone's My Lai.

24th May. – The market is a busy scene – everyone is in dead earnest – little time is lost in friendly greetings; vendors of fish run about with potsherds full of snails or small fishes or young birds smoke-dried and spitted on twigs, or other relishes to exchange for cassava roots, potatoes, vegetables, or grain, bananas, flour, palm-oil, fowls, salt, pepper; each is intensely eager to barter food for relishes, and makes strong assertions as to the goodness or badness of everything: the sweat stands in beads on their faces – cocks crow briskly, even when slung over the shoulder with their heads hanging down, and pigs squeal. Iron knobs, drawn out at each end to show the goodness of the metal, are exchanged for cloth of the Muabé palm. They deal fairly, and when differences arise they are easily settled by the men interfering or pointing to me: they appeal to each other, and have a strong sense of natural justice. With so much food changing hands amongst the three thousand present much benefit is derived; some come from twenty to twenty-five miles. It is a scene of the finest natural acting imaginable. The eagerness with which all sorts of assertions are made – the eager earnestness with which apparently all creation, above, around, and beneath, is called on to attest the truth of what they allege – and then the intense surprise and withering scorn cast on those who despise their goods. Little girls run about selling cups of water for a few small fishes to the half-exhausted wordy combatants. A stranger in the market had ten human under jaw-bones hung by a string over his shoulder: on inquiry he professed to have killed and eaten the owners, and showed with his knife how he cut up his victim. When I expressed disgust he and others laughed. Two nice girls were trying to sell their venture, which was roasted white ants.

18th June. – Dugumbé arrived. He has a large party and 500 guns. He is determined to go into new fields of trade, and has all his family with him, and intends to remain six or seven years, sending regularly to Ujiji for supplies of goods.

15th July. – Dugumbé's horde tried to deal in the market in a domineering way. It was a hot, sultry day, and when I went into the market I saw Adie and Manilla, and three of the men who had lately come with Dugumbé. I was surprised to see them with their guns, and felt inclined to reprove them, as one of my men did, for bringing weapons into the market, but I attributed it to their ignorance, and, it being very hot, I was walking away to go out of the market, when I saw one of the fellows haggling about a fowl, and seizing hold of it. Before I had got thirty yards out, the discharge of two guns in the middle of the crowd told me the slaughter had begun: crowds dashed off from the place, and threw down their wares in confusion, and ran. At the same time as the three opened fire on the mass of people near the upper end of the market-place volleys were discharged from a party down near the creek on the panic-stricken women who dashed at the canoes. Fifty or more of these were jammed in the creek, and men and women, wounded by the fire poured into them, leaped and scrambled into the water, shrieking. A long line of heads in the river showed that great numbers had struck out for an island a full mile off. Shot after shot continued to be fired. Some of the long line of heads disappeared quietly; whilst other poor creatures threw their arms high, as if appealing to the great Father above, and sank. One canoe took in as many as it could hold, and all paddled with hands and arms: three canoes, got out in haste, picked up sinking friends, till all went down together, and disappeared. One man in a long canoe, which could have held forty or fifty, had clearly lost his head; he had been out in the stream before the massacre began, and now paddled up the river nowhere, and never looked to the drowning. By-and-bye all the heads disappeared; some had turned down stream towards the bank, and escaped.

After the terrible affair in the water, the party of Tagamoio, who was the chief perpetrator, continued to fire on the people. I counted seventeen villages burning this morning. I asked the question of Dugumbé and others, 'Now for what is all this murder?' All blamed Manilla as its cause, and in one sense he was the cause; but the wish to make an impression in the country as to the importance and greatness of the new comers was the most potent motive. It made me sick at heart. No one will ever know the exact loss on this bright sultry summer morning. It gave me the impression of being in Hell. The Arabs themselves estimated the loss of life at between 330 and 400 souls.

The slaughter was peculiarly atrocious, inasmuch as we have always heard that women coming to or from market have never been known to be molested: even when two districts are engaged in actual hostilities, 'the women', say they, 'pass among us to market unmolested', nor has one ever been known to be plundered by the men.

2 p.m. – An old man, called Kabobo, came for his old wife; I asked her if this were her husband, she went to him, and put her arm lovingly around him, and said 'Yes'. I gave her five strings of beads to buy food, all her stores being destroyed with her house; she bowed down, and put her forehead to the ground as thanks, and old Kabobo did the same: the tears stood in her eyes as she went off. Tagamoio caught 17 women, and other Arabs of his party, 27; dead by gunshot, 25. The heads of two headmen were brought over to be redeemed by their friends with slaves.

The open murder perpetrated on hundreds of unsuspecting women fills me with unspeakable horror: I cannot think of going anywhere with the Tagamoio crew; I must either go down or up Lualaba, whichever the Banian slaves choose.

LJ 1870

1   *Thoughts on Slavery,* 1774.
2   Coupland, p. 256.
3   *Wilberforce,* Sir R. Coupland, Collins, London, 1945, p. 249.
4   MT 32–33.

CHAPTER 8

The Livingstone Touch

All Livingstone represents has come into question today: the Victorians have been taught to cringe, as we point from their rhetoric to their results. True, our revaluations of the heroic still spare courage and endurance. But a *missionary*? The anthropologists explode. A *Christian*? The young shrug. A *colonist*? The Marxists shudder. A *saint*? The Freudians smile. An *explorer*? 'Of what?' say the new Africans. 'He was a tourist:' and proceed to rub his image off the blackboard.

But, however erratically, Livingstone could write and through his writing declare vividly three claims on the attention of time: his passion for Africa, his subjection to Christ, and his natural leadership. He appears through these as one of the great originals who create new possibilities in history. In Shelley's sense (and in Hegel's) he is an artist; and if that is granted one may hope to finesse the neglect of his family that worries some, on the grounds that 'since marriage began the great artist has been known as a bad husband' etc.

145

A lot of Livingstone comes simply from his being a Scot. As a people the Scots have been tough, democratic individualists, punctilious in honour, hard-working, handy, quick-witted, accustomed to hardship, and very familiar, through endless emigration, with finding themselves lords of the softer circumstance. If not overtaken by the bottle or worse, they are a formidable people.

Livingstone was a Christian too; but, as Highlander and Hebridean, he had no obligation to be a Calvinist, nor was he. Characteristically, if he was a churchman at all, he was an Independent or Congregationalist. This was an old puritan sect which had rejected the centralizing spirit of Calvin and Knox, and would have each church responsible for its own conduct. The mission at Kuruman was founded by a Congregationalist, and Livingstone sought a natural (if temporary) home there:

> 'Friends advised me', he writes, 'to join the London Missionary Society on account of its perfectly unsectarian character.' It "sends neither episcopacy nor presbyterianism nor independency, but the Gospel of Christ, to the heathen". This exactly agreed with my idea of what a Missionary Society ought to do; but it was not without a pang that I offered myself, for it was not quite agreeable, to one accustomed to work his own way, to become, in a measure, dependent on others.'[2]

His spiritual life seems to have consisted of prayer, observance of the Sabbath and the conduct of simple, Sunday services in the vernacular. The services were Church of England. He had with him at his death what Waller calls 'his Bible and Church-service', the latter presumably the Book of Common Prayer. Of these early glimpses of his worship, one comes from the Kalahari and two from his halcyon days with Sekeletu in mid-1853:

> The Bakalahari, who live at Motlatsa wells, have always been very friendly to us, and listen attentively to instruction conveyed to them in their own tongue. Like most others, they listen with respect and attention, but, when we kneel down and address an unseen Being, the position and the act often appear to them so ridiculous that they cannot refrain from bursting into uncontrollable laughter. After a few services they get over this tendency. I was once present when a missionary attempted to sing among a wild heathen tribe of Bechuanas, who had no music in their composition; the effect on the audience was such that the tears actually ran down their cheeks.
>
> MT 157

> At our public religious services in the *kotla*, the Makololo women always behaved with decorum from the first, except at the conclusion of the prayer. When all knelt down, many of those who had children, in following the example of the rest, bent over their little ones; the children, in terror of being crushed to death, set up a simultaneous yell, which so tickled the whole assembly there was often a subdued titter, to be turned into a hearty laugh as soon as they heard Amen. Long after we had settled at Mabotsa, when

preaching on the most solemn subjects, a woman might be observed to look round, and seeing a neighbour seated on her dress, give her a hunch with the elbow to make her move off; the other would return it with interest, and then three or four would begin to hustle the first offenders, and the men to swear at them all, by way of enforcing silence.

The numbers who attended at the summons by the herald, who acted as beadle, were often from five to seven hundred. The service consisted of reading a small portion of the Bible and giving an explanatory address, usually short enough to prevent weariness or want of attention. So long as we continue to hold services in the *kotla*, the associations of the place are unfavourable to solemnity. This will appear more evident when it is recollected that, in the very spot where we had been engaged in acts of devotion, half an hour after, a dance would be got up; and these habits cannot be at first opposed without the appearance of assuming too much authority over them. It is always unwise to hurt their feelings of independence. Much greater influence will be gained by studying how you may induce them to act aright, with the impression that they are doing it of their own free will.

MT 187

I gave many public addresses to the people of Sesheke under the out-spreading camel-thorn tree, which serves as a shade to the *kotla* on the high bank of the river. It was pleasant to see the long lines of men, women, and children winding along from different quarters of the town, each party following behind their respective head men. They often amounted to between five and six hundred souls, and required an exertion of voice which brought back the complaint for which I had got the uvula excised at the Cape. They were always very attentive; and Moriantsane, in order, as he thought, to please me, on one occasion rose up in the middle of the discourse, and hurled his staff at the heads of some young fellows, whom he saw working with a skin instead of listening. My hearers sometimes put very sensible questions on the subjects brought before them; at other times they introduced the most frivolous nonsense, immediately after hearing the most solemn truths. Some begin to pray to Jesus in secret as soon as they hear of the white man's God, with but little idea of what they are about; and no doubt are heard by Him who, like a father, pitieth his children. Others, waking by night, recollect what has been said about the future world so clearly, that they resolve not to listen to the teaching again, as certain villagers in the south, who put all their cocks to death because they crowed the words, 'Tlang lo rapeleng' – 'Come along to prayers'.

MT 235

There is certainly room – though not here – for a close study of Livingstone's religious impulse, for it brings us to the heart of Christianity's effectiveness as a homogenizer of love and will. He is a man of prayer and the Bible; neither church nor sacraments seem of great appeal to him. For instance, I find no mention of the bread and wine, and therefore assume his chief communion was a discipline of the imagination, especially through prayer. How does this work?

It is all too easy at this stage to make Christian assumptions that alienate non-Christians, and vice versa. I shall follow Freud's theories as distancing without devaluing the phenomenon. In describing these processes, Freud considers them normal, and I hope I may look to Christians for charity enough to bear with his neutral hypothesis as compatible with and merely another way of putting the manner in which God may operate.

There is a total submission to a man: we are confronted with such prayers as this:

> *19th March.* – Birthday. My Jesus, my king, my life, my all; I again dedicate my whole self to Thee. Accept me, and grant, O Gracious Father, that ere this year is gone I may finish my task. In Jesus' name I ask it. Amen, so let it be.
>
> LJ 1872

In Freud's view, a boy's dilemma of love and hate for his father (in rivalry for his mother) is resolved by identifying himself with and so, as it were, becoming his father, exactly in the same manner as, in play, he is seen to identify himself with so many other things. The boy now has *within himself* a complete father-son relationship: now he can be the father giving commands, now he can be the son receiving them. If his mental energies are low, all that emerges, as he grows up, is a mild conscience and possibly a conventional religion. If they are high, however, the introjected father may be projected with hallucinatory force as a giant being, both loved and dreaded. Any adoption of the Judaeo-Christian religion with its apotheosis of Father and Son will now be one of great intensity. Notice, particularly, the alternating father-son relationship: now I am utterly obedient as the son – the position of prayer – and now no less assured as the good-son-who-is-the-father – the position of witness, or of fearless obedience to the father's will.

The syndrome was given historic definition in Christian eyes by Jesus, whose life becomes the model for all good sons of the persuasion. To Freud the belief, while 'entirely normal' (by which I think he means very common), is one deriving from exceptional passivity towards the father. He concludes that

> this identification with God becomes so great in some . . . that they lose the ability to recognize the existence of facts. They end in lunatic asylums. But the man whose super-ego is based upon this supposition and who preserves a full respect for facts and reality, may, if he possesses ability, accomplish great things in the world.[3]

In the presence of Livingstone's life of prayer and witness, this hypothesis explains the rhythm of submission and assertion he constantly displays. It throws light on other features of his life, too. The first is his sensitivity to children, natural to one who felt himself in the position of a trusting child.

Another is his difficulties with colleagues. To Freud, aggression is the other side of passivity, and must find its outlet somewhere. If the father is extremely loved, the covert resentment towards him will often find vent against father-substitutes. Of President Wilson, Freud writes:

> Because of this repressed hostility, he found it difficult to maintain friendly relations with men of superior intellect or position, and preferred to surround himself with women or inferiors.[4]

That begs a lot of questions, nor is Wilson Livingstone; but the inferences are striking.

The overworn 'charisma' can be strictly applied to Livingstone, for it means a gift of God whereby good to others may be performed. This was Livingstone's power of leadership. I am not now concerned with how he handled it, merely with its possession. He was dominant in two ways. The first was unaccountable, although he became increasingly aware of it. A slaving party ran away from him on the shore of Lake Malawi in 1863:

> On our return to the Kongone, we found that H.M.S. Lynx had caught some of these very slaves in a dhow; for a woman told us she first saw us at Mosauka's, and that the Arabs had fled for fear of an *uncanny* sort of Basungu.
>
> ZT 124

Much earlier (1856) he had been vaguely aware of the confidence he aroused:

> One of the discoveries I have made is that there are vast numbers of good people in the world, and I do most devoutly tender my thanks to that Gracious One who mercifully watched over me in every position, and influenced the hearts of both black and white to regard me with favour.
>
> MT 672

His second mode of dominance both flowed from and magnified the first: it was his quick, bold, resourceful reaction to any kind of emergency:

> On one occasion I nearly lost my waggon by fire, in a valley where the grass was only about three feet high. We were roused by the roar, as of a torrent, made by the fire coming from the windward. I immediately set fire to that on our leeward, and had just time to drag the waggon on the bare space there, before the windward flames reached the place where it had stood.
>
> MT 368

Both these modes of dominance fit the Freudian hypothesis and give it further strength. Leadership is the power to assume the position of a good father and thus permit others to regress to that of unconsciously trusting children. It implies in the leader mastery and assurance. Mastery, Livingstone had: he wielded skills almost magical in Africa. Assurance he supplied from being himself assured, and this power he gained, oddly enough, on his knees. I scarcely seek to canonise Livingstone but he sets an example of a saint in a field where the unsainted, both white and black, have long done magnificent service.

These few passages from his prayers, sermons, and reflections display his religion, from its core in prayer to its outward and inflexible continuance in well-doing:

31st December. – We now end 1866. It has not been so fruitful or useful as I intended. Will try to do better in 1867, and be better – more gentle and loving; and may the Almighty, to whom I commit my way, bring my desires to pass, and prosper me! Let all the sins of '66 be blotted out for Jesus' sake.

1st January, 1867. – May He who was full of grace and truth impress His character on mine. Grace – eagerness to show favour; truth – truthfulness, sincerity, honour – for His mercy's sake.

LJ 1866/7

We were invited by Gombwa in the afternoon to speak the same words to his people that we used to himself in the morning. He nudged a boy to respond, which is considered polite, though he did it only with a rough hem! at the end of each sentence. As for our general discourse we mention our relationship to our Father: His love to all His children – the guilt of selling any of His children – the consequence; *e.g.* it begets war, for they don't like to sell their own, and steal from other villagers, who retaliate. Arabs and Waiyau invited into the country by their selling, foster feuds, and war and depopulation ensue. We mention the Bible – future state – prayer: advise union, that they should unite as one family to expel enemies, who came first as slave-traders, and ended by leaving the country a wilderness.

LJ 9 Oct 1866

21st June. – No jugglery or sleight-of-hand would have any effect in the civilization of the Africans; they have too much good sense for that. Nothing brings them to place thorough confidence in Europeans but a long course of well-doing. They believe readily in the supernatural as effecting any new process, for it is part of their faith to ascribe everything above human agency to unseen spirits. Goodness or unselfishness impresses their minds more than any kind of skill or power.

LJ 1872

The spirit of Missions is the spirit of our Master: the very genius of His religion. *A diffusive philanthropy is Christianity itself.* It requires perpetual propagation to attest its genuineness.

LJ 8 Nov 1872

The qualities required in a Missionary leader are not of the common kind. He ought to have physical and moral courage of the highest order, and a considerable amount of cultivation and energy, balanced by patient determination; and, above all these, are necessary a calm Christian zeal and anxiety for the main spiritual results of the work. Before success appeared at the Mission-stations on the West Coast, upwards of forty Missionaries had succumbed to the climate. This may be proof of folly to some, but to others they are telling evidence that our religion has lost none of its pristine power. Nothing in our opinion is wanting to complete the title of many of these men to take rank with the Saints and Martyrs of primitive times.

ZT 572

'The idea that primitive man is deeply religious is nonsense. All the varieties of scepticism, materialism and spiritual fervour are to be found in the range of tribal societies.'[5]

So writes a modern anthropologist. Livingstone looked as close at Africans as any white had done, and reports:

I have found it difficult to come to a conclusion on their character. They sometimes perform actions remarkably good, and sometimes as strangely the opposite. I have been unable to ascertain the motive for the good, or account for the callousness of conscience with which they perpetrate the bad. After long observation, I came to the conclusion that they are just such a strange mixture of good and evil, as men are everywhere else. There is not among them an approach to that constant stream of benevolence flowing from the rich to the poor which we have in England, nor yet the unostentatious attentions which we have among our own poor to each other. Yet there are frequent instances of genuine kindness and liberality, as well as actions of an opposite character. The rich show kindness to the poor, in expectation of services, but a poor person who has no relatives, will seldom be supplied even with water in illness, and, when dead, will be dragged out to be devoured by the hyaenas, instead of being buried. Relatives alone will condescend to touch a dead body. It would be easy to enumerate instances of inhumanity which I have witnessed. An interesting-looking girl came to my waggon one day, in a state of nudity, and almost a skeleton. She was a captive from another tribe, and had been neglected by the man who claimed her. Having supplied her wants, I made inquiry for him, and found that he had been unsuccessful in raising a crop of corn, and had no food to give her. I volunteered to take her; but he said he would allow me to feed her and make her fat, and then take her away. I protested against this heartlessness; and as he said he could 'not part with his child', I was precluded from attending to her wants. In a day or two she was lost sight of. She had gone out a little way from the town, and, being too weak to return, had been cruelly left to perish. On the other hand, I have seen instances in which both men and women have taken up little orphans, and carefully reared them as their own children. By a selection of cases of either kind, it would not be difficult to make these people appear excessively good or uncommonly bad.

MT 510

One must remember Livingstone's object. It was to make Christians (of his own independent quality) from people he called 'savages' not because of their 'delicate tribalisms', which he respected, but because he often found them inexcusably cruel, hard, truculent and inconsiderate:

I had been, during a nine weeks' tour, in closer contact with heathenism than I had ever been before; and though all, including the chief, were as kind and attentive to me as possible, and there was no want of food (oxen being slaughtered daily, sometimes ten at a time, more than sufficient for the wants of all), yet to endure the dancing, roaring, and singing, the jesting, anecdotes, grumbling, quarrelling, and murdering of these children of nature, seemed more like a severe penance than anything I had before met with in the course of my missionary duties. I took thence a more intense disgust at heathenism that I had before, and formed a greatly elevated opinion of the effects of missions in the south, among tribes which are reported to have been as savage as the Makololo. The indirect benefits, which to a casual observer lie beneath the surface are worth all the money and labour that have been expended to produce them.

MT 226

It is essential to distinguish between Livingstone's squeamishness which, like his regular habits, was offended by 'dancing, roaring and singing' etc., and his condemnation of heavy evils, 'quarrelling and murdering', in the fibre of tribal life. The two get mixed up. There is an element of prudery, undoubtedly, but who, familiar with Livingstone's toughness, would deny that grimmer things than the proprieties are in his mind:

I shall not often advert to their depravity. My practice has always been to apply the remedy with all possible earnestness, but never allow my own mind to dwell on the dark shades of men's characters. I have never been able to draw pictures of their guilt, as if that could awaken Christian sympathy. The evil is there. But all around in this fair creation are scenes of beauty, and to turn from these to ponder on deeds of sin, cannot promote a healthy state of the faculties. The human misery and sin we endeavour to alleviate and cure, may be likened to the sickness and impurity of some of the back slums of great cities. One contents himself by ministering to the sick and trying to remove the causes, without remaining longer in the filth than is necessary for his work; another, equally anxious for the public good, stirs up every cess-pool, that he may describe the reeking vapours, and, by long contact with impurities, becomes himself infected, sickens, and dies.

MT 259

Moral evaluations are extremely difficult. In the Gospels themselves, the New Law conflicts with the residues of the Old. The facade of Victorianism has been demolished. Our own standards are fluid. In this confusion, the note of the last extract seems the clue. To Livingstone's perspicacious eye, Europe, America and Africa, high and low, lucky or unlucky, are on the same moral footing. His criterion, whether he knew it or not, is older than Christianity. 'Before the bar of Zeno ... nothing but goodness is good.'[6] To this positive Livingstone always responds:

> We came to a village among fine gardens of maize, bananas, ground-nuts, and cassava, but the villagers said, 'Go on to next village'; and this meant, 'We don't want you here'. I was so weak I sat down in the next hamlet and asked for a hut to rest in. A woman with leprous hands gave me hers, a nice clean one, and very heavy rain came on: of her own accord she prepared dumplings of green maize, pounded and boiled, which are sweet, for she said that she saw I was hungry. It was excessive weakness from purging, and seeing that I did not eat for fear of the leprosy, she kindly pressed me: 'Eat, you are weak only from hunger; this will strengthen you.' I put it out of her sight, and blessed her motherly heart.
>
> LJ 27 Jan 1870

> *27th December.* – A man, ill and unable to come on, was left all night in the rain, without fire. We sent men back to carry him. Wet and cold. We are evidently ascending as we come near the Chambezé. The N.E. clouds came up this morning to meet the N.W. and thence the S.E. came across as if combating the N.W. So as the new moon comes soon, it may be a real change to drier weather.
>
> 4 p.m. – The man carried in here is very ill; we must carry him tomorrow.
>
> *29th December.* – Our man Chipangawazi died last night and was buried this morning. He was a quiet good man.
>
> LJ 27 Dec 1872

> *21st August.* – Gave people an ox, and to a discarded wife a cloth, to avoid exposure by her husband stripping her. She is somebody's child!
>
> LJ 21 Aug 1872

As usual, we were caught by rains after leaving Soana Molopo's, and made our booths at the house of Mozinkwa, a most intelligent and friendly man belonging to Katema. He had a fine large garden in cultivation, and well hedged round. He had made the walls of his compound, or courtyard, of branches of the banian, which, taking root, had grown to be a live hedge of that tree. Mozinkwa's wife had cotton growing all round her premises, and several plants used as relishes to the the insipid porridge of the country. She cultivated also the common castor-oil plant, and a larger shrub which also yields a purgative oil. Here, however, the oil is used for anointing the heads and bodies alone. We saw in her garden likewise the Indian bringalls, yams, and sweet potatoes. Several trees were planted in the middle of the yard, and in the deep shade they gave, stood the huts of his fine family. His children, all by one mother, very black but comely to view, were the finest negro family I ever saw. We were much pleased with the frank friendship and liberality of this man and his wife. She asked me to bring her a cloth from the white man's country, but, when we returned, poor Mozinkwa's wife was in her grave, and he, as is the custom, had abandoned trees, garden, and huts to ruin. They cannot live on a spot where a favourite wife has died, probably because unable to bear the remembrance of the happy times they have spent there, or afraid to remain in a spot where death has once visited the establishment. If ever the place is re-visited, it is to pray to her, or make some offering. This feeling renders any permanent village in the country impossible.

MT 314

One does not expect a doctor to be prudish but Livingstone is nonplussed (or pretends to be) by African nudity, especially (though not only) among the Batonga of the middle Zambezi:

Great numbers of them came from all the surrounding villages, with presents of maize and *masuka*, and expressed great joy at the first appearance of a white man, and harbinger of peace. The women clothe themselves better than the Balonda, but the men walk about without the smallest sense of shame. They have even lost the tradition of the figleaf. I asked a fine large-bodied old man, if he did not think it would be better to adopt a little covering. He looked with a pitying leer, and laughed with surprise at my thinking him at all indecent: he evidently considered himself above such weak superstition. I told them that on my return I should have my family with me, and no one must come near us in that state. 'What shall we put on? we have no clothing.' It was considered a good joke when I told them that, if they had nothing else, they must put on a bunch of grass.

In musing over the peculiar habit indicated in the name 'Baenda pezi' (Go-nakeds), we conjectured that it might be an order similar to that of Free-masons, but no secret society can be found among the native Africans. A noble specimen of the *Baenda pezi* order once visited us and gained our esteem, though the full dress in which he stood consisted only of a tobacco-pipe, with a stem two feet long wound round with polished iron. He brought a liberal present. 'God made him naked,' he said, 'and he had therefore never worn any sort of clothing.' This gentleman's philosophy is very much like that of some dirty people we have known, who justified their want of fastidiousness by saying, 'fingers were made before forks'. Early next morning we had another interview with our naked friend, accompanied this time by his wife and daughter, bearing two large pots of beer, with which to refresh ourselves before starting. Both the women, as comely and modest-looking as any we have seen in Africa, were well-clothed, and adorned, as indeed all their women are. Some wear tin ear-rings all round the ear, and as many as nine often in each ear. The men rub their bodies with red ochre. Some plait a fillet two inches wide, of the inner bark of trees, and shave the hair off the lower part of the head, an inch above the ears being bare; the hair, on the upper part, having been well smeared with red ochre in oil, the fillet is bound on to it, and gives the head the appearance of having on a neat forage-cap. Some strings of coarse beads, and a little polished iron-wire round the arms, the never-failing pipe, and a small pair of iron tongs to lift the lighted coal, constitute the entire clothing of the most dandified young men of the *Baenda pezi*. All their other faculties seem fairly developed; but, as neither ridicule nor joking could awaken the sense of shame, it is probable that clothing alone would arouse the dormant feeling. Girls of eight or ten years, nearly naked, were clothed and taken into the Mission-house at Kolobeng as nurses to the children. In a fortnight after, they hastily covered their bosoms, even if one only passed through the sitting-room in which they slept. Among Zulus the smaller the covering, the more intense the shame on accidental exposure.

ZT 237

The Griquas and Bechuanas were in former times clad much like the Caffres, if such a word may be used where there is scarcely any clothing at all. A bunch of leather strings about eighteen inches long hung from the lady's waist in front, and a prepared skin of a sheep or antelope covered the shoulders, leaving the breast and abdomen bare: the men wore a patch of skin, about the size of the crown of one's hat, which barely served for the purposes of decency, and a mantle exactly like that of the women. Now, these same people come to church in decent though poor clothing, and behave with decorum.

MT 108

The last sentence precipitates the whole question of how much harm the century of colonialism and Christianity Livingstone inaugurated has done to Africa. Has Christianity, with its load of sin and guilt, offended an innocence the west itself is only beginning to recover? By an irony history alone could create, independent Africa seems destined to collect our neuroses as we shed them. The *Argus* correspondent writes from Nairobi in July, 1972:

After independence two years ago district commissioners began insisting that bare-bosomed traditional dancers wear brassieres, particularly when important people were watching them.
Many African women purchased bras for dance nights, carefully storing them away when the dancing finished.
Some local administrators went further – and insisted that traditional scanty grass skirts be replaced by thicker, imitation grass skirts, made from nylon.

Many would-be dancers added them to their wardrobes.

Then some administrators insisted that heavy linen bloomers be worn under the imitation grass skirts.

With sighs all round, the somewhat less joyful dancers bought bloomers ... In Parliament last week some back-bench MPs demanded that all traditional dancers be forced to wear Government-designed uniforms ...

Would Livingstone approve? I am afraid he would.

But the Africa he found was not happy, and his documentation of its pathos can do nothing more valuable than correct the myth that it was. The tyranny of the spear, the fragility of justice, the gangrene of slavery, the despair of peace are known from sources other than Livingstone, who himself palliates the horrors of the first two. What takes one's breath away is the confidence of his solution: Christianity, Colonies, Commerce. To this extent he was the child of his cotton-picking age. His master-plan matured step by step. Its coherence and goodwill appear in the following extracts. Of its consequences, a little more will have to be said later.

We were the very first white men the inhabitants had ever seen and we were visited by prodigious numbers. Among the first who came to see us was a gentleman who appeared in a gaudy dressing-gown of printed calico. Many of the Makololo, besides, had garments of blue, green, and red baize, and also of printed cottons; on inquiry, we learned that these had been pur-chased, in exchange for boys, from a tribe called Mambári, which is situated near Bihé. As they had a number of old Portuguese guns, which Sebituane thought would be excellent in any future invasion of Matebele, he offered to purchase them with cattle or ivory, but the Mambari refused everything except boys about fourteen years of age. The Makololo declare they never heard of people being bought and sold till then, and disliked it, but the desire to possess the guns prevailed, and eight old guns were exchanged for as many boys; these were not their own children, but captives of the black races they had conquered. I have never known in Africa an instance of a parent selling his own offspring. The Makololo were afterwards incited to make a foray against some tribes to the eastward; the Mambari bargaining to use their guns in the attack for the captives they might take, and the Mako-lolo were to have all the cattle. They went off with at least two hundred slaves that year. During this foray the Makololo met some Arabs from Zanzibar, who presented them with three English muskets, and in return received about thirty of their captives.

In talking with my companion over these matters, the idea was suggested that, if the slave-market were supplied with articles of European manu-facture by legitimate commerce, the trade in slaves would become impossible. It seemed more feasible to give the goods, for which the people now part with their captives, in exchange for ivory and other products of the country, and thus prevent the trade at the beginning, than try to put a stop

to it at any of the subsequent steps. This could only be effected by estab-
lishing a highway from the coast into the centre of the country.

                                                                    MT 92

A 'picho' was called to deliberate on the steps proposed. In these
assemblies great freedom of speech is allowed; and on this occasion one of
the old diviners said, 'Where is he taking you to? This white man is throwing
you away. Your garments already smell of blood.' It is curious to observe
how much identity of character appears all over the world. This man was a
noted croaker. He always dreamed something dreadful in every expedition,
and was certain that an eclipse or comet betokened the propriety of flight.
But Sebituane formerly set his visions down to cowardice, and Sekeletu only
laughed at him now. The general voice was in my favour; so a band of
twenty-seven were appointed to accompany me to the west. These men were
not hired, but sent to enable me to accomplish an object as much desired by
the chief and most of his people as by me. They were eager to obtain free and
profitable trade with white men. The prices which the Cape merchants could
give, after defraying the great expenses of a long journey hither, being very
small, made it scarce worth while for the natives to collect produce for that
market; and the Mambari, giving only a few bits of print and baize for
elephants' tusks worth more pounds than they gave yards of cloth, had
produced the belief that trade with them was throwing ivory away. The
desire of the Makololo for direct trade with the seacoast coincided exactly
with my own conviction, that no permanent elevation of a people can be
effected without commerce.

                                                                    MT 228

The promotion of commerce ought to be specially attended to, as this,
more speedily than anything else, demolishes that sense of isolation which
heathenism engenders, and makes the tribes feel themselves mutually
dependent on, and mutually beneficial to, each other. My observations on
this subject make me extremely desirous to promote the preparation of the
raw materials of European manufactures in Africa, for by that means we
may not only put a stop to the slave-trade, but introduce the negro family
into the body corporate of nations, no one member of which can suffer
without the others suffering with it. Success in this, in both Eastern and
Western Africa, would lead, in the course of time, to a much larger diffusion
of the blessings of civilization than efforts exclusively spiritual and
educational.

                                                                    MT 28

As far as I am myself concerned, the opening of the new central country
is a matter for congratulation only in so far as it opens up a prospect for the
elevation of the inhabitants. As I have elsewhere remarked, I view the end of
the geographical feat as the beginning of the missionary enterprise. I take the
latter term in its most extended signification, and include every effort made

for the amelioration of our race; the promotion of all those means by which God in His providence is working, and bringing all His dealings with man to a glorious consummation.

If the reader has accompanied me thus far, he may perhaps be disposed to take an interest in the objects I propose to myself, should God mercifully grant me the honour of doing something more for Africa. As the highlands on the borders of the central basin are comparatively healthy, the first object seems to be to secure a permanent path thither, in order that Europeans may pass as quickly as possible through the unhealthy region near the coast. When we get beyond the hostile population we reach a very different race. On the latter my chief hopes at present rest. All of them, however, are willing and anxious to engage in trade, and, while eager for this, none have ever been encouraged to cultivate the raw materials of commerce. Their country is well adapted for cotton; and I venture to entertain the hope that by distributing seeds of better kinds than that which is found indigenous, and stimulating the natives to cultivate it by affording them the certainty of a market for all they may produce, we may engender a feeling of mutual dependence between them and ourselves. I have a two-fold object in view, and believe that, by guiding our missionary labours so as to benefit our own country, we shall thereby more effectually and permanently benefit the heathen. We ought to encourage the Africans to cultivate for our markets, as the most effectual means, next to the Gospel, of their elevation.

MT 673

Senhor Ferrao received us with his usual kindness, and gave us a bountiful breakfast. During the day the principal men of the place called, and were unanimously of opinion that the free natives would willingly cultivate large quantities of cotton, could they find purchasers. They had in former times exported largely both cotton and cloth to Manica and even to Brazil. 'On their own soil', they declared, 'the natives are willing to labour and trade, provided only they can do so to advantage: when it is for their interest, blacks work very hard.' We often remarked subsequently that this was the opinion of men of energy; and that all settlers of activity, enterprise, and sober habits had become rich, while those who were much addicted to lying on their backs smoking, invariably complained of the laziness of the negroes, and were poor, proud, and despicable.

ZT 36

It is perhaps a failing in a traveller to be affected with a species of home-sickness, so that the mind always turns from the conditions and circum-stances of the poor abroad to the state of the lowly in our native land; but so it is. When we see with how much ease the very lowest class here can subsist, we cannot help remembering, with sorrow, with what difficulty our own poor can manage to live – with what timid eagerness employment is sought – how hard the battle of life; while so much of this fair earth remains unoccupied, and not put to the benevolent purpose for which it was intended by its Maker.

ZT 263

In this light, a European colony would be considered by the natives as an inestimable boon to intertropical Africa. Thousands of industrious natives would gladly settle round it, and engage in that peaceful pursuit of agriculture and trade of which they are so fond, and, undistracted by wars or rumours of wars, might listen to the purifying and ennobling truths of the Gospel of Jesus Christ. The Manganja on the Zambesi, like their countrymen on the Shire, are fond of agriculture; and, in addition to the usual varieties of food, cultivate tobacco and cotton in quantities more than equal to their wants. To the question, 'Would they work for Europeans?' an affirmative answer may be given, if the Europeans belong to the class which can pay a reasonable price for labour, and not to that of adventurers who want employment for themselves.

ZT 199

Hindsight may smile but could foresight have imagined what would swarm in when the land was swept clean of slavery? Livingstone makes two mistakes. Instead of confining himself, as he usually does, to the penetration of missions, his do-gooding heart is tempted to off-load whites onto Africa's highlands. He could not foresee that the slums from which he proposed to rescue them in Europe would become the locations of the blacks,[7] nor that a more delicate bane than slavery would accompany the process. He would have been dismayed to learn that the chief business of the first ecumenical council since Nicaea (A.D. 325) in which whites were in a minority – that of the Anglican Churches at Limuru, Kenya, in 1972 – had been racism.

His second mistake was a sinister mistrust of educated blacks. Not for the first time one meets a gnarl in Livingstone's character conflicting with facile liberal assumptions. Consider the implications of this curious sequence of thoughts between 24th May and 10th July, 1872, in the Last Journals:

I would say to missionaries, Come on, brethren, to the real heathen. Leaving the coast tribes, and devoting yourselves heartily to the savages, as they are called, you will find, with some drawbacks and wickedness, a very great deal to admire and love. Educated free blacks from a distance are to be avoided: they are expensive, and are too much of gentlemen for your work. You may in a few months raise natives who will teach reading to others better than they can, and teach you also much that the liberated never know. A cloth and some beads occasionally will satisfy them, while neither the food, the wages, nor the work will please those who, being brought from a distance, naturally consider themselves missionaries.

LJ 24 May 1872

Livingstone can be judged only by the Christian standards he himself appeals to. In this instance he must have had in mind some such knotty scripture as 'Thou hast hid these things from the wise and prudent and hast revealed them unto babes', etc. This explains but it does not excuse his thought. How other than through 'educated, free *and Christian* blacks' can the Africa of his dreams emerge –

> The crowds of well-dressed, devout, and intelligent-looking worshippers, in both West and South Africa form a wonderful contrast to the same people still in their heathen state. In Sierra Leone, Kuruman, and other places, the Sunday, for instance, seemed as well observed as it is anywhere in Scotland. The sight produced an indelible impression on the mind ... because wherever Christianity spreads it makes men better.
>
> ZT 602

– or, *mutatis mutandis*, of ours?
But we have followed him into a field wider than the Livingstone touch can control. It is essentially a small-scale, person-to-person relationship, and this seems to make its example so valuable. He comes closest to defining it when he calls it 'the magic power of kindness', and he has faith in it, although

> this charm may not act at once, nor may its effects always be permanent; the first feeling of the wretched, of whatever colour, may be that of distrust, or a suspicion that kindness is a proof of weakness.

Obviously it includes generosity and consideration, but he often stresses an intellectual respect that one must call dialogue:

> When I can get the natives to agree in the propriety of any step, they go to the end of the affair without a murmur. I speak to them and treat them as rational beings, and generally get on well with them in consequence.
>
> MT 436

In action, this becomes:

> In our relations with this people we were simply strangers exercising no authority or control whatever. Our influence depended entirely on persuasion; and, having taught them by kind conversation as well as by public instruction, I expected them to do what their own sense of right and wrong dictated. We never wished them to do right merely because it would be pleasing to us, nor thought ourselves to blame when they did wrong. We saw that our teaching did good to the general mind of the people by bringing new and better motives into play. Five instances are positively known to me in which by our influence on public opinion war was prevented; and where, in individual cases, we failed, the people did no worse than they did before we came into the country. In general they were slow in coming to a decision on religious subjects; but in questions affecting their worldly affairs they were

keenly alive to their own interests. They might be called stupid in matters which had not come within the sphere of their observation, but in other things they showed more intelligence than is to be met with in our own uneducated peasantry. They are remarkably accurate in their knowledge of cattle, sheep, and goats, knowing exactly the kind of pasturage suited to each; and they select with great judgment the varieties of soil best suited to different kinds of grain. They are also familiar with the habits of wild animals, and in general are well up in the maxims which embody their ideas of political wisdom.

MT 19

Its most famous instance is the discussion with the Rain-doctor:

I am not aware of ever having had an enemy in the tribe. The only avowed cause of dislike was expressed by a very influential and sensible man, the uncle of Sechele. 'We like you as well as if you had been born among us; you are the only white man we can become familiar with; but we wish you to give up that everlasting preaching and praying; we cannot become familiar with that at all. You see we never get rain, while those tribes who never pray as we do obtain abundance.' This was a fact; and we often saw it raining on the hills, ten miles off, while it would not look at us 'even with one eye'. If the Prince of the power of the air had no hand in scorching us up, I fear I often gave him the credit for doing so.

As for the rain-makers, they carried the sympathies of the people along with them, and not without reason. With the following arguments they were all acquainted, and in order to understand their force we must place ourselves in their position, and believe, as they do, that all medicines act by a mysterious charm. The term for cure may be translated 'charm' *(alaha)*.

Medical Doctor. – Hail, friend! How very many medicines you have about you this morning! Why, you have every medicine in the country here.

Rain Doctor. – Very true, my friend; and I ought; for the whole country needs the rain which I am making.

M. D. – So you really believe that you can command the clouds? I think that can be done by God alone.

R. D. – We both believe the very same thing. It is God that makes the rain, but I pray to him by means of these medicines, and, the rain coming, of course it is then mine. It was I who made it for the Bakwains for many years, when they were at Shokuane; through my wisdom, too, their women became fat and shining. Ask them; they will tell you the same as I do.

M. D. – But we are distinctly told in the parting words of our Saviour that we can pray to God acceptably in His name alone, and not by means of medicines.

R. D. – Truly! but God told *us* differently. He made black men first, and did not love us, as he did the white men. He made you beautiful, and gave you clothing, and guns, and gun-powder, and horses, and waggons, and many other things about which we know nothing. But toward us he had no heart. He gave us nothing, except the assegai, and cattle, and rain-making;

and he did not give us hearts like yours. We never love each other. But God has given us one little thing, which you know nothing of. He has given us the knowledge of certain medicines by which we can make rain. *We* do not despise those things which you possess, though we are ignorant of them. We don't understand your book, yet we don't despise it. *You* ought not to despise our little knowledge, though you are ignorant of it.

M. D. – I don't despise what I am ignorant of; I only think you are mistaken in saying that you have medicines which can influence the rain at all.

R. D. – That's just the way people speak when they talk on a subject of which they have no knowledge. I use my medicines, and you employ yours; we are both doctors, and doctors are not deceivers. You give a patient medicine. Sometimes God is pleased to heal him by means of your medicine: sometimes not – he dies. When he is cured, you take the credit of what God does. I do the same. Sometimes God grants us rain, sometimes not. When he does, we take the credit of the charm. When a patient dies, you don't give up trust in your medicine, neither do I when rain fails. If you wish me to leave off my medicines, why continue your own?

M. D. – I give medicine to living creatures within my reach, and can see the effects though no cure follows; you pretend to charm the clouds, which are so far above us that your medicines never reach them. The clouds usually lie in one direction, and your smoke goes in another. God alone can command the clouds. Only try and wait patiently; God will give us rain without your medicines.

R. D. – Mahala-ma-kapa-a-a!! Well, I always thought white men were wise till this morning. Who ever thought of making trial of starvation! Is death pleasant then?

M. D. – Could you make it rain on one spot and not on another?

R. D. – I wouldn't think of trying. I like to see the whole country green, and all the people glad; the women clapping their hands and giving me their ornaments for thankfulness, and lullilooing for joy.

M. D. – I think you deceive both them and yourself.

R. D. – Well, then, there is a pair of us.

MT 23

Humour, being the gift of a kind super-ego, cannot rub off, but Livingstone has a constant supply of it, from broad to dry.

The laugh of the women is brimful of mirth. It is no simpering smile, nor senseless loud guffaw; but a merry ringing laugh, the sound of which does one's heart good. One begins with ha, Héé, then comes the chorus in which all join, Haééé! and they end by slapping their hands together, giving the spectator the idea of great heartiness. When first introduced to a Chief, if we have observed a joyous twinkle of the eye accompanying his laugh, we have always set him down as a good fellow, and we have never been disappointed in him afterwards.   ZT 503

I had a long talk with Moamba, a big, stout, public-house-looking person, with a slight outward cast in his left eye, but intelligent and hearty. He was very anxious to know why we were going to Tanganyika; for what we came; what we should buy there; and if I had any relations there. He then showed me some fine large tusks, eight feet six in length. 'What do you wish to buy, if not slaves or ivory?' I replied, that the only thing I had seen worth buying was a fine fat chief like himself. He was tickled at this.

LJ 23 Feb 1867

I left Sekeletu at Naliele, and ascended the river. He furnished me with men, besides my rowers, and among the rest a herald, that I might enter his villages in what is considered a dignified manner. This it was supposed would be effected by the herald shouting out at the top of his voice, 'Here comes the lord; the great lion;' the latter phrase being 'tau e tona', which in his imperfect way of pronunciation became 'sau e tona', and so like 'the great sow', that I could not receive the honour with becoming gravity, and had to entreat him, much to the annoyance of my party, to be silent.

MT 221

29th July. – Visited Sheikh bin Nassib, who has a severe attack of fever; he cannot avoid going to the war. He bought a donkey with the tusk he stole from Lewalé, and it died yesterday; now Lewalé says, 'Give me back my tusk'; and the Arab replies, 'Give me back my donkey'.

LJ 1872

As we came away from Monina's village, a witch-doctor, who had been sent for, arrived, and all Monina's wives went forth into the fields that morning fasting. There they would be compelled to drink an infusion of a plant named 'goho', which is used as an ordeal. This ceremony is called 'muavi', and is performed in this way. When a man suspects that any of his wives have bewitched him, he sends for the witch-doctor, and all the wives go forth into the field, and remain fasting till that person has made an infusion of the plant. They all drink it, each one holding up her hand to heaven in attestation of her innocency. Those who vomit it are considered innocent, while those whom it purges are pronounced guilty, and put to death by burning. I happened to mention to my own men the water-test for witches formerly in use in Scotland: the supposed witch, being bound hand and foot, was thrown into a pond; if she floated, she was considered guilty, taken out, and burned; but if she sank and was drowned, she was pronounced innocent. The wisdom of my ancestors excited as much wonder in their minds, as their custom did in mine.

MT 621

While humour may be non-transferable, the species of gentleness called humouring can be learned:

An old man, who said he had been born about the same time as the late Matiamvo, and had been his constant companion through life, visited us; and as I was sitting on some grass in front of the little gipsy tent mending my camp stool, I invited him to take a seat on the grass beside me. This was peremptorily refused: 'he had never sat on the ground during the late chief's reign, and he was not going to degrade himself now.' One of my men handed him a log of wood taken from the fire, and helped him out of the difficulty. When I offered him some cooked meat on a plate, he would not touch that either, but would take it home. So I humoured him by sending a servant to bear a few ounces of meat to the town behind him.

MT 322

In his last years, weak with sickness, Livingstone could no longer display among his men the daring that gave him power and enabled him always to lead gentleness from strength. He was very conscious of the loss:

If slaves think you fear them, they will climb over you. I clothed mine for nothing, and ever after they have tried to ride roughshod over me, and mutiny on every occasion!

LJ 12 Apr 1871

He speaks, in the last phase, of his 'peace plan' obviously a kind of Gandhism, which he practised but could not finally endorse:

The pugnacious spirit is one of the necessities of life. When people have little or none of it, they are subjected to indignity and loss. My own men walk into houses where we pass the nights without asking any leave, and steal cassava without shame. I have to threaten and thrash to keep them honest, while if we are at a village where the natives are a little pugnacious they are as meek as sucking doves. The peace plan involves indignity and wrong. I give little presents to the headmen, and to some extent heal their hurt sensibilities. At least it is appreciated, and produces profound hand-clapping.

LJ 16 Dec 1872

He never lost his assurance in respect of outsiders:

11th March. – I had a long, fierce oration from Amur, in which I was told again and again that I should be killed and eaten – the people wanted a 'white one' to eat! I needed 200 guns; and 'must not go to die'. I told him that I was thankful for advice, if given by one who had knowledge, but his vehement threats were dreams of one who had never gone anywhere, but sent his slaves to kill people. I left this noisy demagogue, after saying I thanked him for his warnings, but saw he knew not what he was saying.

LJ 1871

28th November. – Chiwé presented a small goat with crooked legs and some millet flour, but he grumbled at the size of the fathom cloth I gave. I offered another fathom, and a bundle of needles, but he grumbled at this too, and sent it back. On this I returned his goat and marched.

LJ 1872

One must conclude with him, however, in the plenitude of his powers, at the Murchison Falls on the Shire River in 1863:

Five Zambesi men, who had been all their lives accustomed to great heavy canoes, were very desirous to show how much better they could manage our boat than the Makololo; three jumped into her when our backs were turned, and two hauled her up a little way; the tide caught her bow, we heard a shout of distress, the rope was out of their hands in a moment, and there she was, bottom upwards; a turn or two in an eddy, and away she went, like an arrow, down the Cataracts. One of the men in swimming ashore saved a rifle. The whole party ran with all their might along the bank, but never more did we see our boat.

The five performers in this catastrophe approached with penetential looks. They had nothing to say, nor had we. They bent down slowly, and touched our feet with both hands. 'Ku kuata moendo' – 'to catch the foot' – is their way of asking forgiveness. It was so like what we have seen a little child do that they were only sentenced to go back to the ship, get provisions, and, in the ensuing journey on foot, carry as much as they could, and thus make up for the loss of the boat.

ZT 478

Such solutions look simple but their quality should not be underrated. It needs another white to offset Livingstone's wisdom in handling men. Fist and whip were H. M. Stanley's way (according to Coupland) but he testifies how deeply he was impressed by Livingstone's gentleness. ' "You bad fellow, you very wicked fellow, you blockhead, you fool of a man" were the strongest terms he employed, where others would have clubbed or clouted.' The irascible Stanley 'had come close to moral greatness', Coupland concludes, 'and he was startled, captivated, subjected by it'. Stanley himself says:

I defy anyone to be in his society long without thoroughly fathoming him, for there is no guile in him and what is apparent on the surface is the thing that is in him. I grant he is not an angel but he approaches to that being as near as the nature of a living man will allow . . .

I do not wish to leave Livingstone with wings nor to obscure his example any longer with words other than his own. It is hard to choose a final illustration of the Livingstone touch but much of it is to be seen in action in his last encounter with the hostile Chiboque, in 1854:

Having reached the village of Njambi, one of the chiefs of the Chiboque, we intended to pass a quiet Sunday; and our provisions being quite spent, I ordered a tired riding-ox to be slaughtered. As we wished to be on good terms with all, we sent the hump and ribs to Njambi, with the explanation that this was the customary tribute to chiefs in the part from which we had come, and that we always honoured men in his position. He returned thanks, and promised to send food. Next morning he sent an impudent message, with a very small present of meal; scorning the meat he had accepted, he demanded either a man, an ox, a gun, powder, cloth, or a shell. We replied, we should have thought ourselves fools if we had scorned his small present, and demanded other food instead; and even supposing we had possessed the articles named, no black man ought to impose a tribute on a party that did not trade in slaves. The servants who brought the message said that, when sent to the Mambari, they had always got a quantity of cloth from them for their master, and now expected the same, or something else as an equivalent, from me.

We head some of the Chiboque remark, 'They have only five guns'; and about mid-day, Njambi collected all his people, and surrounded our encampment. Their object was evidently to plunder us of everything. My men seized their javelins, and stood on the defensive, while the young Chiboque had drawn their swords and brandished them with great fury. Some even pointed their guns at me, and nodded to each other, as much as to say, 'This is the way we shall do with him'. I sat on my camp-stool, with my double-barrelled gun across my knees, and invited the chief to be seated also. When he and his counsellors had sat down on the ground in front of me, I asked what crime we had committed that he had come armed in that way. He replied that one of my men, Pitsane, while sitting at the fire that morning, had, in spitting, allowed a small quantity of the saliva to fall on the leg of one of his men, and this 'guilt' he wanted to be settled by the fine of a man, ox, or gun. Pitsane admitted the fact of a little saliva having fallen on the Chiboque, and in proof of its being a pure accident, mentioned that he had given the man a piece of meat, by way of making friends, just before it happened, and wiped it off with his hand as soon as it fell. In reference to a man being given, I declared that we were all ready to die rather than give up one of our number to be a slave; that my men might as well give me as I give one of them, for we were all free men. 'Then you can give the gun with which the ox was shot.' As we heard some of his people remarking even now that we had only 'five guns', we declined, on the ground that, as they were intent on plundering us, giving a gun would be helping them to do so.

This they denied, saying they wanted the customary tribute only. I asked what right they had to demand payment for leave to tread on the ground of God, our common Father? If we trod on their gardens we would pay, but not for marching on land which was still God's and not theirs. They did not attempt to controvert this, because it is in accordance with their own ideas, but reverted again to the pretended crime of the saliva.

My men now entreated me to give something; and after asking the chief if he really thought the affair of the spitting a matter of guilt, and receiving an answer in the affirmative, I gave him one of my shirts. The young Chiboque were dissatisfied, and began shouting and brandishing their swords for a greater fine.

As Pitsane felt that he had been the cause of this disagreeable affair, he asked me to add something else. I gave a bunch of beads, but the counsellors objected this time, so I added a large handkerchief. The more I yielded, the more unreasonable their demands became, and at every fresh demand, a shout was raised by the armed party, and a rush made around us with brandishing of arms. One young man made a charge at my head from behind, but I quickly brought round the muzzle of my gun to his mouth, and he retreated. I pointed him out to the chief, and he ordered him to retire a little. I felt anxious to avoid the effusion of blood; and though sure of being able with my Makololo, who had been drilled by Sebituane, to drive off twice the number of our assailants, I strove to avoid actual collision. My men were quite unprepared for this exhibition, but behaved with admirable coolness. The chief and counsellors, by accepting my invitation to be seated, had placed themselves in a trap; for my men very quietly surrounded them, and made them feel that there was no chance of escaping their spears. I then said, that, as one thing after another had failed to satisfy them, it was evident that *they* wanted to fight, while *we* only wanted to pass peaceably through the country; that they must begin first and bear the guilt before God: we would not fight till they had struck the first blow. I then sat silent for some time. It was rather trying for me, because I knew that the Chiboque would aim at the white man first; but I was careful not to appear flurried, and, having four barrels ready for instant action, looked quietly at the savage scene around. The chief and counsellors, seeing that they were in more danger than I, were perhaps influenced by seeing the air of cool preparation which some of my men displayed at the prospect of a work of blood.

The Chiboque at last put the matter before us in this way: 'You come among us in a new way, and say you are quite friendly: how can we know it unless you give us some of your food, and you take some of ours? If you give us an ox we will give you whatever you may wish, and then we shall be friends.' In accordance with the entreaties of my men I gave an ox; and when asked what I should like in return, mentioned food, as the thing which we most needed. In the evening Njambi sent a very small basket of meal, and two or three pounds of the flesh of our own ox! with the apology that he had no fowls, and very little of any other food. It was impossible to avoid a laugh at the coolness of the generous creatures. I was truly thankful nevertheless that, though resolved to die rather than deliver up one of our number to be a slave, we had so far gained our point as to be allowed to pass on without having shed human blood.

In the midst of the commotion, several Chiboque stole pieces of meat out of the sheds of my people, and Mohorisi, one of the Makololo, went boldly into the crowd and took back a marrow-bone from one of them. A few of my Batoka seemed afraid, and would perhaps have fled had the affray actually begun, but upon the whole I thought my men behaved admirably. They lamented having left their shields at home by command of Sekeletu, who feared that, if they carried these, they might be more disposed to be overbearing in their demeanour to the tribes we should meet. We had proceeded on the principles of peace and conciliation, and the foregoing treatment shows in what light our conduct was viewed.

My people were now so much discouraged that some proposed to return home; the prospect of being obliged to return when just on the threshold of the Portuguese settlements distressed me exceedingly. After using all my powers of persuasion, I declared to them that if they returned I would go on alone, and went into my little tent with the mind directed to Him who hears the sighing of the soul; and was soon followed by the head of Mohorisi, saying – 'We will never leave you. Do not be disheartened. Wherever you lead we will follow. Our remarks were made only on account of the injustice of these people.' Others followed, and with the most artless simplicity of manner told me to be comforted – 'they were all my children; they knew no one but Sekeletu and me, and they would die for me; they had not fought because I did not wish it; they had just spoken in bitterness of their spirit, and when feeling that they could do nothing; but if these enemies begin, you will see what we can do.' One of the oxen we offered to the Chiboque had been rejected because he had lost part of his tail, as they thought that it had been cut off and witchcraft medicine inserted; and some mirth was excited by my proposing to raise a similar objection to all the oxen we still had in our possession. The remaining four soon presented a singular shortness of their caudal extremities, and though no one ever asked whether they had medicine in the stumps or no, we were no more troubled by the demand for an ox! We now slaughtered another ox, that the spectacle might not be seen of the owners of the cattle fasting, while the Chiboque were feasting.

MT 339–353

1   He must mean here any worship involving external regulation, even that, presumably limited, of the
    Independents and Congregationalists themselves.
2   MT 6.
3   *Thomas Woodrow Wilson*, S. Freud and W. C. Bullitt, Wiedenfeld and Nicholson, London, 1967,
    p. 37.
4   ibid. p. 52.
5   *Natural Symbols,* Mary Douglas, Cressett Press, London, 1970, p. x.
6   *Stoic, Christian and Humanist*, Gilbert Murray, George Allen and Unwin, London, 1940, p. 98.
7   Cf. Shaw's 'Every square yard of West End means a new acre of East End'.

Chapter 9

Venus in Black

Livingstone's character originates (on the Freudian hypothesis) from a slight
shift in boyhood towards passivity to the father, developing into a faint homo-
sexuality. Such a trend is a common deviation from centre and does not
unbalance the character from what is socially acceptable and applauded. Dis-
tinctive, yes; abnormal no.

From this position, and corresponding to the drive of the person concerned,
sublimations are possible which, under constant self-discipline, can forego sex
almost entirely, meaning by sex, of course, copulation. Such avoidance is an
obvious feature of Livingstone's life in Africa. One does not expect a Victorian
to discuss his sex-life: Livingstone either censors his interest entirely or betrays
it verbally by heavily humorous embarrassment or by the use of words such as
'low', 'degraded', etc., in deference to the peculiar defences of his times. His

integrity in this matter has not been questioned, nor has any evidence been produced of a 'secret life'. I therefore take this extract to be sincere and reliable:

> Although the Makololo were so confiding, the reader must not imagine
> that they would be so to every individual who might visit them. Much of my
> influence depended upon the good name given me by the Bakwains, and that
> I secured only through a long course of tolerably good conduct. No one ever
> gains much influence in this country without purity and uprightness. The
> acts of a stranger are keenly scrutinized by both young and old, and seldom
> is the judgment pronounced, even by the heathen, unfair or uncharitable. I
> have heard women speaking in admiration of a white man, because he was
> pure, and never was guilty of any secret immorality. Had he been, they
> would have known it, and, untutored heathen though they be, would have
> despised him in consequence. Secret vice becomes known throughout the
> tribe; and while one unacquainted with the language may imagine a pecca-
> dillo to be hidden, it is as patent to all as it would be in London, had he a
> placard on his back.
>
> MT 513

Within this framework, Livingstone shows a lively interest at least in the
opposite sex, and yields us the benefit of a shrewd look at the charms, status,
vanities, work and sufferings of the African woman in her original setting:

> The Watusi are the cattle herds of all this Unyanyembé region. They are
> very polite in address. The women have small compact, well-shaped heads
> and pretty faces; colour, brown; very pleasant to speak to; well-shaped
> figures, with small hands and feet; the last with high insteps, and springy
> altogether.
>
> LJ 21 Mar 1872

> It is difficult to conceive in what their notion of beauty consists. The
> women have somewhat the same ideas with ourselves of what constitutes
> comeliness. They came frequently and asked for the looking-glass; and the
> remarks they made – while I was engaged in reading, and apparently not
> attending to them – on first seeing themselves therein, were amusingly
> ridiculous. 'Is that me?' 'What a big mouth I have!' 'My ears are as big as
> pumpkin-leaves.' 'I have no chin at all.' Or, 'I would have been pretty, but
> am spoiled by these high cheek-bones.' 'See how my head shoots up in the
> middle!' laughing vociferously all the time at their own jokes. They readily
> perceive any defect in each other, and give nicknames accordingly. One man
> came alone to have a quiet gaze at his own features once, when he thought I
> was asleep: after twisting his mouth about in various directions, he remarked
> to himself, 'People say I am ugly, and how very ugly I am indeed!'
>
> MT 192

The Makololo ladies are liberal in their presents of milk and other food, and seldom require to labour, except in the way of beautifying their own huts and court-yards. They drink large quantities of *boyáloa*, which, being made of sorghum, in a minute state of subdivision, is very nutritious, and gives that plumpness of form which is considered beautiful. They dislike being seen at their potations by persons of the opposite sex. They cut their woolly hair quite short, and delight in having the whole person shining with butter. Their dress is a kilt reaching to the knees; its material is ox-hide, made as soft as cloth. It is not ungraceful. A soft skin mantle is thrown across the shoulders when the lady is unemployed, but when engaged in any sort of labour she throws this aside, and works in the kilt alone. The ornaments most coveted are large brass anklets as thick as the little finger, and armlets of both brass and ivory, the latter often an inch broad. The rings are so heavy that the ankles are often blistered by the weight pressing down; but it is the fashion, and is borne as magnanimously as tight lacing and tight shoes among ourselves. Strings of beads are hung around the neck, and the fashionable colours being light green and pink, a trader could get almost anything he chose for beads of these colours.

MT 186

A young woman, dressed in the highest style of Makonde fashion, punting as dexterously as a man could, brought a canoe full of girls to see us. She wore an ornamental head-dress of red beads tied to her hair on one side of her head, a necklace of fine beads of various colours, two bright figured brass bracelets on her left arm, and scarcely a farthing's worth of cloth, though it was at its cheapest.

ZT 440

A man, who accompanied us to the Falls, was a great admirer of the ladies. Every pretty girl he saw filled his heart with rapture. 'Oh, what a beauty! never saw her like before; I wonder if she is married?' and earnestly and lovingly did he gaze after the charming one till she had passed out of sight. He had four wives at home, and hoped to have a number more before long, but he had only one child; this Mormonism does not seem to satisfy; it leads to a state of mind which, if not disease, is truly contemptible.

ZT 307

Livingstone cannot approve of polygamy but his approach to it is pragmatic rather than moralistic. He notices that the Makololo make off with all the pretty girls of their tributary tribes along the Zambezi, and he relishes the comedy of their various affiliations:

Before Ben Habib started for Loanda, he asked the daughter of Sebituane in marriage. This is the plan the Arabs adopt for gaining influence in a tribe. The daughter named Manchunyane, was about twelve years of age. As I was the bosom friend of her father, I was supposed to have a voice in her disposal, and, on being asked, objected to her being taken away, we knew not whither, and where we might never see her again. As her name implies, she was only a little black, and, besides being as fair as any of the Arabs, had quite Arab features; but I have no doubt that Ben Habib will renew his suit more successfully on some other occasion. In these cases of marriage, the consent of the young women is seldom asked. A maidservant of Sekeletu, however, pronounced by the Makololo to be goodlooking, was at this time sought in marriage by five young men. Sekeletu, happening to be at my waggon when one of these preferred his suit, very coolly ordered all five to stand in a row before the young woman, that she might make her choice. Two refused to stand, apparently, because they could not brook the idea of a repulse, although willing enough to take her, if Sekeletu had acceded to their petition without reference to her will. Three dandified fellows stood forth, and she unhesitatingly decided on taking one who was really the best looking. It was amusing to see the mortification on the black faces of the unsuccessful candidates, while the spectators greeted them with a hearty laugh.

MT 508

The Makololo ladies have soft, small, delicate hands and feet; their foreheads are well shaped and of good size; the nose not disagreeably flat, though the *alae* are full; the mouth, chin, teeth, eyes, and general form are beautiful, and, contrasted with the West-Coast negro, quite ladylike. They are a light warm brown complexion, have pleasant countenances, and are remarkably quick of apprehension. They dress neatly, wearing a kilt and mantle, and have many ornaments. Having maidservants to wait on them and perform the principal part of the household work, abundance of leisure time is left them, and they are sometimes at a loss to know what to do with it. Unlike their fairer and more fortunate sisters in Europe, they have neither sewing nor other needlework, nor pianoforte practice, to occupy their fingers, nor reading to improve their minds; few have children to attend to, and time does hang rather heavily on their hands. The men wickedly aver that their two great amusements, or modes for killing time, are sipping beer, and secretly smoking bang, or Indian hemp, here known as matokwane. Although the men indulge pretty freely in smoking it, they do not like their wives to follow their example, and many prohibit it. Nevertheless, some women do smoke it secretly, and the practice causes a disease known by a minute eruption on the skin, quite incurable unless the habit be abandoned.

Sebituane's sister, the head lady of Sesheke, wore eighteen solid brass rings, as thick as one's finger, on each leg, and three of copper under each knee; nineteen brass rings on her left arm, and eight of brass and copper on her right, also a large ivory ring above each elbow. She had a pretty bead necklace, and a bead sash encircled her waist. The weight of the bright brass rings round her legs impeded her walking, and chafed her ankles; but, as it was the fashion, she did not mind the inconvenience, and guarded against the pain by putting soft rag round the lower rings.

The practice of polygamy, though intended to increase, tends to diminish the tribe. The wealthy old men, who have plenty of cattle, marry all the pretty young girls. An ugly but rich old fellow, who was so blind that a servant had to lead him along the path, had two of the very handsomest young wives in the town; one of them, the daughter of Mokele, being at least half-a-century younger than himself, was asked, 'Do you like him?' 'No,' she replied; 'I hate him, he is so disagreeable.' The young men of the tribe, who happen to have no cattle, must get on without a wife, or be content with one who has few personal attractions. This state of affairs probably leads to a good deal of immorality, and children are few. By pointed inquiries, and laying oneself out for that kind of knowledge, one might be able to say much more; but if one behaves as he must do among the civilized, and abstains from asking questions, no improper hints even will be given by any of the native women we have met.

Polygamy, the sign of low civilization, and the source of many evils, is common, and, oddly enough, approved of even by the women. On hearing that a man in England could marry but one wife, several ladies exclaimed that they would not like to live in such a country: they could not imagine how English ladies could relish our custom; for, in their way of thinking, every man of respectability should have a number of wives, as a proof of his wealth. Similar ideas prevail all down the Zambesi. No man is respected by his neighbour who has not several wives. The reason for this is, doubtless, because, having the produce of each wife's garden, he is wealthy in proportion to their number.

ZT 283

The person whom Nyakoba appointed to be our guide came and bargained that his services should be rewarded with a hoe. I had no objection to give it, and showed him the article; he was delighted with it, and went off to show it to his wife. He soon afterwards returned, and said that, though he was perfectly willing to go, his wife would not let him. I said, 'Then bring back the hoe'; but he replied, 'I want it'. 'Well, go with us, and you shall have it.' 'But my wife won't let me.' I remarked to my men 'Did you ever hear such a fool?' They answered, 'Oh, that is the custom of these parts; the wives are the masters'. And Sekwebu informed me that he had gone to this man's house, and heard him saying to his wife, 'Do you think that I would ever leave you?' then, turning to Sekwebu, he asked, 'Do you think I would leave this pretty woman? Is she not pretty?' Sekwebu had been making inquiries among the people, and had found that the women indeed possessed a great deal of influence. When a young man takes a liking to a girl of another village, and the parents have no objection to the match, he is obliged to come and live at their village. He has to perform certain services for the mother-in-law, such as keeping her well supplied with firewood; and when he comes into her presence he is obliged to sit with his knees in a bent position, as putting out his feet towards the old lady would give her great offence. If he becomes tired of living in this state of vassalage, and wishes to return to his own family, he is obliged to leave all his children behind – they belong to the wife. This is only a more stringent enforcement of the law the practice which prevails so very extensively in Africa, known to Europeans as 'buying wives'. Such virtually it is, but it does not appear quite in that light to the actors. So many head of cattle or goats are given to the parents of the girl, 'to give her up', as it is termed, *i.e.* to forgo all claim on her offspring, and allow an entire transference of her and her seed into another family. If nothing is given, the family from which she has come can claim the children as part of itself: the payment is made to sever this bond.

MT 622

Mokalaosé has his little afflictions, and he tells me of them. A wife ran away, I asked how many he had; he told me twenty in all: I then thought he had nineteen too many. He answered with the usual reason, 'But who would cook for strangers if I had but one?'

LJ 12–14 Aug 1866

The Makololo were eager to travel fast, because they wanted to be back in time to hoe their fields before the rains, and also because their wives needed looking after. Indeed Masiko had already been obliged to go back and settle some difference, of which a report was brought by other wives who followed their husbands about twenty miles with goodly supplies of beer and meal. Masiko went off in a fury; nothing less than burning the offenders' houses would satisfy him; but a joke about the inevitable fate of polygamists, and our inability to manage more than one wife, and sometimes not even her, with a walk of a good many miles in the hot sun, mollified him so much, that a week afterwards he followed and caught us up without having used any weapon more dangerous than his tongue.

ZT 484

Their ideas of right and wrong differ in no respect from our own, except in their professed inability to see how it can be improper for a man to have more than one wife. A year or two ago several of the wives of those who had been absent with us petitioned the Chief for leave to marry again. They thought that it was of no use waiting any longer, their husbands must be dead; but Sekeletu refused permission; he himself had bet a number of oxen that the Doctor would return with their husbands, and he had promised the absent men that their wives should be kept for them. The impatient women had therefore to wait a little longer. Some of them, however, eloped with other men; the wife of Mantlanyane, for instance, ran off and left his little boy amongst strangers. Mantlanyane was very angry when he heard of it, not that he cared much about her deserting him, for he had two other wives at Tette, but he was indignant at her abandoning his boy . . .

. . . Some of the reports which the men had heard from the Batoka of the hills concerning their families, were here confirmed. Takelang's wife had been killed by Mashotlane, the headman at the Falls, on a charge, as usual, of witchcraft. Inichikola's two wives, believing him to be dead, had married again; and Masakasa was intensely disgusted to hear that two years ago his friends, upon a report of his death, threw his shield over the Falls, slaughtered all his oxen, and held a species of wild Irish wake, in honour of his memory: he said he meant to disown them, and to say, when they come to salute him, 'I am dead. I am not here. I belong to another world, and should stink if I came among you.'

We remained the whole of the 7th beside the village of the old Batoka chief, Moshobotwane, the stoutest man we have seen in Africa. We gave him a present, and a pretty plain exposition of what we thought of his bloody forays among his Batoka brethren. A scolding does most good to the recipient, when put alongside some obliging act. He certainly did not take it ill, as was evident from what he gave us in return; which consisted of a liberal supply of meal, milk, and an ox. He has a large herd of cattle, and a tract of fine pasture-land on the beautiful stream Lekone. The women of this village were more numerous than the men, the result of the chief's marauding. The Batoka wife of Sima came up from the Falls, to welcome her husband back, bringing a present of the best fruits of the country. Her husband was the only one of the party who had brought a wife from Tette, namely, the girl whom he obtained from Chisaka for his feats of dancing. According to our ideas, his first wife could hardly have been pleased at seeing the second and younger one; but she took her away home with her, while the husband remained with us.

In the evening, when all was still, Takelang, fired his musket, and cried out, 'I am weeping for my wife: my court is desolate: I have no home'; and then uttered a loud wail of anguish.

ZT 247–291

Livingstone's courtesy is nowhere more apparent than in these matters, which must have strained his moral sensibilities as much as they gratified his eyes:

18th March. – A very beautiful young woman came to look at us, perfect in every way and nearly naked but unconscious of indecorum, a very Venus in black.

LJ 1868

He may measure people by the standards of Victorian Christianity but he never fails to regard them as people, and the last thing he cares about is their colour.

None of these gentlemen had Portuguese wives. They usually come to Africa, in order to make a little money, and return to Lisbon. Hence they seldom bring their wives with them, and never can be successful colonists in consequence. It is common for them to have families by native women. It was particularly gratifying to me, who had been familiar with the stupid prejudice against colour, to view the liberality with which people of colour were treated by the Portuguese. Instances, so common in the south, in which half-caste children are abandoned, are here extremely rare. They are acknowledged at table, and provided for by their fathers, as if European. The coloured clerks of the merchants sit at the same table with their employers, without any embarrassment. The civil manners of superiors to inferiors is probably the result of the position they occupy – a few whites among thousands of blacks; but nowhere else in Africa is there so much goodwill between Europeans and natives as here.

MT 371

While on our journey north-west, a cheery old woman, who had once been beautiful, but whose white hair now contrasted strongly with her dark complexion, was working briskly in her garden as we passed. She seemed to enjoy a hale, hearty old age. She saluted us with what elsewhere would be called a good address, and answered each of us with a frank 'Yes, my child'. Another motherly-looking woman, sitting by a well, began the conversation by 'You are going to visit Muazi, and you have come from afar, have you not?' But in general women never speak to strangers unless spoken to, so anything said by them attracts attention. Muazi once presented us with a basket of corn. On hinting that we had no wife to grind our corn, his buxom spouse struck in with roguish glee, and said, 'I will grind it for you; and leave Muazi, to accompany and cook for you in the land of the setting sun'. As a rule the women are modest and retiring in their demeanour, and, without being oppressed with toil, show a great deal of industry. The crops need about eight months' attention. Then when the harvest is home, much labour is required to convert it into food as porridge, or beer. The corn is pounded in a large wooden mortar, like the ancient Egyptian one, with a pestle six feet long and about four inches thick. The pounding is performed by two or even three women at one mortar. Each, before delivering a blow with her pestle, gives an upward jerk of the body, so as to put strength into the stroke, and they keep exact time, so that two pestles are never in the mortar at the same moment. The measured thud, thud, thud, and the women standing at their vigorous work, are associations inseparable from a prosperous African village. Boys and girls, by constant practice with the pestle, are able to plant stakes in the ground by a somewhat similar action, in erecting a hut, so deftly that they never miss the first hole made. Let any one try by repeatedly jabbing a pole with all his force to make a deep hole in the ground, and he will understand how difficult it is always to strike it into the same spot.

Another part of the work of women is in the preparation of beer. The malted grain is sun-dried and pounded into meal, then cooked or brewed. A merry-making often implies that all who come to make merry shall bring their hoes and let off the excitement of the liquor by a substantial day's hoeing. At other times, a couple shut themselves up in their huts, on pretence of sickness, and drink the whole brew themselves. But a more common mode is to invite all the friends and relatives of the woman whose beer is to be drunk, and they rejoice in the entertainment, and praise the good-wife's ale, as so good that the 'taste reaches right to the back of the neck', or in proper native gourmand's phrase declare the feast to be so good that every step they take homewards will cause their stomachs to say 'tobu, tobu, tobu'. Bless their hearts, let them rejoice in the fruits of their labour! We confess, however, that we have never witnessed the plenty which their land yields, without turning in imagination to the streets and lanes of our own cities, and lamenting that the squalid offspring of poverty and sin has not more pleasant lives in this world, where there is so much and to spare.

ZT 541

The wife of Pitsane was busy making a large hut, while we were in the town: she informed us that the men left house-building entirely to the women and servants. A round tower of stakes and reeds, nine or ten feet high, is raised and plastered; a floor is next made of soft tufa, or ant-hill material and cowdung. This plaster prevents the poisonous insects, called tampans, whose bite causes fever in some, and painful sores in all, from harbouring in the cracks or soil. The roof, which is much larger in diameter than the tower, is made on the ground, and then, many persons assisting, lifted up and placed on the tower, and thatched. A plastered reed fence is next built up to meet the outer part of the roof, which still projects a little over this fence, and a space of three feet remains between it and the tower. We slept in this space, instead of in the tower, as the inner door of the hut we occupied was uncomfortably small, being only nineteen inches high, and twenty-two inches wide at the floor. A foot from the bottom it measured seventeen inches in breadth, and close to the top only twelve inches, so it was a difficult matter to get through it. The tower has no light or ventilation, except through this small door. The reason a lady assigned for having the doors so very small was to keep out the mice!

The children have merry times, especially in the cool of the evening. One of their games consists of a little girl being carried on the shoulders of two others. She sits with outstretched arms, as they walk about with her, and all the rest clap their hands, and stopping before each hut sing pretty airs, some beating time on their little kilts of cowskin, others making a curious humming sound between the songs. Excepting this and the skipping-rope, the play of the girls consists in imitation of the serious work of their mothers, building little huts, making small pots, and cooking, pounding corn in miniature mortars, or hoeing tiny gardens. The boys play with spears of reeds pointed with wood, and small shields, or bows and arrows; or amuse themselves in making little cattle-pens, or in moulding cattle in clay; they show great ingenuity in the imitation of various-shaped horns. Some too are said to use slings, but as soon as they can watch the goats, or calves, they are sent to the field. We saw many boys riding on the calves they had in charge, but this is an innovation since the arrival of the English with their horses. Tselane, one of the ladies, on observing Dr. Livingstone noting obser-vations on the wet and dry bulb thermometers, thought that he too was engaged in play; for on receiving no reply to her question, which was rather difficult to answer, as the native tongue has no scientific terms, she said, with roguish glee, 'Poor thing, playing like a little child!'

ZT 293

Professor Westphal, whose help over Livingstone's languages I have already acknowleged, amused me by his opinion of Livingstone's home life. He says 'Mrs. Livingstone's life must have been a lonely one, because her husband's contacts were with men, only men, to an African, being true friends, while women are creatures to whom he does not show any great affection. I am sure that in this respect Livingstone was an African, and that his relationships with his wife, while not exactly African, were Dickensian, Baptist, and severely formal.' I find, however, the evidence more in favour of his being a feminist: he reports with approval an unspoilt Africa in which women's rights seem perfectly natural:

The Bechuanas could never understand the changes which took place in the Boer commandants. 'Why, one can never know who is the chief among these Boers. Like the Bushmen, they have no king.' The idea that any tribe of men could be so senseless as not to have an hereditary chief was so absurd to these people, that, in order not to appear equally stupid, I was obliged to tell them that we English were so anxious to preserve the royal blood, that we had made a young lady our chief. This seemed to them a most convincing proof of our sound sense.

MT 38

Sebituane installed his daughter Mamochisáne into the chieftainship long before his death, but, with all his acuteness, the idea of her having a husband who should not be her lord did not seem to enter his mind. He wished to make her his successor, probably in imitation of some of the negro tribes with whom he had come into contact; but, being of the Bechuana race, he could not look upon the husband except as the woman's lord, so he told her all the men were hers, she might take any one, but ought to keep none. In fact, he thought she might do with the men what he could do with the women; but these men had other wives; and according to a saying in the country, 'the tongues of women cannot be governed', they made her miserable by their remarks. One man whom she chose was even called her wife, and her son the child of Mamochisane's wife; but the arrangement was so distasteful to Mamochisane herself, that, as soon as Sebituane died, she said she never would consent to govern the Makololo so long as she had a brother living. Three days were spent in public discussion on the point.

Mamochisane, however, upheld Sekeletu's claims, and at last stood up in the assembly and addressed him with a womanly gush of tears: 'I have been a chief only because my father wished it. I always would have preferred to be married and have a family like other women. You, Sekeletu, must be chief and build up your father's house.'   MT 179

The women are accustomed to transact business for themselves. They accompany the men into camp, sell their own wares, and appear to be both fair traders, and modest sensible persons. In other places they bring things for sale on their heads, and, kneeling at a respectful distance, wait till their husbands or fathers, who have gone forward, choose to return, and to take their goods, and barter for them. Perhaps in this particular, the women here occupy the golden mean between the Manganja hill-tribes and the Jaggas of the north, who live on the mountain summits near Kilimanjaro. It is said that at the latter place the women do all the trading, have regular markets, and will on no account allow a man to enter the market-place.

ZT 192

One of the Makalaka had speared an ox belonging to one of the Makololo, and being unable to extract the spear, was thereby discovered to be the perpetrator of the deed. The culprit was bound hand and foot and placed in the sun to force him to pay a fine, but he continued to deny his guilt. His mother, believing in the innocence of her son, now came forward, with her hoe in hand, and, threatening to cut down any one who should dare to interfere, untied the cords with which he had been bound and took him home. This open defiance of authority was not resented but referred to Sekeletu at Linyanti.

MT 234

The Chief brought a small present of meal in the evening, and sat with us for a few minutes. On leaving us he said that he wished we might sleep well. Scarce had he gone, when a wild sad cry arose from the river, followed by the shrieking of women. A crocodile had carried off his principal wife, as she was bathing. The Makololo snatched up their arms, and rushed to the bank, but it was too late, she was gone. The wailing of the women continued all night, and next morning we met others coming to the village to join in the general mourning. Their grief was evidently heartfelt, as we saw the tears coursing down their cheeks. In reporting this misfortune to his neighbours, Muana-Moesi said 'that white men came to his village; washed themselves at the place where his wife drew water and bathed; rubbed themselves with a white medicine (soap); and his wife, having gone to bathe afterwards, was taken by a crocodile; he did not know whether in consequence of the medicine used or not'. This we could not find fault with. On our return we were viewed with awe, and all the men fled at our approach; the women remained; and this elicited the remark from our men, 'The women have the advantage of men, in not needing to dread the spear'.

ZT 122

In one village we found all the men engaged in celebrating, with dancing and singing, a ceremony for two girls of twelve or fourteen, analogous to the *boguera* which among the Bechuana and Makololo forms the young men into bands or regiments for life. The Bechuana call it *boyale* when the novices are girls, and here the ceremony is named *moari*, evidently a cognate word. These girls were dressed with a profusion of beads, and painted over the head and face with pipeclay, which gave them the appearance of wearing an ancient helmet with chin-straps. The women were so eager in the dance and in teaching their young protegées to perform their part in it properly, that they paid no attention to the entreaties of the men to go and grind meal, and clothe themselves with the cloth the strangers had brought. Whence these customs, and from whom a number of laws which are recognised for thousands of miles, have been derived, no one can divine. They seem to have made an indelible impression on the native mind, and abide in it unchanged, from age to age. The *boguera* has something of the Jewish ceremony of initiation, but it is a political, not a religious institution. It cannot be traced to Arab origin, and is spoken of, by those who have undergone it, under the breath, and with a circumlocution which shows that they regard it in a very serious light.

ZT 518

The patriarchal injustices of polygamy are magnified in the presence of slavery. Livingstone's emotional balance is remarkable in stories such as these:

31st May. – Old Kapika sold his young and good-looking wife for unfaithfulness, as he alleged. Her heart was evidently sore: for a lady to come so low down is to her grievous. She had lost her jaunty air and was, with her head shaved, ugly; but she never forgot to address her captors with dignity, and they seemed to fear her. The sight of such a lady in the chain-gang shocked the ladies of Lunda, who ran to her, and having ascertained from her own mouth that she was a slave now, clapped their hands on their mouths in the way that they express wonder, surprise, and horror: the hand is placed so that the fingers are on one cheek and the thumb on the other.

The case of the chieftainess excited great sympathy; some brought her food, Kapika's daughters brought her pombe and bananas; one man offered to redeem her with two, another with three slaves, but Casembe, who is very strict in punishing infidelity, said, 'No, though ten slaves be offered she must go'. He is probably afraid of his own beautiful queen should the law be relaxed. Old Kapika came and said to her, 'You refused me, and I now refuse you'. There is a very large proportion of very old and very tall men in this district. The slave-trader is a means of punishing the wives which these old fogies ought never to have had.

LJ 1868

In the morning we were loudly accosted by a well-dressed woman who had just had a very heavy slave-taming stick put on her neck; she called in such an authoritative tone to us to witness the flagrant injustice of which she was the victim that all the men stood still and went to hear the case. She was a near relative of Chirikaloma, and was going up the river to her husband, when the old man (at whose house she was now a prisoner) caught her, took her servant away from her, and kept her in the degraded state we saw. The withies with which she was bound were green and sappy. The old man said in justification that she was running away from Chirikaloma, who would be offended with him if he did not secure her.

I asked the officious old gentleman in a friendly tone what he expected to receive from Chirikaloma, and he said, 'Nothing'. Several slaver-looking fellows came about, and I felt sure that the woman had been seized in order to sell her to them, so I gave the captor a cloth to pay to Chirikaloma if he were offended, and told him to say that I, feeling ashamed to see one of his relatives in a slave-stick, had released her, and would take her on to her husband.

She was evidently a lady among them, having many fine beads and some strung on elephant's hair: she has a good deal of spirit too, for on being liberated she went into the old man's house and took her basket and calabash. A virago of a wife shut the door and tried to prevent her, as well as to cut off the beads from her person, but she resisted like a good one, and my men thrust the door open and let her out. A second wife – for old officious had two – joined the first in a furious tirade of abuse, the elder holding her sides in regular fishwife fashion till I burst into a laugh, in which the younger wife joined. I explained to the different headmen in front of this village what I had done, and sent messages to Chirikaloma explanatory of my friendly deed to his relative, so that no misconstruction should be put on my act.

Akosakone, the name of the lady whom we had liberated, soon arrived at the residence of her husband, who was another brother of Machemba. She behaved like a lady all through, sleeping at a fire apart from the men. The ladies of the different villages we passed condoled with her, and she related to them the indignity that had been done to her. Besides this she did us many services: she bought food for us, because, having a good address, we saw that she could get double what any of our men could purchase for the same cloth; she spoke up for us when any injustice was attempted, and, when we were in want of carriers, volunteered to carry a bag of beads on her head. On arriving at Machemba's brother, Chimseia, she introduced me to him, and got him to be liberal to us in food on account of the service we had rendered to her. She took leave of us all with many expressions of thankfulness, and we were glad that we had not mistaken her position or lavished kindness on the undeserving.

LJ 26 Jun 1866

I noticed a very pretty woman come past quite jauntily about a month ago, on marriage with Monasimba. Ten goats were given; her friends came and asked another goat, which being refused, she was enticed away, became sick of rheumatic fever two days afterwards, and died yesterday. Not a syllable of regret for the beautiful young creature does one hear, but for the goats: 'Oh, our ten goats!' – they cannot grieve too much – 'Our ten goats – oh! oh!'

LJ 6 Dec 1870

Beauty, cruelty, laughter – this is not a bad note on which to leave Livingstone and his Africa. It is no better and no worse, different and in a deeper
sense no different from the rest of the world. He sees the unrepressed and irre-
pressible joy of its life, its 'elastic individuality, aesthetic receptivity ... and its
unique blend of warmth, sensitivity, nonsense, vitality and elegance'.

But accompanying this (which he liked well enough to spend his life with) is
his record of its callousness. He senses an indifference to pain and liberty not
merely among the corrupted and enslaved but in all, exploited and exploiting
alike. To this, as rain to parched earth, he took his doctrine and example.
Possibly a flood of brotherly love has supervened since he left but, until there is
wider evidence of this, it is as crass for the African states to topple his statues,
erase his name and ignore his books as it would be to proscribe rain. He pierces
the crust of colour, race, class, culture, creed, power and platform to the roots
of kindness, practised – and unpractised. His prayer-driven life had only one
criterion, 'love is the deeds of love', *deus est mortali iuvare mortalem*, the
divine is for one human being to help another.

In the long, hopeful view his life can be read as a parable of the white
presence in Africa. He makes no apology for being there. The Africans recognised that what he had to give was indispensable, and he was welcomed.
Grossly outnumbered always, his security was the reward of his humanity.
Technologically, his advantages were huge but technology is nothing in itself,
he said: the ineluctable battle is for the mind and heart. He respected the *amour-
propre* of tribalism: he was spared the neo-liberal, colour-conscious narcissisms
that have succeeded it. One wonders what he would have done about that.
Martyred on, I suppose.

Love is a two-way traffic. There is as much work to be done now towards
the whites as towards the blacks, and perhaps an African Livingstone is already
keeping his journals on the Reef.

When Livingstone reached 'the annihilation of his hopes' on the Zambezi, at
the Caborabasa Rapids, his Shona canoemen said to him *Kwapera basa*, the
work is finished. If he could stand there in 1975, when the world's fifth largest
source of hydro-electric power will be ready to serve all the territories he had
opened up south of the Equator, I think he would shake his head and say
quietly *Basa rozogundika* – The work is just beginning.